# JOTTINGS

OF

# A YEAR'S SOJOURN IN THE SOUTH;

OR

FIRST IMPRESSIONS

OF THE

# COUNTRY AND ITS PEOPLE;

WITH

A GLIMPSE AT SCHOOL-TEACHING

IN

THAT SOUTHERN LAND,

AND

REMINISCENCES OF DISTINGUISHED MEN.

BY

A. DE PUY VAN BUREN.

"To thee, perchance, this rambling strain
Recalls our summer walks again;
The wild unbounded hills we ranged,
While oft our talk its topic changed,
And, desultory as our way,
Ranged, unconfined, from grave to gay."

BATTLE CREEK, MICHIGAN.

1859.

Review and Herald Print:
Battle Creek.

TO

MAJOR W. W. WILDY,
JOHN S. PAUL AND H. BARKSDALE,

WORTHY SOUTHERN PLANTERS AND GENTLEMEN,

THE PLEASURE AND DELIGHT OF A SOJOURN IN WHOSE HOMES WE SHALL LONG CHERISH IN PLEASING REMEMBRANCE,

**THIS VOLUME**

IS MOST RESPECTFULLY INSCRIBED

BY THEIR FRIEND

THE AUTHOR.

# PREFACE.

In presenting this volume to the public we do not suppose that we are adding to the number of

"Books which are books;"

we have not entertained a doubt but what we shall have the old trick of Diluvian Noah memory played upon us—that our little "Dove-of-a volume" will come back to us from its disappointed errand. "Then why do you send it out on this mission?" For pretty much the same reason that Noah did the dove—on an errand of discovery. We expect, if it reaches a certain *terra incognita*—a land unknown to us—nothing short of fame. If not, we are consigned to the dusty immortality of the shelves. The author may write, but it is the people that make the book. But between him and the people lurks the critic-cat, ever ready to pounce upon, and devour whatever passes from the one to the other. Should this volume succeed in reaching its destination, to its recipients we have a word to say:

First, we propose to let these pages go for what they are worth; we certainly would prefer not to say another word about them; would give more to be in your presence *incognito*, when you had finished reading this volume, and hear the praise or censure, that you would give without reading a preface, in which the author has explained a way for you to praise him. Because if you praised at all, it would be from merit *found.* Yet the nature of the work calls for a few words in prelude.

The book is what it purports to be, "Jottings of a Year's Sojourn in the South"—our first impressions of the country and its people, given in a style more or less sketchy. A large share of the work was first presented to the public, in a series of sketches and jottings, through the columns of the Battle Creek (Michigan) *Journal*; and at the close of their publication in that paper, we were urged by many friends to put them in the more durable form of a book. Hence, having yielded to their solicitations and our own vanity, the reader is in possession not only of such a volume as the original sketches would have formed, but one of twice the size. Our intention has been to give him a pleasant volume filled with the pleasant memories of a pleasant land.

In regard to praising the South—which we have a most inalienable right to do, when and wherever we think she deserves it—we have certainly written with perfect disregard to political prejudice, as if Slavery did not exist in our Southern Border.

We are not like IAGO—

"Nothing, if not critical."

But we have given our impressions, if glowingly at times, we trust truthfully.

There is a poetic period in our early life, and a most happy one it is, too. And there are poetic hours in one's after life—moods full of nature, into which one often falls, and in which the truths of a scene impress one with their full charm. If there are any scenes in these Jottings that are thought to be drawn *coleur de rose*, we would say that they have been taken on the spot, in moods we have described, when we received their impressions *coleur de nature;* and besides they were new scenes to us, and written during the full glow of first conceptions. Moreover, many of the subjects and scenes we have noticed, will sustain some considerable glow of enthusiasm.

For the reminiscences we do not claim completeness of portrait—merely give them as reminiscences, and only claim for them the merit of their being valuable from the fact that they are what the people remembered of their distinguished men; and they take their tone and color from the manner in which we have heard them spoken of. We are indebted for much that is valuable in these reminiscences, to Hon. H. BARKSDALE, of Oak Valley, Banks of the Yazoo.

To the Messrs. WHITE and SMITH, of the *Review* and *Herald* office, we are also much indebted for many acts of kindness during our connection with their office, and to the lady of the latter for many timely hints in revising and correcting this work, as it passed through the press.

A. DE PUY VAN BUREN.

*Farm-Home, Battle Creek,*
*October* 30*th*, 1859.

---

## ONE WORD.

There are some typographical errors in this work, which have escaped our attention in reading proof, such as "whining machinery," for whirring machinery, "vulgars," for and the *vulgus*, "physiological reading," for physiognomical reading, "Cote," for Cato, and others which we trust will sufficiently explain themselves.

# CONTENTS.

---

## CHAPTER VIII.



## CHAPTER IX.



## CHAPTER X.



## CHAPTER XI.



## CHAPTER XII.



## CHAPTER XIII.



## CHAPTER XIV.



## CHAPTER XV.



## CHAPTER XVI.



## CHAPTER XVII.

# JOTTINGS

OF

# A YEAR'S SOJOURN IN THE SOUTH.

## CHAPTER I.

> "Go, and beneath yon Southern sky
> A plaided stranger roam. * * *
> * * * * * *
> Go, and to check thy wandering course,
> Quaff from the fountain at the source."
>
> SCOTT.

My trunks had been packed, the "good-byes" had been given, and I had couched down, for it was getting deep into the evening, to take a little rest, previous to my leaving home on the 12 o'clock train.

An hour before midnight my brother awoke me; we went over to the depot, and soon the train came rumbling in from the east. There was one "good bye" yet to be given—the final one to my brother—and all of the others that had been given, were in it. Uttering this, was parting from friends and home again, and all at once. The bell rang the good bye was said—my brother left the cars. As he left, he said something to me that then appeared of not much consequence, but which, lingering in my mind, I afterwards realized to be this good advice:—

"Make no man your confidential friend; trust none, and none will deceive you."

On we went. I was alone among strangers. The first moment I felt all the sadness of leaving home weighing upon me. I essayed to throw it off—it yielded an instant, then came back with heavier force. A gentleman by my side, who had observed our parting, tried to engage in conversation, as if to cheer me up; but it was dull talking with me. I however rallied at length, and began to talk; but every now and then I felt all the love of home one ever feels on leaving it.

Ah! this is the time when one rightly estimates and loves brothers—sisters—parents—home. But away we go from them.

"Galesburgh!" shouts the conductor as we come near that place. A rustle among the passengers; *one* man gets off, and on we go again.

"Kalamazoo!" cries out the conductor; satchels are siezed, *three* or *four* get off, several get on, and away we speed.

"Paw Paw!" "Decatur!" "Dowagiac!" "Niles!" are each cried out in succession, almost ere the sound of the preceding one had died away.

This is not traveling, but only stopping at places. I have traveled this road once, in the old, slow, rocking stage-coach, when time and distance had their tedium, and when the winding of the stage-horn heralded your coming into these villages, or into the newer ones that had sprung up here in this western land, almost with the magic of wild flowers, along the old territorial road.

But now, instead of the twanging stage-horn, the shrill piping of the steam-car, as we rush with the speed of the wind from place to place, warns the villager and the expectant traveler, of its coming—warns for relay *men*, not horses; steam has been harnessed in iron bands and

"Chain'd to the flying car."

But here we are! We have outstripped the night and overtaken the dawn of day at Michigan City; the people have just risen and come about the depot rubbing their eyes.

Those large outspreading flats and marshes that preface your entrance into Chicago, tire the vision; but when you arrive at that city, the eye finds glad and delightful objects to rest on, along Michigan Avenue, that most neat, tasteful and elegant street of residences. Its shrubbery was in its autumn hues. The dwellings seemed to vie with each other in beauty of structure, style and ornamental finishings.

Morning came in, in all its glory, as we rode along this avenue. Seeing this fine street, all aglow with the purple and gold of sunrise, like reading a beautiful line of poetry, affects one as a joy forever.

Getting out of the cars in that "Mammoth Cave"—the Central Depot—one would think that the builders of Babel had just found out that they could not understand each other, and had met here in "confused conclave" to reconcile the jargon of their tongues; but failing to accomplish it, each one was screaming at the top of his voice to be heard.

In half an hour, myself, effects and fortunes, were embarked upon the Illinois Central train for St. Louis.

Now for a ride over the heaven-wide prairies of Illinois. In an hour or two, like a vessel on the bosom of calm old Ocean, we were moving on o'er a vast and boundless plain. The old Scotch tourist was right when he said that "Nature kept these magnificent prairies to whip creation with."

We passed some fine villages, that looked like "sweet Auburns" scattered over this *interminable* prairie; for we rode all day and all night till the next morning, over prairie, prairie, nothing but prairie! and most of the route, without a *lady* in the car. It was like a spring without flowers—autumn without her rosemaries, hollies and myrtles. But though we had slow traveling, we had kind conductors over this Prairie State.

Crossing the ferry at Illinoistown, we were soon whirled up into the city of St. Louis, and stepped out of the hack and into the Planter's House just as grey morning was streaking the dappled east.

St. Louis was settled in 1664—six years earlier than Detroit. In 1820 it had some five thousand inhabitants; now it claims one hundred and twenty thousand. Its commerce, as an inland town, rivals the world. It is the natural depot of the vast and fertile regions watered by the Missouri, the upper Mississippi, the Illinois and their tributaries. Its levee is a limestone bank, solidly paved for over two miles, and its whole length is alive with the stir and strife of business.

By mistake I had gone to the Planter's House while my trunks had been checked to the Barnum House. Both buildings are of massive structure. As soon as it was daydawn I went in search of my trunks. Found them at Barnum's—one injured very much.

Solidity and grandeur characterize this city. Its high and grand buildings tower above you, as you walk along its narrow streets. But I don't know where I have met a more intellectual, business, healthy looking people than are passing and re-passing me in throngs. Ladies of beauty, in all the splendor of dress, and countenances flushed with health. After breakfast, with an old citizen, I went about the city, not undertaking to "do it," for it is six miles long and five wide, but to get a glimpse of the interior.

The City Hall is a splendid edifice of brick; so is Veranda Hall, with its veranda style. The Presbyterian Church is a large, well finished building, occupying an eligible site on the high grounds of the city, surrounded with ornamental trees. The Unitarian Church is of tasteful architecture. The Court House is after the style of the capitol at Washington. My friend remarked that he had heard TOM BENTON make many a speech in it.

As we passed by the St. Louis University—a Catholic school—I thought of IGNATIUS LOYOLA, the founder of the Jesuits, and that celebrated maxim of his: "Give me the teaching of the child, and I care not who preaches to him."

But the Roman Catholic Cathedral attracted my attention most. This is a very large and splendid pile. It has a peal of six bells in its steeple, the three largest of which weigh nearly three thousand pounds each. The front of the building is of polished free-stone, with a portico of four massive, Doric columns. The interior is splendidly finished and furnished, containing several elegant paintings of celebrated masters. I spent an hour or more in it. Here, as I leaned against one of its massive pillars, and looked about me and saw the meaning of those hitherto unmeaning terms, the "nave," the "transept," and the "choir," I thought of all I had read about these venerable piles; how they were all built at one time throughout Europe, and, 'tis said, under the supervision of one man; and that they were the expression of the Gothic idea in Architecture; while SHAKSPEARE, afterwards, gave expression to the same idea in poetry.

And then that thrilling and unequal passage of CONGREVE'S, which Dr. JOHNSON calls the most poetical paragraph in the whole range of the drama—finer than any one in SHAKSPEARE. It is where the awe of the place overcomes ALMERIA—

"LEONARD. Hark!

"ALMERIA. No; all is hushed and still as death. 'Tis dreadful!
How reverend is the face of this tall pile,
Whose ancient pillars rear their marble heads
To bear aloft its arched and ponderous roof,
By its own weight made steadfast and immovable,
Looking tranquility! It strikes an awe
And terror on my aching sight; the tombs
And monumental caves of death look cold,
And shoot a chillness to my trembling heart.
Give me thy hand, and let me hear thy voice;
Nay, quickly speak to me, and let me hear
Thy voice—my own affrights me with its echoes."

While here, the dead were brought in. The priest, the ceremony, the boys swinging burning incense about the coffin, the mumbling and strict silence of all present; how strange, and yet with what devotion! The Catholics have no infidels among them. Is it not strange that the higher, purer, better the religion is, the more infidels it has?

I noticed many a fine and costly building devoted to benevolent and religious purposes, aside from the grand churches that ornament the city.

We had gone down to the river, in the morning, to select a steamer for Vicksburgh, Mississippi. The levee, as we have said, is a paved limestone bank, running along the river for nearly three miles, and almost all this distance I saw a dense and nearly double row of steamers, with the places of their destination painted on canvas and hoisted above their fore-castles.

Surely, thought I, all the "carrier pigeons" of the great valley of the west are waiting here for their messages. While I stood gazing, and doubting which one I should choose, I asked a gentleman to point me out a first-class steamer that was going down the river to-day.

He pointed up the river and said, "There is the Minne-ha-ha; she starts out, at noon, for New Orleans."

"Minne-ha-ha!" That's beautiful! To sail down the Mississippi in the "Laughing water!" How much Indian romance there will be in it! But she was some way up stream. I had to wait the mending of a broken trunk, so she sailed off and left me. The "James E. Woodruff" sailed in the afternoon. I was soon "ticketed" and aboard of her. She did not go, though, till the next day in the afternoon.

The officers on board of these steamers think of the traveler as Cortes did of the Mexicans—that truth is too precious for them. You must bide your time and learn to wait. But if you are not in haste—your board is free—one has enough to occupy his time walking about the city seeing its curiosities; or they can sit here, on deck, and look at this mass of men, mules and horses—

"Drays, carts, cabs and coaches, roaring all—

goods of all kinds, and even more; some carried on board the steamer, some taken off; all stir, noise, bustle, tustle, pulling, hauling, rallying, hallooing, doing all things and everything; lifting, dragging, lugging, tugging, urging, driving and whipping cattle, horses, mules, sheep, hogs—"*et id omne genus*," aboard.

Sitting in the fore-castle of the steamer, and looking out upon all this confused scene, I longed for a term to express a thousand things at once—that would syllable forth in *one* word all I saw and heard. I longed to give expression to something unutterable, till "melee" occurred. I uttered it aloud and felt relieved.

I remember that I noticed on the doors and walls of the Central depot, Chicago, this placard: "*Beware of pick-pockets and watch-stuffers!*" But these steamboats lying along this levee, especially when the passengers come aboard, the day they are to start, should be conspicuously placarded with such warnings. Gangs of thieves prowl about them, and when you are at breakfast, or any of your meals, or out of your state-room, unless it is locked, as it should be when you leave it, they steal into it, and rifle the room of anything valuable, even breaking open carpet-bags.

This morning, on board the "Woodruff," a fine gold watch, and porte-monnaie, with considerable gold in it, was stolen from one of the state-rooms. On the "Alleghany," lying near us, the same morning, a carpet-bag was broken open and rifled of its contents. The owner of the watch and porte-monnaie applied to our Captain ; he referred him to the Detective Police. This officer was found. The story was told.

"My friend," said he, "this is an ower true tale." Not a morning passes but what I hear the story of some of these passengers being robbed—watches, money, or valuables stolen from them." He said it was useless to search the boat while lying along the levee.

> "'Tis true—tis a pity,
> And pity 'tis, 'tis true,"

that the Detective Police, though Argus-eyed, would be eluded and baffled in detecting and apprehending these thieves, or getting back the stolen treasures.

## CHAPTER II.

"'Twas an Autumn morning, as the clock struck ten,
That we left St. Louis, on our route again;
Gazing on the river, thick with yellow mud,
And dreaming of disaster, fire, and fog, and flood—
Of boilers ever bursting, of snags that break the wheel,
And sawyers, ripping steamboats through all their length of keel,
While on our journey southward, in our gallant ship,
*Floating, steaming, panting down the Mississip.*"

MACKAY.

We left St. Louis at 12 o'clock, November 5th. We were "bannered" away by the waving of handkerchiefs of friends on the other steamers and the levee.

Passing Jefferson Barracks, down the river "aways," I could not but think with sadness of the early death of young MASON, STEWART and ANDRUS, of Battle Creek, Michigan. Here they lie buried, with

"No tomb to plead their remembrance."

They were enjoying the happiness of a farm-life, in their own Peninsular State, when the "pibroch"* for the Mexican war sounded near their homes. Young and ambitious, they were influenced by a love of military glory—they went to the war. And thus far had they got on their return home, when they found that the

"Paths of glory lead but to the grave."

"*Requescat in pace*"—friends of my early days.

Our passage down the Mississippi was a slow one, long drawn out. The river was nearly at low water mark, and we "sounded" our way along, dodging sand-bars, rafts, snags and sawyers. The current is wayward and impetuous, and so crooked that the "needle of the compass turns round and round, pointing East, West, North and South, as it marks the bearings of your craft," showing those tremendous bends in the stream, which nature appears to have formed to check the headlong current and keep it from rushing too madly to the Ocean. But in its impetuosity it frequently grows impatient of the "round-about course," and "*ploughs*" through the bend, making what is termed a "cut-off."

The *poetical* name of the Mississippi is the Father-of-waters. But the word is found in the Choctaw language, and is rendered thus: "Mïssa"—"old big," and "Sippah"—"strong." Hence, Mississippi means, "Old-big-strong"—a name eminently characteristic of the river. And he

> "That has been
> Where the wild will of the Mississipi tide
> Has dashed him on a sawyer,"

will think the Choctaw was right when he called it the "Old-big-strong."

The "Iron Mountains," on the Mississippi shore, where there lies embedded enough wealth in ore to supply the United States with iron for the next two or three centuries, are a wild, picturesque range of bluffs, looking like decayed old castles along the haunted Rhine, half hid by trailing shrubs and clambering vines, rich with many-colored leaves.

> "It was rugged, steep and wild,
> Where naked cliffs were rudely piled;
> And ever and anon between
> Lay velvet tufts of loveliest green;

And the honeysuckle loved to crawl
Up the low crag, and ruined wall.
And still they seemed like shattered towers,
The mightiest work of human powers."

The Illinois side is low and sandy, a forest rising up in the distance.

Our passengers are from all places. Here we have the Marseillese, talking about Parisian life, Napoleon the Great, and Louis the XIV. One would think France had but two great men, and *they* were the two, to hear him talk. In fact, she has but two—Napoleon and Louis XIV are the only ones she has immortalized in painting and sculpture.

"I speak very correct English, better that most 'Mericans themself," says he, showing the true Yankee dispatch in curtailing his sentences.

Here we have the Mississippian and lady, whose accent on many words bespeak them Southrons; the Tenneseean, who never says Tennes*see*, as we of the North do, but accenting the first syllable, says, *Ten*nessee.

That young lady—a Southern blonde—has just returned from a four years' sojourn in Scotland, and is going home to Memphis. The one by her side, of stately figure, is an actress from Philadelphia, going to New Orleans.

Here we have a young German of dress, a true child of the mist, who has made a tour of the United States and is now going to spend the winter in Cuba.

There you see two or three gentlemen from Kentucky and Arkansas, listening to a Pennsylvania Dutchman's story about how he opposed the tariff in CLAY times, fearing "that if they got it into operation they'd run the darned old thing right through his barn." He was like many good honest farmers who had been bewildered with the fabulous accounts of the "locomotive," but have since seen it, and now the wonder ceases.

That gentleman with the sandy whiskers and moustache, is the proprietor of the St. Charles Hotel in New Orleans.

"And thereby hangs a tale."

He was a poor Yankee boy, who left his home in New England to seek his fortune in the great West, and finally wandered off to New Orleans, and is now by sheer industry and economy, proprietor of one of the first hotels in America.

Those nabobs in the old world, whose fortunes seek them, would be startled at the accounts of fortunes sought and made by the industry and thrift of young Americans. And many an American boy, now hawking his penny papers about the streets of our cities, may yet stand unshadowed by the side of the richly possessed nabobs of Europe. That little ragged urchin that offers his apples to our rich German at "two pennies apiece," may yet smoke a "meerschaum" with him sailing down his castled Rhine.

Here is a Kentuckian, who has been telling me about the CLAY family. His father lived a neighbor to the "Sage of Ashland," and although opposed to him in politics all his life, yet he always loved him. It was true that the children were inclined to insanity. He met JOHN in St. Louis last Fall; he hated to go home, the old lady and the boys made such a "fuss" about that "affair of his horse-trainer." It is well known that JOHN CLAY shot his groom in the streets of Lexington.

Mrs. CLAY was a very domestic lady; and JAMES B. had incurred the displeasure of the Kentuckians, and the ridicule and sarcastic wit of GEORGE D. PRENTICE, for rebuilding his father's house. It was the property of Kentucky on the death of her noblest son.

As if to complete the variety of our passengers, we have that rare specimen of *homo genus*, who, whether on the banks of the Mississippi, Sacramento or Ganges, is noted for his industry and thrift—a *live Yankee*. He is going South to teach school, or to "get up" a class in music, or peddle eight-day clocks; and should he fail in these he has a reserve in a large supply of "Prof. HASKELL'S Electric Oil."

We were entertained this evening by the singing and piano-playing, at the other end of the cabin, of our "SIDDONS," whom we have mentioned. We laid by last night, afraid to venture among the shallows.

A rainy morning. We have stopped at Cape Girardeau to take in some flour. It is a small town lying on the slopes of the bluffs. It has some fine buildings—mills, a convent, and a grand University building, situated on the apex of a beautiful terraced eminence. Students were walking about the ground.

In a talk with a planter from Kentucky, going to New Orleans to sell his tobacco, about our buying of England all our railroad iron, he remarked, pointing to the "Iron Mountains" on the Missouri side, "There we have inexhaustible treasures of it, and that which is better, too. We are fools, and the dupes of greater fools; our bargains are made for us by other men, and we've got to stand it."

We are gradually approaching the region of perpetual summer; and I am getting acquainted with that class of people that live on the borders of it—the real Southrons.

Here I am listening to a Louisiania planter and a Michigan farmer, talking about BUCHANAN, wheat and cotton; then to a bustling Eastern man, talking to a Western pioneer.

The skies are clear again, and we have gone upon the hurricane deck "prospecting." Missouri walls up the

Mississippi yet with castellated bluffs, but the monotonous sand-bars, and young growth of cotton-wood continues on the other side, while the great "Father-of-waters" goes rolling on in grand sweeps around the bends and islands, in his course South.

Here sits the actress, our "SIDDONS," pensively musing with a book in her hand; a JULIET thinking of her ROMEO; or is she musing on the tale of romance told by these rude, ivy-covered rocks—these

"Battled towers and donjon keeps!"

Was not that HINDA'S bower on that one peering above the rest? And is she not watching HAFED, as he climbs the steep ascent, leaping from rock to rock, till he gets on that jutting crag from which

"When she saw him rashly spring,
And midway there in danger cling,
She threw him down her long black hair,
Exclaiming breathless, There, love! there!"

But I am seated now, and we are talking with our pretty tourist from Scotland. Who can think of that country and not of her SCOTT, the wizard of the North? She had visited Melrose Abbey, and following Sir WALTER'S directions, she had gone at night.

"If thou wouldst view fair Melrose aright,
Go visit it by pale moonlight;
For the gay beams of lightsome day
Gild but to flout the ruins gray."

And she had seen Abbotsford, "that romance of stone and mortar," and Dryburgh, and had visited Sir WALTER'S tomb, and MIADA'S, too.

But, here we are on a sand-bar! Backing off, we take a turn and plough through in another direction. The air is soft and balmy. How pleasant to have the warm Southern breezes kissing your cheeks, while your friends at home are shivering in the cold November winds.

We passed the "graves," and left the Alleghany stranded on one of them. We had been playing "hide and seek" with her among the islands, bends and curves in the river, all the way from St. Louis. But now we have left her, poor thing! in distress. She remained there, stranded, for nearly twenty-four hours. We got to Cairo by sunset, and there laid by all night.

This morning it is truly in the "fogs" of Egypt. This town has a criminal reputation. The inhabitants are called "Thugs," and travelers tell hard stories about their "robbing," and now and then a man's "being heard of no more," after he had sought their hospitality.

From the limestone bluffs, at Alton, commences what is called the American bottoms, and continues to the mouth of the Ohio. The people here call this bottom, or lower part of Illinois, Egypt, from its near resemblance to ancient Egypt. It is a great country for corn; its capital, or principal town, is Cairo; and in point of intelligence, the darkness of Egypt covers the land.

We left the Alleghany here. We have got the "tag" now, and we will keep it unless the sand-bars hold us as they did her yesterday, and she gets it as we did, and runs away.

But we are leaving the limestone bluffs of Missouri. The last stone bluffs are seen in descending about thirty miles above the mouth of the Ohio, and below the mouth of the river, the alluvion, the river flats, broadens from thirty to forty miles in width, still expanding to the Balize, where it is three times that width. And three-fifths of this alluvion is either dead swamps of cypress forest, or stagnant lakes, or creeping bayous, or impenetrable cane-brakes, a great part of it inundated.

From St. Louis to the mouth of the Ohio, on the West side of the river, the bluffs are generally near it, seldom diverging from it more than two miles. These are mostly perpendicular masses of limestone, sometimes shooting up into towers and pinnacles, presenting, as JEFFERSON observes, at a distance, the appearance of the battlements and towers of an ancient city.

At the Cornice rocks, and the cliffs above St. Genevieve, they rise between two and three hundred feet above the level of the river. They are imposing spectacles in the distance. We might mention among them that gigantic mass of rocks, forming a singular island in the river, called the "Grand Tower," and the shot towers of Herculaneum. Two striking peculiarities of this river are often unobserved.

First, no person who descends it receives on his first trip a clear and adequate idea of its grandeur, and the amount of water that it carries. When he sees it descending from the Falls of St. Anthony, that it swallows up one river after another, with mouths as wide as itself, without affecting its width at all; when he sees it receiving in succession the mighty Missouri, which changes the color of the waters, making them muddy—

> "So the Mississippi, lucent to the brim,
> Wedded to Missouri, takes her hue from him,
> And is pure no longer,——"

the broad Ohio, St. Francis, Arkansas and Red, all of them of great depth, length and volume of water—absorbing them all, and retaining a volume apparently unchanged, and, strange to relate, even growing narrower;

when he sees all this he begins to estimate the force, fury, overwhelming power and increasing depth of the current as it sweeps and rolls on to the great Gulf.

The other peculiarity is the uniformity of its "meanders"—the points and bends in its course. One would think that the deep and frequent draughts it had taken—an accumulating force with no increasing width—that this would cause it irregularly to sway from side to side, like a drunken POLYPHEMUS. But what is most remarkable, there is "method in this madness." The curves are often described as with the decision of a compass. Having performed this sweep, or half-circle, the current is precipitated across its own channel, and describes another curve of the same regularity on the opposite shore. Thus the great "Father-of waters" goes on in a grand waltz to the ocean. The curves are so regular, that boatmen and Indians formerly calculated distances by them, instead of estimating their progress by the mile or league.

Opposite these bends there is always a sand-bar, matched in its convexity to the concavity of the curve. Here on this bar you see those young cotton-wood groves in their most striking appearance. The trees rising from the shore, showing the present year's growth, while those of the second, third, fourth, fifth, and so on, recede and rise higher in regular gradations, with foliage varying in hues from the pale to the deep and deeper green, till they gain the ancient wood.

"'Tis a scene that would delight a Shenstone."

Then in the middle of the stream you often find beautiful islands. One would think them the charming haunts of river nymphs, they have such an aspect of beauty as they appear at a distance swelling from the stream, clothed in their woody grandeur; and when sunset gilds them they look

"Like emeralds chased in gold."

As we sailed out from among these "fairy isles" we often came suddenly in sight of the "silvery sand-bars," the resort of innumerable geese, cranes, pelicans and water-fowl.

The whole river scene I have described is most poetically and truthfully delineated by LONGFELLOW in his EVANGELINE. In fact, it is one of the fine poetical descriptions of a scene which one rarely finds, that it will do to read on the spot:

"Day after day they glided down the turbulent river;
Now through rushing chutes, among green islands, where plum-like
Cotton-trees nodded their shadowy crests, they swept with the current,
Then emerged into broad lagoons, where silvery sand-bars
Lay in the stream, and along the wimpling waves of the margin,
Shining with snow-white plumes large flocks of pelicans waded."

But there goes the "gong!" I must leave the contemplation of this broad and magnificent river, winding on toward the tropics amid landscape scenes so delightful for the eye to roam over, and hasten down to dinner.

It is like sitting down to a banquet to take seat at one of these tables. One wants the faculty of Sir WALTER SCOTT in describing a feast, to give an idea of the repasts on board one of these steamers.

Some rich soup leads—but let our Marseillese describe them:

"You have grand table on the Mississippi steamers—grand table—better than I get at the Astor House or St. Charles, New Orleans; grand table. I travel up and down this river quite often, for the good living you get on these steamboat. But you have *miserable* poor brandy and wine; miserable poor. It makes one feel bad, very bad, to get drunk in America; but mighty pleas*ont* in France; mighty pleas*ont*."

A Mississippi steamer is a miniature world afloat, or as our Kentuckian expresses it, "Should the world be deluged again, it would only be necessary, by way of preserving the human family, to save one of these Mississippi steamers as a 'nest-ark,' which generally contains, not only the animal kingdom represented in 'pairs' but the human family by nations."

One not only finds its passengers of a many-placed variety, but the various parts that men "act" in life you find here represented, the serious, gay and comic.

B., our Kentuckian, is a true son of COMUS. He does our song-singing, fluting, violining and story-telling. He is a medley. His entertainment this evening began with some piece of spirit and sentiment, or a hymn. Then, "OLD UNCLE NED," followed by some boatman's song.

After this came in passages from HAMLET or RICHARD III. He is endeavoring to draw the auditors from our "Actress," who is entertaining the other end of the cabin with singing and music from the piano.

We have, of course, among the variety, the "suspicious character," and they appear to be among those that are so much attached to the card-table. Several of them seem to express the gambler in his genuine character. Though our New York city merchant tells me they have not the real gambler aboard; still the wine and brandy they invariably have to grace their table, makes their playing look like the game in its most earnest phase.

But at the other end of the cabin, cards are played in a gay and more amusing manner. Our Yankee has been over with the ladies "whisting." Their part of the cabin is prohibited us, unless we pay five dollars extra, or travel with a lady. "He must needs be a bold rider that leaps the fence of custom." But once tell a Yankee of anything desirable, and his ingenuity will get it at the lowest possible figure.

The application of steam to locomotion, and the magnetic telegraph, appear to have supplied the latest wants of mankind up to this date. And though

> "Man wants but little here below,
> He'll not want that little long,"

if he only makes his need known to an ingenious Yankee, who is the only man now-a-days that believes in the Latin maxim, "*Nil mortilibus arduum est*,"—nothing is impossible for mortals. And in whatever enterprise he engages he bears

> "That banner with the strange device"—
> *Eureka!*

This is the Sabbath on the great "Father-of-waters." Could we catch sight of Father HENIPEN and his two companions, as they were dropping down the river in their frail canoe, we would hail the good old Jesuit and invite him on board to preach for us. A sermon, though Jesuitical, would be better than none. But I think the wonder excited by our steamer would rather frighten the old Father from a sermon into curiosity and amazement.

It appears that we have almost every other profession on

board to-day save that of the clergyman. The passengers seem to be conscious that it is the Sabbath, and show some slight change in their appearance. Even B. is more quiet; yet you can see that mirth and jollity are "pent up" in him, for he seems uneasy, and frequently in a low humming of some song, a whole line escapes audibly, by way of relief.

It has rained during the night, and continues this morning. The great canvass curtain has been let down about the fore-castle to keep the rain from beating in on the freight.

Arkansas is on our right, and Tennessee on our left. The landscape grows broader and more level, the shores lower and more monotonous. I have had a long talk with S. of Philadelphia, on Religion and Phrenology. He believes the latter and is sceptical on the former. He had better change—give his belief to Religion and his scepticism to Phrenology.

About four this morning we reached Memphis. Many of our passengers stop here. I shall miss some of them very much. A few days' acquaintance here has made it seem as if we had known each other for a year or more.

I arose and went out to the fore-castle; it was not daylight yet; nothing but a dim, obscure outline of buildings could be discerned. By endeavoring to find some form and comeliness to them, gazing in the dark, I found the effort hurt my eyes. We sailed away with such an impression of Memphis as the Daguerrean would get from his subject on smoked tin. The recollection of sailing along by these scenes and places in the night is like the faint remembrance one has of places he has visited in his dreams. Trees looked less nipped by the frost here.

Came to Helena, a "snatch" of a village, with a bad reputation, lying on the banks of the river, on the Arkansas side. We often meet men and boys in small boats and skiffs, darting by us across the stream.

We were much amused this noon, at table, by a stalworth Kentuckian. His uncombed hair, coarse boots, and brusque appearance, described him oddly among the rest. The waiter had given him beef steak as he directed, which he began to eat, but shortly desisted. He looked over to the rest, apparently to see how they got along with theirs. One could evidently see that he was in trouble—that he had either lost his appetite, or that there was a wrong somewhere. He tried his steak again, essayed to masticate it, stopped, threw down his knife and fork, looked up toward the waiter, who was some distance from him, and cried out, loud enough to startle the whole table: "Here, waiter, take this 'ere beef; it's tougher'n thunder! Give me something I can eat!"

A heavy fog rests on the river this morning, and hems in sight. Just as we arose from the breakfast table we were almost staggered from our feet. The steamer in the dense fog had run against the bank. She staggered back and reeled like a drunken sailor, then sheered off and went on again. We all rushed to the fore-castle, but the fog was there and nothing more. They tell us they had the first frost here last night, November 10th.

Here on the Mississippi side planters' houses appear in sight, sitting in a covert of green trees, with negro cabins neatly white-washed in rows near by them.

> "Along the shores of the river
> Shaded by China-trees, in the midst of luxuriant gardens,
> Stood the houses of planters, with their negro cabins and dove-cots."

The river is low, and even here we sound our way along. "Quarter less twain!" cries the man with the line below. "Quarter less twain!" echoes some one on the hurricane deck to the pilot at the wheel. "Quarter more twain!" &c., &c., all cried out to the pilot who steers the boat accordingly.

But we "caught a Tartar" last night. He has made more stir and noise since he came on board than we have had in the whole trip before. He is a rattling, garrulous talker on politics, or any other subject. He is among us like "the boy that puts the chip on the shoulder," then urges some one to knock it off, which leads to contention and blows. I fear some of us will part in a quarrel.

About noon Vicksburgh appeared in sight, ten miles off, resting on a hill-side. But we have lost sight of it in going round this bend. There it is again! lying like a thing of romantic beauty on the side of hills that slope to the river. "From the foot of this irregular side of the summit, the dwellings are scattered in the most picturesque manner. Upon every green knoll, rise of ground or accessible cliff, you see cottages of every style and form, seated in nests of flowers and evergreens. The streets, some of them terraces in the hill-side, are parallel with the river, and rise one above the other, so that the galleries of the houses on one often project over the tops of those on the other." The principal business streets have many fine, commodious blocks of brick and stone. They were not crowded, but had the quiet, composed air of the city mart. The levee is not paved, but covered, to-day, with goods, swarms of carts and drays, and moving things. It is truly a walk up-hill to get into the city.

Beyond the business streets we came to those of residences. Here the air was "balm and rosemary;" the gardens were radiant with flowers, and green with perennial shrubs and trees. The arbor vitæ shot up, trimmed in the shape of a cone; the orange myrtle fashioned in the shape of a huge pine-apple, and others trimmed in various other shapes, stood, with their smooth, symmetrical tops, here and there, amid those of nature's untrimmed, luxuriant growth, with their boughs loosed in the wind. Seated amid these were the residences. And hid in a covert of them were those "bird nests"—bowers and summer-houses, clambered over, scented and thatched by the jessamine and woodbine.

Which of these, thought I, is "Club Castle," once the home of S. S. PRENTISS, that brilliant star that shot from the Northern into the Southern hemisphere, dazzling all eyes till it set in its noon-day splendor. They told me many interesting stories about him here. How suddenly he acquired fame among them. The sunshine shed upon their law by his transcendent genius; the wizard power and brilliancy of his eloquence. While he resided in this city, he was in the flower of his forensic fame—in the full freshness of his unmatched faculties.

Finding here an old resident of Michigan, I went with him to a private boarding-house. On paying my bill the next morning, I found, as I often had before on my trip, that

"Thereby hung a tale."

Fifty cents more! But I had got over the apex of exorbitant charges when the barber on the steamboat charged me forty cents for shaving my upper lip. Thinking that he undoubtedly regarded me as some eastern prince, I paid him without a murmur.

At noon I took the trig, excellent little "Packet Steamer, Home," that runs between Vicksburgh and Yazoo City, on the Yazoo river, for Satartia. Leaving the turbid Mississippi, with a current of a mile in width, for this gentle stream of only thirty rods' breadth, was an agreeable change. Its banks are willow-skirted, and the trees in many places are tall, and leaning over the stream from each side, nearly half arch it.

> "Over our heads the soft, tenebrous boughs of the willow
> Met in dusky arch, and trailing mosses in mid air waved,
> Like banners that hung on the walls of ancient cathedrals."

The scenery seemed to me Arcadian, as we sailed up this winding passage of green, and now and then caught glimpses of cotton plantations through the opening willows along the banks. It was getting night, and the sombre-green shade on each side of us grew deeper and deeper as day departed. The banks began to be busy with their dusky images, and now and then a fragment of old tradition about this river, would come across my mind, which fancy would seize, enlarge upon and shape to her liking. I saw the dark forms of the Yazoo warriors moving about among the trees on either side, and "wreaths of smoke ascending through the foliage, betrayed the half-hidden wigwam." But the light from the windows of a plantation house dispelled all fancy's sombre imagery, and left me with the actual fact that the Yazoo Indians disappeared from this valley more than a century ago.

Twelve miles above the mouth of this river are the Yazoo hills, and four miles higher the site of Fort St. Peter, an ancient French settlement, which these Yazoo Indians destroyed in 1729; and they in their turn have long since been unheard of.

On this river and the country which it waters, was laid the scheme of the famous "Yazoo Speculation," which will long be remembered by its unfortunate victims. This speculation aroused the eloquence, and incited the taunts, invectives, and withering sarcasm of JOHN RANDOLPH.

I have met on board the "Home," the gentleman, a Mississippi planter, whose carpet-bag was rifled on board the "Alleghany," the morning that the watch and porte-monnaie were stolen from the "Woodruff;" also a young man from New York, who has come South to teach.

But here we are at Satartia. Let me see—Satartia, Yazoo county, Mississippi, is put down in my memorandum as the terminus of my journey. That journey was commenced at 12 o'clock at night, and, after twelve days' travel, it is finished at 12 o'clock at night. What am I to divine from this, save that I left off as I begun? That is, that I am the same cold, forbidding Northerner, here in the warm heart of the sunny South, that I was twelve days ago when I left home.

An old negro, whose hair was as silvery as the moonlight that fell upon it, took one of my trunks, and placing it on his head, told me to follow him and he'd take me to the tavern. We were soon at the door, and after thumping awhile, both of us by turns, a plump, dapper little man opened it, struck a light, and invited me in. My second trunk was brought, the charge asked, and answered, "Three bits." Three bits! what's that? Mine host replied, "Tis tree sheeling." Paid the old negro his three bits, was shown to my room, and—and—I'm tired and weary—good night.

## CHAPTER III.

> "Nothing seemed so pleasant to hope for or to keep,
> Nothing in the wide world so beautiful as sleep."
>
> MACKAY.

That most luxurious of sleepers, SANCHO PANZA, and who was grateful enough to "benison" the man who invented the luxury he loved so much to indulge in, probably never slept any sounder than we did last night. If we remember right, not the scattered fancy of a dream disturbed our repose. Our long, wearying journey had prepared us admirably for this rest.

It was a beautiful morning in the sunny South as we walked out, thinking to find Satartia a lively village of considerable size. Seeing only a few houses in sight we walked on, supposing we were in the suburbs, to find more of the town, but soon walked out of it. We went back to the tavern-porch and surveyed it—it is not half of a place. The houses are all poor and shabby, and have no shade to hide their tatters. The old negro told me, last night, that he had lived here thirty years. He, no doubt, has seen the rise, progress and dilapidation of the town. It had flourished once with the trade and traffic of four or five stores. Those were its "palmy days." Now it has only two stores—poor, low buildings; a tavern, dentist, doctor and shoemaker.

But "mine host" makes up much for what the place lacks. He has as many occupations as HUMPHREY CLINKER had titles. His like cannot be found. He is landlord, landlady, *fille de chambre*, cook, waiter, bar-tender, porter, hostler, and does all the village tailoring, patching and mending. He is a Scotchman, born in Quebec, thence emigrated to Mackinaw, thence to Prairie du Chien, thence to St. Louis in 1820, when it had only four thousand inhabitants, thence to Vicksburgh, Mississippi, thence to Satartia; and here the good people in Satartia, and the planters about it, are determined he shall pass the remainder of his days as their good and kind "publican." Should any of my Northern friends come to Mississippi, and stop at Satartia, my word for it, endorsed with a day and a half's hospitality and good fare, they will find "UNCLE MAC" their trustworthy and kind-hearted landlord.

After breakfast, which was plain and good, I called upon several Satartians, whose names had been given me as principal men in this place, but I could ascertain nothing in regard to schools; they'd had none here, time out of mind; and they knew of no place in the country where a teacher was wanted.

As I had yet to go ten or twelve miles into the country, to my friend's, Major W., I asked if I could get a horse and carriage for that purpose. There was but one carriage owned in town, and that could not be got. The people here traveled mostly on horseback. Could I have a horse and saddle, then? Not one to be found. The horses were all in use, or they were like JOHN-A-DUCK's mare, "they'd let nobody ride them but JOHN-A-DUCK." In this dilemma, a young gentleman visiting here from New Orleans, informed me that one of Mr. H.'s negroes was in town, and, as he was going to Major W.'s plantation, I could send a letter by him, informing him of my arrival. A note was written and sent.

The next morning a little negro boy came on a mule, bringing me a horse and saddle. Leaving my trunks with

"UNCLE MAC," I mounted my horse and followed my little guide. He "wasn't going to take me," he said, "round by the carriage road through the uplands, twelve miles, but was going through by the shortest way, along the valley." It was the bridle-path, three or four miles nearer, from Satartia.

But ere we had got out of sight of town we were overtaken by a young man on horseback. He was an overseer, in search of a place. Said his name was HAYNE. I asked him if he was kin to ROBERT Y. HAYNE, of South Carolina. "Yes, he was. He had the pure blood of the HAYNES in him." And when I praised that young orator, who, like the great champion of debate whom he so ably withstood in the United States Senate, was gifted with a little of that spirit that would raise mortals to the skies, he raised himself in his stirrups and spurred his horse with pride as he said, "Yes *sir*, he gin WEBSTER *jessie*."

But riding under these trees through the woods we find our hats brushed off by the limbs occasionally, and our heads combed in rather too brusque a manner. Leaving the river we came into a portion of valley wood-land, about midway in which we met several horsemen with rifles on their shoulders, and powder-pouches strung around them, on a hunt, attended by a bevy of hounds. They had "started" a deer, and were in pursuit of him. They wished to know if we had seen him. Being informed that we had not, they spurred their horses on to the chase again.

Our little sable guide rides ahead and opens the gates, when we come out of the woods to them, and often tells us we are getting off the track, by following some of the many trails that branch off from the main path. We passed through several door-yards, by log plantation-houses, and along plantations yet snowy with cotton-flakes, and speckled with negroes. This was a novel sight to me.

My day-dream of years was here realized—to see the sunny South with its fields of "mimic snow."

I remember the first cotton-field I ever saw. It was in OLNEY'S old Geograpy. The overseer stood with his arms folded, whip in his hand, off a little way from the negroes hoeing in the cotton-field. The big white blossoms hung, like snow-balls, among the green leaves, from the little plants. It was really—this cotton-field in a book—a *picture*-sque scene for my school-boy eyes; and how much pleasanter it was for the negroes to be hoeing in such a pretty field, than it was for me to hoe my "stint" in the garden, so many rows of corn or potatoes, every Saturday afternoon when there was no school.

But here was a picturesque scene, drawn by an "old master"—Nature. The cotton was higher; in many places over the heads of the negroes; and they were picking instead of hoeing it; and the overseer was on horseback, or in some fields was walking round among the negroes. But he had the same broad-rimmed hat on, and the same whip in his hand, and he was overseeing the same negroes. But yet how different! The painter's best representations of the world are pleasing things; but the world that is not painted is the most interesting to see. My only trouble was, I was so much absorbed in these scenes around me, that I would forget that I was on horseback, and often found myself grasping at the saddle-bow, or the pony's mane to keep myself aboard. Then again, at the loud laugh of the negroes, or at some of them darting up suddenly from among the cotton rows, or from out the corners of the fence, my little craft would start so quick, and "shy off," that he would leave me "half seas over."

After something over an hour's ride we came to Major W.'s plantation. It is in the valley. Here is the old plantation-house, in which the family formerly resided, but which is now occupied by the overseer, and here are the "quarters," the negro cabins. The family live in the uplands, some two miles from here; their home is called the "Ridge House." The "old house" sits on a green knoll that overlooks the whole plantation. It is built of logs, and is unchinked on the inside; the clefts between the logs are battened on the outside, with cypress shakes. The roof comes down low in front and rests on posts, thus forming a porch the whole length of the building. In this porch Major W. can sit and read his *Picayune*, *Delta*, *Crescent*, or *Day Book*, while he can see below him any thing that transpires on any part of his plantation. This open porch continues in an open hall that divides the house into two rooms, one at each end.

The negro cabins are of logs. They are a part of them a few rods to the left of the house, on this knoll that runs out from it, like a terrace in the bluffs that rise behind them. And part of them are perched a little higher up, on little cliffs and knolls, looking at a distance like great rooks' nests that had dropped down from the wood above them. It is not often that Nature has terraced down these bluffs with graded steps, so that you can ascend by means of them from the valley to the uplands. She has generally sloped them down at a sweep, or knocked off the tops of them, and tumbled them down below, forming a broken, irregular descent. Here you follow a carriage path around the foot of the knoll on which the house sits, and which then goes winding through the bed of the ravine, between two towering bluffs, till it reaches the uplands.

Having arrived at the gate, at the foot of the sloping lawn, in front of the house, I was met by Major W.'s two oldest sons. They showed me much attention, respect and kindness. The eldest, a recent graduate from Nashville Military Academy, had just returned from a hunt; his horse yet saddled, with the bridle thrown loosely over his neck, was cropping the Bermuda grass on the side of the knoll; his hounds lay here and there, on the side of the slope, resting after the chase. The other son was acting overseer for the time being. They excused their delay in not sending a servant sooner to me at Satartia—their father was from home with the carriage, and the horses were away, and they had to wait till their return.

"But walk in, Mr. VAN BUREN; this rain and mist will wet you through." We walked up the sloping knoll to the house. The air was rather cool, and the house so open that I felt even chilly by their fireside. It was near noon. My first meal with a planter I shall never forget. We had "corn-dodgers," pork, some butter, sweet potatoes and coffee. But the fare, though rather coarse, was a banquet in the cheerful way it was given. The rain had now increased, and it was deemed best that I should stay here all night. I found part of a library in the room, and an old set of college books. The uncle, who works his slaves in conjunction with Major W., has a room here, and these are his books. He, too, is a graduate of the Nashville Military Academy. He is an intelligent young man, has read many books, in conversation is agreeable, in manners a very pleasant gentleman.

Dr. H., physician of the immediate neighborhood, joined us at night-fall; and while the rain was pattering on the roof, and dripping off the eaves, we conversed the time away around the cheerful fireside. Dr. H. is a native of Indiana; has been here four years as a practicing physician; likes the South well, but thought the inconvenience of getting about here, and, at first, the loneliness of a planter's life, and all of the many things that you would miss here that you enjoyed at home, were apt to induce a disease on a Northerner that baffled the skill of the physician and all his drugs. A disease as incident to the stranger in India, in Europe, on the banks of the Hudson, as on the Yazoo; and though it had baffled ESCULAPIUS and all of his disciples ever since, there was an unfailing specific remedy for it, and that remedy every one found at home. Then if I should get this disease, my remedy would be to take "home-path-ie" doses, and continue them till I got to Battle Creek, Michigan.

In the morning Master HARRY W. came after me; his mother requesting me to come to the family house. We reached the uplands by the ascent of the winding path referred to above. The road to the "Ridge House" is mostly on the crest of a ridge.

The first thing I observed in the woods, as new to me, was the long moss hanging in dingy gray streamers from the limbs of the trees. The whole tree-top, like the head of MEDUSA, before MINERVA changed her beautiful locks, hung thick with long, flowing tresses. These streamers are five or six feet long. To see all the trees draped with them, it gives the woods a lovely mournfulness—a beautiful gloom. Some Southern poet has given this fine description of this moss:

"There is a little tangled moss that grows
Within our Southern clime,
And in the fanning breezes hangs and flows,
Like flakes of hoary rime.
Far in the wild woods' lone recesses,
Where the brown shadows seem
Like living things, its undulating tresses
From the long branches stream."

The oak and hickory predominate here, along these ridges; the cane grows green and luxuriant in the ravines. The bay, or cucumber tree, was pointed out to me. It looked like our bass-wood, but its leaves, which had fallen from the tree, and now carpeted the ground with their rich pale yellow, were three times as large as those of the bass-wood tree. The frosts come much later here than at the North, though part of the

"Forest has been rifled
By the gusty thieves,
And the book of nature
Is getting short of leaves."

A few moments' ride through the woods, and we were alighting from our horses at the gate of the "Ridge House." Here I met a cordial reception from Mrs. W., a lady of true Southern frankness—of a generous and spirited nature, and whose countenance expresses much of the feeling of her heart. She is an Arkansas lady, passed her early life at Little Rock, at a time when the Indian "border feuds" made it necessary for Government to keep military stations along the lines, one of which was at the capital of Arkansas. The society of Little Rock had many military officers in it, hence it had a tinge of "border chivalry." I have heard her often speak of dancing with some of our military chieftains, who had acquired a fame in the "feuds" of our Southern border—men who tripped

"The light footstep in the dance,
But firm their stirrup in the lists."

A relation of her family has some celebrity as a literary writer. She is also a kin of Mrs. James K. Polk. Soon a very pretty young lady came into the room, whom she presented to me as Miss Mattie W., her daughter. The rest of the family are small. I met here an interesting young lady from the North, Miss Bessie G., their teacher. She had the bloom of the Northern rose in her cheek. She came South, as she afterwards told me, "for the romance of the thing."

The family had been expecting me for some time. I had brought letters of introduction to them from my friend, Miss E. M. P., of New York, who had resided with them as a teacher, and who had told me much about them and the South; so that they had the preface to an acquaintance with me in my letters, and I had a page or two of acquaintance with them through my friend, when we met.

The young ladies were about going to church when I arrived. After a few moments' conversation they excused themselves, and were soon in their riding habits. Their horses were brought to the door, and after being gaily seated in their saddles, they reined their palfreys round, and with the boldness of DIE VERNONS, galloped away through the woods to church. This, no doubt, was something of the "romance of life" that Miss G. was enjoying South.

Speaking of Miss, let me further add:—I have observed that, instead of saying Miss G., they say, Miss BESSIE; calling a young lady by her christened name prefixed with Miss. Also, in speaking of a married lady, instead of saying Mrs., they say, Mistress. And, in addressing, or speaking to a person at a little distance, especially if they are not answered the first time, they use the fine explosive monosyllable, "Ho!" Thus, Ho, Mr. H.! Ho, Miss FANNIE!

Here I begin to see Southern life and observe Southern manners. Manners! How soon we notice them in another people—notice only as they vary from our own. We compare ourselves with others and mark the difference. And there is this about painting the manners of a people—first impressions are the best, because the truest. One is apt to observe less of the strange and novel, as he bides with another people, from the fact that he adopts more or less of their manners, and hence does not notice them, unless he has the individuality of an ARETHUSA, and can move among them intact. One might say that everything is different here from Northern life, and in order to become Southernized, one must go into pupilage—become a learner, and often, no doubt, a blunderer.

First, the table. This I find here with greater variety of meats than at the old plantation-house. Here we have excellent ham, boiled whole, a surloin of venison, and a dainty steak from "old Bruin," occasionally. Butter is not so common as it is on our Northern tables, and wheat bread is rare, or used in much smaller quantities. Corn bread is the Southron's staff of life. This I find on the table here of three kinds; the "muffin," which is the size of, but better than our best biscuit; the "egg-bread," which is "cousin-german" to our Johnny-cake, and the famed "corn-dodger," which is oval, and about the size of one's hand. The sweet potatoe is richer than any of its Irish, pink-eyed cousins; and we have the cousins, too. Coffee is here preferred to tea, but you can have tea, or milk, if you wish. One of the servants acts as "aid" to the waiter at table, bringing in warm viands to her, thus keeping "fresh supplies" on hand during the meal.

But the young ladies have returned from church, and say they have heard the "blind preacher" WIRT so finely describes. An old, blind, itinerant preacher, discourses to them in a church, some two miles away in the woods, among the hollies and evergreens. The preacher, sermon, rural scenery and all, would have inspired, they thought, the glowing pen of a WIRT:

## CHAPTER IV.

"Ridge, knoll, ravine, confusedly hurled,
The formation of an earlier world."

SCOTT.

I ought to have written to my friends at home ere this. EMERSON, I think, says, friends first, business next. And while I am thinking of an apology for one, the long list of others that are waiting for letters from me, come thronging across my mind, till I am not a little confused. In fact, I fear ere I get through to the last, that the apology will return like "NOAH'S dove," on impatient wing to the South.

While sojourning a few days at the "Ridge House," I had taken views on horseback of much of this part of Mississippi. This, besides being cavalierish, is the only way we "peers of the realm" have of riding here; for the rains make such sad havoc with the roads that a heavy shower of three or four hours, and you find your carriage half-spoke deep in mud or clay loam. And then, the ladies claim the carriage, at all times. A planter told me that he paid six hundred dollars for his carriage in Philadelphia, and though he had had it two years he had never rode a rod in it. You often meet the fair of the South, also, upon their palfreys, galloping through the woods.

Our horses are much more spirited than theirs, and the reason of it is obvious. They drive with more urging, longer distances, and over worse roads, and take less care of their horses, than we do. The planter, like the Bedouin, has his horse, of which he is not only sole proprietor, but no one is allowed to ride him but himself. Wherever he wishes to go, on a short trip, or a long journey over the country, this noble steed carries him on his back. But the Arab surpasses him in his love for his horse, which next to that for "Allah," is the "Mecca of his heart." Neither does he share his tent with him, nor part of his fare, but is oftener turned out shelterless, in the chilling blasts of a Southern winter, with nothing but his moiety of corn, and its dry leaves and "shucks." The carriage-horses belong to the planter's wife. They are seldom used for any purpose save on drives for her and her daughters. Each son has also his horse and trappings, the little children often riding some steady and well-behaved mule.

Riding out in a carriage a short time since with Mrs. W., she rallied me about my driving—holding the reins so tight. I told her we "held in" our horses. She replied, they "let theirs go."

Some number of miles from home we came to a "pass," different, but not less difficult than that of "Thermopylæ." I stopped the horses on its margin, and surveyed it. There was no way of getting round it. We must go through or go back. I asked her if we should not, like the Greeks, before going to battle, consult the oracles. She replied that I might if I felt alarmed, consult my goddess, DIANA, but let her have the reins and she would drive through. I drove through safe.

The upsetting of a carriage is nothing uncommon. The upland roads are not so bad; aside from being rougher, those in the valley are the most formidable. The nimble steeds of your Northern liveries would soon become "jaded" in a drive over these roads after a rain. Roads are the paths made to facilitate one's travel about the country—they lead to its improvement—to wherever man has erected a dwelling or built a town. But I should prefer a "cut off," or take it like a Yankee, "cross lots," climb fences, and risk the perils of "bush and briar;" or, were I mounted, run the break-neck hazards of a steeple-chase over hedge and ditch, to the heavy, treacherous plodding of these roads during the wet seasons.

What I had seen of the country in my first travel over it, was not only novel, but interesting to me. My mind had been filled with the different scenes and pictures of this new land, which, had I the descriptive power to transfer to these pages, as they first impressed me, I should be more satisfied that I had given a *true* description of this part of the South.

In the formation of Mississippi, the hill and mountain were not thought of, or if they were, they had all been lavished on the Alleghanies and Andes, the Cordilleras and Rocky. But everything else was, from the level to the "*ultima thule*" of the rough. The uplands are a coarse, geological network of ridges, ravines and gulleys, which certainly would have ill adapted it to husbandry, had not the plastic hand of nature formed here and there, among them, those beautiful oases—the cotton plantations.

The road often takes you round, following the ridge, like one of SANCHO PANZA'S stories, two miles or more, when it would be shortened to thirty rods could you cross the ravine. But as in reading one is often delighted with beautiful passages, figures and similes scattered along his way, so in riding along one of these roads you are often delighted in passing by forest scenery in all its leafy richness, and broad plantations with their beautiful cotton meadows.

Aside from the plantation the country goes to woodland, pasture and waste. You pass occasionly old plantations, worn out and deserted, overgrown with sedge and poverty stricken weeds.

By referring to the map of this State you will find that the Yazoo and Big Black run nearly parallel to the Mississippi. Mid-way, running between these, is a large ridge, or back-bone of land. From this there are ribs or ridges running out on either hand to the rivers. It is the same between the Mississippi and Yazoo. The rains dripping off these ridges, mingling with the soil as they go, turn torrents of muddy water into the gullies, which tumble it headlong into the rivers. Hence there are no clear streams here. They are all roily and of lazy current. How much of the beauty of the country is in the clear waters of its lakes and streams. I have seen no naiades sporting along the banks of Southern streams. Nor have I found here those playmates of my boyhood—bubbling runnels and whimpering brooks.

I think that courtly old angler—Izaak Walton—would find the pleasure in angling along these streams half gone. Such as he sings of in his "Angler's wish"—

> "I in these flowry meads would be;
> These *crystal* streams should solace me;
> To whose harmonious bubling noise
> I with my angle should rejoice."

But he that only *feels* the bite of the fish loses the better part of the sport. Let those politicians, who, disliking clearness, seek the troubled waters, fish here; give me clear streams.

I have only described the uplands. The valley-land is along the rivers, and, is either timbered lands clear'd off, or natural prairie. It is the richest soil of the South.

It is said that the earth is an old nurse, and that every thing shows that she is decrepid and wearing out. But these valleys that have produced a rich crop of cotton, year after year, for more than half a century, are as fertile to-day, and yield as large a crop of cotton, without fertilizing, as they did when first cultivated.

Nothing is more beautiful than to view this long, winding valley from some high bluff of the uplands, that wall it in on both sides of the river. Far along, as far as the eye can reach, you see both up and down the stream, from a half to two miles wide, nothing but fields of "mimic snow," doted here and there with planters' residences, set in green trees and shrubs, which, with the neat, whitewashed, negro cabins, ranged in rows near them, look like trim villas scattered along the vale. Much of the valley is yet open forest-land.

The upland is finely timbered, like the best oak openings of the North. The cypress grows in immense brakes in the swamps, and is their most valuable building timber. It is floated down the Yazoo and the Mississipi, in large rafts, by lumbermen, to New Orleans. There are large pine forests in many parts of the State.

That beautiful and richest leafed of all trees—the magnolia—you find here, standing among the gum, the oak, and the hickory, like a rich prince among his vassals. The holly too is here. The high leaves have no prickles on them, while the lower ones have. Hence SOUTHEY sings of it—

> "Gentle among my friends I'd be,
> Like the high leaves of the holly tree."

These evergreen hollies and magnolias standing among the common trees, seem like beautiful pledges of another spring, to the leafless forest, and one loves to catch the emblem and carry it out to an immortal spring time in the paradise of the blest.

I have often rein'd my horse from the road up to these lovely trees and stood and admired them.

The mistletoe rather took me by surprise. I had forgotten that I would find it here.

This bough—for that is all there is of it—like the fabled account of the bird of paradise, never touches the earth. It grows upon the tops of trees. You can see their evergreen plumes, perched here and there all through the woods, upon the high and leafless branches of the trees. Where they are thick they often kill the tree. They are said to be propagated by the birds.

The cane grows in luxuriance all through the woods; but the cattle and deer feed it down, save in the ravines, that are inaccessible to them. Here it shoots up into a rank, dense, deep-green growth. This cane affords pasturage for the cattle in the winter. The planter raises no grasses, no clovers. What little fodder he needs is supplied by the blades of corn his negroes pick from the corn stalks, and the corn "shucks" which he feeds his cows. Millet is raised in some places.

The apple tree does not do well here. A worm troubles it much. Its fruit is coarser than ours. Pears are raised in some localities plentifully. The peaches, they tell me, rival the famed ones of Jersey.

The planters' houses are mostly alike in style of building. They are long, log, story-and-a-half structures, verandaed in front and rear, with an open hall in the middle. They are elevated from the ground for coolness in summer, and retreat back from the road, like the old English cottage, spreading out broad lawns in front of them. They are generally surrounded with beautiful trees and shrubbery, much of it in evergreen, making even the rudest log building look romantic.

In thus adorning their grounds about their dwellings, and in cultivating a rich variety of flowers in their gardens, the planters exhibit fine taste.

But there is one plant he cultivates, which, if it does not exhibit his taste, does his wealth; and that, in common parlance, is called the cotton plant. Mississippi is a cotton growing State. She stands, among the other States, unrivaled in this field. This little plant is the wealth of the Ind to her. It has many enemies among the vermin, freshet and blight. But the season is kind to it; it is as tender over it as a lover over his mistress; not allowing the winds of March to visit it too roughly, nor the cold storms of December to hinder its being gathered in.

They are the whole year attending to it. One crop is scarcely secured ere another is planted. It brings the planter about forty dollars per acre. Think of seven hundred acres—that is not a large plantation—yielding him more than BUCHANAN'S salary. Planters make more money than Presidents. The modern adage—"Cotton is king"—that one often hears in reference to the influence this little plant gives to the planter, in home and foreign trade, is, in the *richest* sense of the word, true.

Finally, what strikes one as novel here, aside from the forest with its peculiar Southern trees—the plantation with its vast and almost interminable fields of cotton—is, you see no farm-land, no farm-home, with its orchards laden with fruit, with its small and well fenced fields of the various grains, grasses and clovers; you see nothing of the farming North, save the corn-field, and that, with a crop of such luxuriant growth that you would notice it as novel too.

Place Michigan where she was twenty years ago, in the rude days of her pioneer life, with her log houses, scattered here and there, three or four, and sometimes seven or eight miles apart, over the Southern portion of her territory, and give each a farm of from one to ten thousand acres, with from three hundred to three thousand acres cultivated on it, and you have something of an idea how Mississippi is settled.

I have thus given a crude sketch of this part of the South. I have only seen it in fall and winter. What it will be in full leaf and bloom, spring and summer will tell.

It is said the South, like CALYPSO, has a smile and a charm for every one of her defects; and not only detains her guests seven years, but usually the threescore and ten.

In regard to myself, after a sojourn of some months, I like her very much. I like her warm-heartedness and hospitality, which, though proverbial, is not all in the proverb. I like her beautiful climate, which has all the mildness of the temperate zone. I like her fine country, which has all the luxuriance of the tropics.

I have drawn a sort of geographical map of the country over which my adventures were made in search of a school, previous to giving their narrative, that you may better understand it when given.

---

## CHAPTER V.

"Half the ease and comfort he enjoys,
Is when surrounded by slates, books and boys."
CRABBE.

There was a species of the *homo genus* that PLATO did not include when he defined man—"A biped without feathers;" and which DIOGENES illustrated by stripping the plumes from a "rooster," and presenting it as PLATO'S man.

Neither did BUFFON include it, when he classified the animal kingdom, giving man his proper place.

BACON came nearer including this "*sui generis*" when he said "Man was science added to nature." And the great LUTHER actually dignified him, by giving him a position not second to that of the minister of the gospel. Of the various descriptions and portraits given of him we have space only for one.

"He was tall but exceedingly lank, with narrow shoulders, large arms and legs, hands that dangled a mile out of his sleeves, feet that might have served for shovels, and his whole frame most loosely hung together. His head was small, and flat at top, with huge ears, large green, glassy eyes, a long snipe nose, so that it looked like a weather-cock perched upon his spindle-neck to tell which way the wind blew. To see him striding along the profile of a hill, on a wintry day, with his clothes bagging and fluttering about him, one might have mistaken him for the Genius of Famine descending upon the earth, or some scarecrow eloped from a cornfield."

To complete the picture, let us draw his house.

"It was a low building of one large room, rudely constructed of logs; the windows partly glazed and partly patched with leaves torn from old copy-books. It was most ingeniously secured at vacant hours, by a withe twisted in the handle of the door, and stakes set against the window shutters, so that though a thief might get in with perfect ease, he would find some embarrassment in getting out."

This portrait is given as one, of course, of the common kind, drawn too by a writer who owes so much of his celebrity as a charming author, to one not much inferior, perhaps, to him that sat for the pen-portrait we have given.

But why this personage should be the subject of burlesque, and have his common faults portrayed by the humorist, for the amusement of mankind, I never could determine. Though we could give an instance, in our own land, in which one of these humble individuals has shaped and moulded the character of such men as the distinguished BUCKINGHAM, SALSTONSTALL, the great WEBSTER, the statesman CASS, the historian BANCROFT, both the EVERETTS, ALEXANDER and EDWARD—the American CICERO. They were all prepared for the parts they have acted, and are acting, by the individual of whom we speak.

He has ever been supposed to be a composition of useful drudgery, petty tyranny, indifferent respectability, some considerable learning, and any amount of patience and endurance. And his occupation has seldom received a higher name than—Knowledge made accessible by means of the birch. Though like the great Athenian, wherever he goes, he is followed by a crowd of the youth of the land, eager to catch his words of wisdom; yet, like that great and good Greek, though a benefactor and most useful man, his earnest and unwearied labor is ill requited; oftener by the "hemlock," than by deserved reward.

I am not a misanthrope and accuse mankind of being ungrateful—I know *people* are—to their benefactors; but I am one of the class I have been trying to portray—a pedagogue; and with the learned PAUL I would "magnify mine office"—have better school-houses, those more fitted to the great importance of their use. And I would do it for the same reason that CICERO defended the literature and learning of Rome—for my country—for its freedom and prosperity.

"The English alphabet is a more powerful weapon for its protection, than the bayonet. The school-teacher is a more efficient man for its defense, than the soldier. And those little school-houses, scattered all over our land, are better than forts and arsenals for securing its freedom and prosperity."

How many of this class have sought the South, I know not. But I know that the long catalogue has another name on it this morning. There is another one on the list of those whose services, like the Roman poet's hero—

> " Half with Phœbus grace did find,
> And 'tother half was whistled down the wind."

By many Northern teachers, the Roe's egg is supposed to be lacking to their temple of fame, one wreath wanting in their chaplet, till they are won in the South. Besides, a sojourn here would always be remembered as a fine episode in their lives.

I had sought the South, not so much to win this "pedagoguic laurel," as to find a healing balm in its mild and healthy climate for my injured health.

Having ascertained that the school I was to take charge of, on my arrival here, was yet in session, and rather than wait a month or two for its term to close, with a little of the bitter of uncertainty about getting it at all, to make waiting unpleasant, I concluded, during the while, to go out in search of a school, and thus see more of the country and people.

"There are some men who carry letters of recommendation in their faces, which are received and credited on presentation." But rather than trust to my face alone, as a rcommendation to the South, especially at a time when she was in no little "huff" with the North, I carried them in "little four nooked billets," with which my friend, before mentioned, had favored me.

Having ordered my horse, this morning, I mounted him —taking seat in a Mexican saddle, which was like sitting between the two humps on a camel's back—and started out to deliver my letters of introduction to the several planters to whom they were directed. Major W. was not at home—hence I went alone.

Leaving the Ridge House, I rode along on a level road; a fine open wood on one side, and in it I saw, not over half a mile from the family mansion, a small wood-colored school-house, modestly retired from the road, seated on a little eminence, in the midst of a beautiful wooded landscape.

It was Bellevue Academy; built by Major W. and some of his neighbors.

Here Miss G. was urging the little Southron youth along the flowery path of knowledge.

On the other side of the road was an old deserted plantation, lying with its broad rolling acres to the sun; covered with sedge, and tall, ragged weeds.

But it was a relief to look to my right, having passed the wood, to see a corn-field with its tall rustling stalks bending over with their long unhusked ears. The corn was what we of Michigan call the white and yellow dent, but it grew much taller.

Something over a mile brought me to an old weather-beaten, two-story shell of a house, though on a commanding site, and with some pretensions to cornice and finishings on the outside. It was on the deserted plantation. I began to question my directions' being right, that this was Dr. J.'s residence. It looked so forsaken and tenantless, and as I hallooed,

> "Methought an answer met my ear,—
> Yet was the sound so low and drear,
> So hollow and so faintly blown,
> It might be echo of my own."

I heard nothing but my own voice resounding in the vacant hall and apartments; and as I waited, in vain, for some one to come to the door, to see them moving about in the house, or among the trees, I began to fear, that if I waited too long, I should see something unreal; and was reining my horse around, to depart, when I saw a boy come limping through the hall. He came up, looking at me with such a fine pair of black eyes, and with such an intelligent face, that I resumed myself and asked him, if Dr. J. did not live here, and was at home.

He did, but he and his lady were away on a visit.

Getting the directions to Mr. H.'s plantation, I rode by a rather small field, thickly flecked with cotton and dotted with negroes, before whom the white flakes vanished like snow before a summer sun.

Passing a rough, log house in a large clump of oaks, I came in sight of the plantation sought. It had more the appearance of thrift about it than many I had seen. I noticed a little log blacksmith's shop hard by the "quarters," which were comfortable log cabins in rows by the roadside. His plantation-house stood amid shade-trees, but each one had just spread its carpet of leaves about it, so that you saw, unhid by the foliage, a plain log building, with the usual porch and open hall in the middle.

Mr. H. is a very frank gentleman; he has a head of fine cast; he reminded me of Senator STUART, of Michigan, though with a complexion of true Southern bronze. I should think him a prompt, business man.

After reading my letter, he told me that should I need any of his assistance in securing a situation as teacher among them, it would be cheerfully given.

At my departure he gave me the names of several gentlemen interested in schools, in Mechanicsburgh—a small village some eight miles distant.

In the afternoon, which is termed evening here, and the forenoon morning, I rode over a part of the country rolling and broken with ridges, but finely wooded with oak and hickory, which were all draped with the long streaming moss, and often thickly hung with trailing festoons of the grape-vine. The primitive beauties of the forest had not been marred, save in the more tillable and level portions of the country, where the plantations spread out their broad and showy fields; yet the green is lacking on the earth, except where the young shoots of the cane, strange weeds, and scattering wild flowers that the cattle and deer have not fed down are growing among the loose and variegated carpet of leaves.

Here, in the lonely woods, a little apart from the roadside, stands quite a large wood-colored church, built of cypress. It is the church in which our young ladies—mentioned a-back—had heard the blind preacher discourse "of that better land far away," last Sabbath. Farther on, away in the field, I saw a large white frame building, looking like a country tavern;—it was a plantation house.

Passing by a little frame building, that had once been a store, but was now occupied by a carpenter from Pennsylvania, who lives here among the planters, and works at his trade—commanding wages at from three to five dollars per day—I heard the sound of an anvil. It had really the brawny smithy's musical ring in it.

On reaching the shop—a low shanty—I saw a white smith at the forge, and a black smith at the bellows. The latter is Major W.'s HORACE who is an apprentice to the trade here.

Between this shop and Mechanicsburgh I passed several plantations—some small and very good looking ones, one larger, with a rail fence straggling round it, fallen down and broken in places, as if discouraged in the idea of enclosing such impoverished fields; and one with a nursery on it. You see no orchards laden with rich fruit near the planter's house. A few scattering apple and peach trees are all the orchards they have.

Mechanicsburgh is a ragged, uninviting town.

> "'Tis not what my fancy painted it—
> I'm sadly taken in."

I claim for it, par excellence, the title of *odd.* I believe I said more than twenty times while riding through it—"How odd!"

The road by which one approaches it, separates into two branches just after you get into the place. One of these branches follows off a crooked ridge, and the other takes an indifferent course—neither straight nor crooked.

The houses are built along these roads—odd looking streets.

Though the place was founded by mechanics, there is nothing square—straight or regular about it—it is built by "hook and by crook."

It has a "Grocery and Provision Store," a wagon and shoe shop, a brick building for an Odd Fellow's Lodge, and a school-house a mile out of town. To that I am going.

Coming in sight, I noticed a building—a little weather-beaten straggler from the village—that had stopped here by the road-side, under a few umbrageous oaks, as if for protection. A stick chimney run up at one end, on the outside, high enough to smoke one of its gables;—some of its window panes were out, and some were patched, and some were budding with jackets and shawls.

Hitching my horse to the fence, I rapped at the door, and—peace to his maves—"Domine SAMPSON" opened it, and gave me one of his earnest, quisitorial stares. But his face was round and fuller, his shoulders broader, and his whole frame more solid. He was not as "lank and spare" as usual. He had just got the new suit Col. MANNERING had given him; it even looked better and more fashionable; his boots were highly polished; he was dressed, in fine, like a Broadway dandy. It was said he changed his "dickey" every day.

A chain was hitched in a button hole of his vest, which led to an opera glass in his pocket. This he took out whenever any of his pupils brought their "sums" to him on their slates, and placing it to his eye, would glance over and correct them.

It was time for recess, of which fact he resolved the pupils by announcing in authoritative tones, "*The boys may go out.*"

At the word, books and slates dropped; some on the desk, and some on the floor; some were caught half way in the descent, and some were knocked off the desk by the pupils hurrying and crowding by in their haste to get out.

After this little "jail delivery," I had a few moments' conversation with the teacher.

He was, he said, giving instructions in the common branches, mostly. He had a few scholars in Trigonometry, yet he did not teach Algebra. He had no black-board, nor other facilities for the learner and teacher. He was teaching in the good old way they used to teach, when they hung witches in Salem, and whipped people for not attending church on Sunday, in Boston. It was glorious, because it had the prestige of time immemorial to sanction it.

Each girl or boy was cyphering on his or her "own hook;" this made them independent; they did not borrow from one another; and when either had done their "sum" or lesson, it was heard, one after another, through to the end of the class, which was scattered all along through the book, and no two on the same page.

Thus he urged his pupils, "Indian file," along the winding trail of knowledge.

I don't know, to use the Domine's own favorite adjective, but what they got along—"*pro-di-gious*"—ly, by this method of teaching. I presume old COTTON MATHER when a school boy, studied the same way; and that ICHABOD CRANE taught by the same method.

He told me, during our short chat, that he was the oldest teacher in the county; having taught in it fifteen years. Here was the prestige of ripe experience that the Domine did not have. But though he had all of the ignorance, he had not a tithe of the latter's learning. Still his head was stored with the reading of many a learned page, and his mind had the discipline from solving many a profound problem in Mathematics.

And it was told me, that, at evening, the "ingle" of his boarding-place was merry with his jokes and repartees, and amused and instructed by his stories, in which he displayed so much wit and learning, that he had the name of being a fine classical scholar.

He was a true son of the Emerald isle—and had the "rich brogue" of his mother tongue in his speech. He was not going to leave his school, as I had been informed. But Mr. C.—he informed me—a planter some eight miles from this place, wished to "get up a school" near his home.

Getting the "bearings" of my course—the "points and bends" in the road—here is where one's Geometry is useful to him, when he is to describe on horse-back, the angles, points and curves—the whole intricate problem of his route, he really needs the "discipline of *Trigonom-*

*etry*," that the Domine told me was so highly essential to one's mind.

After riding a mile or two, I lost my direction. Had not learned my lesson well that the teacher had just given me. Could not tell whether to describe an acute angle, or keep on in the straight road.

Here I am in one of those "brown studies" that my classmate, P., of the "Old Branch," Kalamazoo, Michigan——and here's a sigh for those schoolmates and halcyon school-days—used to get into. He invariably broke down, when about half way through with the description of a problem in Geometry.

One day, determined not to fail again, he not only doubled his diligence, but the time in getting the lesson. And then to make sure he came to me with it, and wanted I should play Prof. S., and hear him go over it once more. I took the book and played the Professor—EUCLID himself could not have beaten him. He went through with it correctly—shouted, "*Eureka!*" and we went in to recite.

P. was called on—"took the board"—his sweetheart was in the class—and, after a fair commencement, he came to one of his usual "dead sets," which he always manifested by scratching his head; and that was the sign for the class to begin laughing, which they did now in earnest.

But he had taken a HANNIBAL oath not to fail on this problem. He looked around, caught the eye of his "dulcena," received inspiration, and, began again. "There's *E*,"—it was on an acute angle—then scratched his head, and—took his seat amid the loudest applause of our class.

No orator on commencement-day ever left the stage with greater acclaim.

Poor E.! here is the acute angle; and I have come to one of your "stands;" but I have no LEGENDRE, nor even the *Domine*, back here, to set me right. I must ride back, I don't know how far—it seemed three miles—and get the directions to Mr. C.'s.

"Keep the straight road," is the answer I received.

After riding over a country undulating with low, sweeping hills, and passing some new plantations, I finally lost sight of both new and old, and night-fall came upon me in the woods.

It soon grew dark, and in vain I looked to the heavens for moonlight or starlight.

The deep forest about me was draped in sombre moss, and the sky overhead was draped in sombre clouds. There was no doubt which road to take now. I gave the reins to my horse and trusted to him to keep *a* road.

Riding so for a long, long while, describing turns and angles in the road, in the dark, and doubting whether I was on the right road or not—going to or from my point of destination—having seen no light or signs of a plantation near, I began to think of being lost in the woods—of spending a night among the wolves.

I never disliked to entertain a thought so bad in my life; it haunted me like a hungry wolf, as I rode along in these mournful, gloomy woods.

But suddenly I saw a light, afar off, glimmering through the trees.

> "How far that little candle throws its beams!"

How far I could not tell, or whether I was riding nearer to it every moment.

When, as suddenly I saw it, it disappeared. It was no time for being poetical, but it was a time when one feels the meaning and deep sentiment of poetry. I question whether Scott ever felt the full force and *truth* of the following lines of his, as I did, as they occurred to me here:

"Oft he looks back, while, streaming far,
His cottage window seems a star,—
Loses its feeble gleam,—and then
Turns patient to the blast again."

I was left alone and could only trust now to the instinct of my horse to keep the road.

Again I caught the light; and it occurred to me rather than lose it, I had better strike a straight line to it. But that would be dangerous. To keep the road was my *dernier resort.*

Thus I rode, losing and catching that light, glimmering through the trees, like the gleamings of hope to cheer me on my lone and dreary way, till it finally disappeared, and I could only urge on my horse in the dark, who was tired, but not as much as his rider.

But I could now perceive, by peering into the darkness, that I was no longer in the woods; an opening seemed to be each side of me, and there also appeared to be the dark form of a fence on either hand. This was a relief though the light was gone. I spurred on my horse. But the plantation might be one of those with fences three or four miles long; and what if it was an old deserted one! This left me deserted of even a cheering thought.

But while busied with these lonely thoughts along my lonely way, my horse suddenly turned off from the road. Trusting to the faithful animal, I gave him the reins, and he was soon walking around among cattle lying in a barnyard, I supposed.

The observing creature had noticed an opening in the fence, and had left the road and gone through it.

I alighted—felt with my cane and found that we were near a fence—palings, it must be, around a house. I hitched my horse to them, and walked along by them, till I came to a corner, described a right angle, and continuing on I found a gate. Felt for a latch, but it was like MUGGINS' feeling for the key-hole—Mrs. MUGGINS must have pulled it inside. Reaching over I found the latch.

Walking into the yard I observed a light shining out from the crevices in the door of a house. I walked up the three or four steps that usually lead to a planter's porch—went to the door and rapped.

---

## CHAPTER VI.

> "Yet various my romantic theme
> Flits winds and shifts—a morning dream;
> Through Southern snowy meads it goes,
> Where Southern wealth around me flows."
>
> SCOTT.

The door was opened by a man of aldermanic dimensions, large gray eyes, and cheeks that needed no swelling whiskers to make them full. The silvery honors had fallen from his head, and their place had been supplied by a thatching made from the auburn locks of youth.

Sitting in one corner of the room, I saw R., the teacher, from New York, that I had met on the "Home," coming up the Yazoo.

This was the plantation of his relative—the gentleman I have described, and to whom he now introduced me.

Mr. D., that was his name, is sixty years of age. He is a native of the Empire State, which he left forty years ago, and came South as a teacher.

He had taught school here in his own neighborhood, where he married a Southern lady of considerable fortune, to which he has added until he has come into possession of the plantation he now owns. During this time he has become a true Southron. His wife dying, some few years ago, left him with a competency for life, enjoying which he will here, though not as a widower, perhaps,

> "Husband out life's taper to its close."

But my first inquiry was, whether I could find lodging for the night, and my second was, like SANCHO'S, "Could my 'Dapple' have 'shelter and provender?'"

To a way-worn traveler, and most especially to a benighted one, there is something that cheers him as he hears a welcome response to his inquiry whether he can find food and shelter for the night; but when it is given in that generous and hospitable manner which says,

> "Guidance and rest and food and fire,
> No stranger may in vain require;"

one feels that he is thrice and four times welcomed.

I need scarcely add that beneath a Southern planter's roof you find this welcome.

There was one other person in the room, of a clever and somewhat intelligent look, whom I soon found to be the overseer. Mr. D. being a widower, and living alone, he had probably associated him as one of the family more than he otherwise would have done. For I saw that he was considered as one of the family.

I supposed I had been out half the night in the woods; I had not quite, yet, though it was deep in the evening, they had not been to supper. They were having a late one. A negro servant girl had just placed it on the table and announced that it was ready as I came in.

I was invited, after a few moments' conversation, to sit down to table with them. The fare was simple—the corn dodger, little wheat biscuit, the size of a door-knob, some butter, hominy and coffee. Of this, after Mr. D. had asked a blessing, I partook with a good appetite.

Our host appeared to be a man of humor, and rallied R., his relative, and myself, about our being Yankee pedagogues; and tried to catch from our conversation some Yankee accent or phrase. He said his overseer had bothered all day over the word "stent," that he had heard R. use; and that he came to him at night to know what he meant by it.

"Why he means, you dunce you," replied Mr. D., "what you mean when you say '*task*.'"

And that he had puzzled the overseer also in telling about some planters having a "*raft*" of slaves. He thought that the pupil ought not to hear the drawling sound, or learn any vulgar phrases from the teacher.

Is it not too often a fact that aside from the poor enunciation and manners of the common school-teacher, which are frequently too bad for the young learner to imitate, his language is the false syntax to all the grammar he teaches. He is a paradox.

During the evening I told Mr. D. I thought he resembled Gen. CASS very much in his looks.

He begged my pardon, for he could not receive my compliment—he'd rather look like any other man. He spoke in bitter terms of him and the "little giant." We replied that Gen. CASS was considered the NESTOR of American Democracy, and the "little giant" its DIOMEDE.

He "reckoned not," or if so, they and their followers were no "kith and kin" of his.

But the North had a man worth them all—MILLARD FILLMORE.

We talked about the political "clans" in our country. Scotland in her days of chieftainship did not surpass us; we had the clan MACGREGOR, MACALPINE, and all the FITZ JAMES and RODERICK DUHS in our political clans, and they were carrying on a fierce and bitter warfare against each other.

But we thought it rather strange, to see, in these "feudal days," a "Lowlander," the follower of a "Highland chief."

He had visited, lately, his native State, New York. And on his way had passed through the Peninsular State, and noticed, he said, a flourishing town on the Central Rail Road, by the name of Battle Creek.

It was a "right smart" place, and characterized by Yankee energy—traffic and thrift.

But he did not like the name; how did it come by it?

Did Gen. CASS ever fight a battle with the Indians on the original town plot?

I gave him the history of its receiving its present name. A battle had been fought on the original site of the place, in its forest days, between the old State surveyors and the Indians;—the latter having attempted to take, by force, provisions from the tent of the former.

That many of its citizens did not like its present name, but as they had not striven for a name merely in building up the town, they had been negligent in having it changed. The situation of the place in a glen or "vale,"

"Where the bright waters meet,"

and the practical character of the town, made it difficult to find a name that would unite the beauty of its locality with its business characteristics, should their fancy seek one.

Pardon this episode on the name of my home in the

North. I have often thought, had it early had the prestige of that "strange spell—a name," it would have been a great benefit to it. And here a far-away Mississippian, who has seen the place, thinks it needs and deserves a better one.

In our evening chat the teacher, R., told me I had run a great risk in not hallooing from my horse, and calling some one to the gate, ere I alighted and came in. That the hounds that the planters usually kept, would in many places, have made it extremely perilous for me to have done so.

He instanced the case of a friend of his, who, attempting to come to the planter's door without first hallooing from the saddle, had barely escaped with his life; the hounds tore his flesh shockingly.

It was the custom here for every one to halloo from the saddle before alighting and coming to the door. The planter was ever ready for a call, and always sent his servant or came himself to meet you at the gate.

He said that it was lucky for me to-night, as I came in, that Mr. D. had no hounds. And, finally, that there was always danger in knocking at the planter's door.

Speaking to our planter host—I find they are apt to be semi-publican—about their wanting teachers, he answered that he knew of no situation anywhere in the country for one.

He "reckoned that if I had come South to teach—'I had been led a dance.'"

This was rather a discouraging close to my first day's adventure in search of a school in the far distant South. It not only cast the adventures of the day in the shade, but threw a shadow over my future prospects.

On retiring for the night, a large room was shown me, in which was a fire briskly burning in a fire-place—a large broad bed—a table with some books and newspapers on it, and an old book-case, on whose shelves papers and books were half arranged or scattered in heaps.

Taking leave of the planter, in the morning, he would take no "sordid ore" for the entertainment he had given me.

His house is the accustomed log building I had observed planters usually lived in. It was surrounded by a paling of cypress shakes, white-washed, which enclosed a small door-yard with no shade. His plantation of over three hundred acres, lay before his door, stretching away in broad rolling fields; some covered with yellow sedge, others bristling with the rustling corn-stalks, and some with long, brown hedge rows, yet "profitably gay" with white blossoms.

I had yet three miles to go, ere reaching Mr. C.'s, to whom I had been directed as the planter who wished "to get up" a school.

They have no name for towns here. They go by the designating terms of the original survey.

Township No. 9, Range 8 West, &c., &c.

The post office in each town has a name, and some of the planters have names to their platations or residences.

Mr. C. was not at home, a lady informed me from the porch of a rough plantation-house. I saw no negro quarters nor cotton-field in sight. One might mistake the house for a farm-house in the North. But you would soon be undeceived, for, turning the corner of the road, I saw lying perdue by the road side, a "Gin-House," which has nothing answerable to it in size and shape, in the whole busy North, or bustling world.

Riding three miles further, I found Mr. C. at one of his neighbor's, building one of these unique looking Gin-Houses. He said he wanted a school very much, but that there was no way of "getting one up," save by riding around among the planters, in his district, and thus find out how many scholars could be obtained. He would head the list by putting down three scholars, each at four dollars per month. They had no school officers. Having failed to elect them last year, a school was now an individual work. They had, he said, an old log school house that would do with some patching and mending. And in regard to "board," the teacher would have to walk some two miles or so, unless he could make arrangements to secure a home with some planter near the school-house.

Having obtained the range of my ride, to find the patrons of the school, I started out to make my round of "calls."

After riding "up hill and down dale," "through bush and brake," back from the main road, along by-paths and no-paths, up steep banks and down steeper ones, amid the tangle-wood of ravines, I found but poor encouragement.

Two planters would send a boy a-piece at Christmas, when cotton-picking was over. One thought of selling his plantation;—"would send two scholars if he stayed."

Having strayed from the "big road," I came up to a small-sized house, sitting on high posts, like those in Siam, to avoid inundation: a planter's wife responded to my halloo—came and opened the gate for me, and, after I had ridden across the inner yard, she opened another gate, for which I thanked her then, and should she ever read these pages, she may consider this line loaded with kind remembrances and my best wishes for her.

She directed me to her husband, at work off in the field. Passing through a lane and into an uncultivated field, I came up to a dense clump of cotton-wood trees; and as I could see no one in sight, I hallooed to the sound of an axe in the midst of them. A man of ordinary size and dress came out with his axe on his shoulder.

I told him my errand.

"Weel, he would do as much as iny mon in supporting a school." He had but one "bairn to send, and ye could ask no more of a mon than to do his best, could ye?"

Certainly not.

"Well, he would send his bairn."

"But," said he, looking at me earnestly and honestly, with one eye—the other was out—"afther ye've worked for a thing, ye want to get it, don't ye?"

Most assuredly.

"Weel, I want a school as much as iny mon, but my bairn must help gather the cotton crop 'fore he can go."

But when will cotton gathering be over?

"Weel, sir, if we are right smart, we'll have niver a cotton-row to pick at 'holl eve, sir, at Christmas, sir."

Whether this planter from the "Green Isle," with his slaves, if he had any, and the help of his "bairn," got through cotton-picking at 'holl eve or not, I never ascertained.

But surely nature is kind to the cotton-planter, or he could not live here a year, with our seasons he would starve at planting.

I had some distance to ride, ere I reached the main road. My directions were to "hold to the path;" it would take me out of the woods safely. I kept it with difficulty; sometimes with doubt, sometimes with fear, for it led me on a will-o'-the-wisp chase, through deep ravines and along dismal looking abysses. At one point I descended from the crest of a ridge following this little path, in its crooks and turns down the steep side to the bottom of a ravine, where I found a little tinkling brook, a tiny hermit stream, born here in the woods near some mossy fountain. Its little babblings were never heard out of this deep woodland dell.

While my horse was drinking of its clear waters, I looked up and saw I should have to climb a steep bank, if I kept the path, as I had been directed. I reached the top of the ridge, after no little fear that my horse would lose his load in the ascent. Most truly,

> "I had passed the glen and scanty rill,
> And climbed the opposing bank, until,
> I gained the top of Blackford hill."

Having gained the bank, I looked down, with a sigh, to the little brook, as I thought that the vandal axe of the forester might yet denude its banks of their shade, and that this lovely little stream would be missing some summer morning.

My last "call" in this vicinity, was at the plantation of Mr. D.

His house stood in the shade of some fine trees. The porch was open, but trellised with clambering vines. The grounds about the house displayed the attention and taste of the planter.

Mr. D., in response to my halloo, came walking down his fine lawn, with his head bare, which reminded me very much, in its shape, of Chief Justice MARSHALL'S, and met me at the gate.

After I had mentioned the subject of my call, he frankly told me he would send to the school if he liked it—would not promise a scholar on any other conditions. Some of his children were away from home at school; he had two or three at home whom he would send to a good school.

But he had been deceived so much in teachers that he had lost confidence in any that he did not know.

I asked him how he had been deceived.

He replied, "In their pretending to be good teachers—

graduates from college—and proving to be, sometimes, ignoramuses."

Were these Northern teachers?

"Yes."

"Was I from the North?"

Yes.

What a fine predicament WHATELY with his *logic*, now placed me in!

The *premiss* was—Northern teachers had deceived him.

I was a Northern teacher, and the conclusion was—I would deceive him.

Worse than that; these teachers were ignoramuses.

I was a teacher, hence—an *ignoramus!*

Reader, did the charlatan WHATELY ever resolve you into such a fix, with his beautiful, laconical, logical, triple reasoning, that makes our common sense, true to the old adage, "a common liar?"

Yet Mr. WHATELY is serious, and honest in laying down these *logical* conclusions.

"Honest IAGO!"

I extricated myself as well as I could from my unpleasant situation, and bidding Mr. D. "good day," reined my horse round for the village of Dover, six miles distant. I had been informed that they wished to hire a teacher for the school in that place.

The road to this town is remarkable for its gates. I passed through eight or ten of them in traveling these six miles.

But their latches are so high—one can reach them from the saddle—and they swing open and shut readily, so that you are saved the trouble of dismounting.

At Dover I saw a blacksmith's shop, about the size of an Irishman's shanty—one, perhaps, *two* buildings, some distance down the road—a decent looking log school-house, and a store about the dimensions of a large sized tin-peddler's box; to which I reined my horse, and gave the usual halloo.

A small, well-dressed man came to the door.

He had a rubicund face, and eyes as black as sloe berries, which told you at a glance, that he was of a merry and social disposition, and withal, an intelligent man.

I asked him if this was Dover, and he was Mr. W.

Being answered in the affirmative, I alighted and went into the store. He briefly told me the situation of their school. Three officers had it under their supervision, and it drew its "annual pension" from the State, when these officers were duly elected. They had just hired a teacher, yet they *might* not agree on terms; they were to see him once more. There was a *possibility* that they might not hire him.

This doubt seemed a pretext that he might enjoy testing the range of my accomplishments.

He could not forego the pleasure—like city ladies a-shopping—of examining the new goods, though he had not the slightest idea of buying any. And he begun at once, as if I was as ready as a clerk to tumble down my intellectual goods for his inspection.

Was I a classical scholar, and so forth, and so on, down to the embellishments of a boarding-school Miss.

The latter acquirements he did not consider so essential; had merely touched upon them because it was better for a teacher to have them.

He next attacked me mathematically. Did I understand Trigonometry, Geometry, Surveying, Algebra, and so on, to the end of the chapter.

Then followed a "fusilaide" on the natural sciences, Chemistry, and so forth, to the end of that chapter.

The close of this "overhaul" of my stock of knowledge, was,

"What were my ideas of government, in a *school*," of course?

They were Democratic. I looked upon every pupil that came to school as being capable of self-government; they ought not to come till they were.

But in managing a school the teacher should hold the reins of government with Spartan firmness, and give his laws with Spartan brevity.

But in regard to managing the different natures, the wayward, the refractory, the timid, and so forth.

Here, we thought, much could be learned from the answer of old Dr. BELAMY to a young clergyman who asked his advice in managing his congregation.

He replied:

"Why; man, can't you take a lesson from a fisherman? In trouting you have a little hook and fine line, and bait it carefully, and throw it out as gently as you can, then sit and wait and humor your fish until you can get him a-shore."

"Now, in fishing for cod, you get a great cod-hook and rope line, and thrash it into the water, and bawl out—

"Bite, or be d——d, to you!"

He then gave me a short paraphrase on the use of mathematical studies.

They were the parade-ground, where the faculties of the mind were drilled and disciplined. The teacher was the mathematical tactician, and the school a little military academy.

During this conference several villagers, lounging about the store, stood by us as listeners.

Mr. W. remarked to me, as I got into the saddle, that

he would write me and let me know, in a few days, whether I could have the school or not.

It was past the mid-after of a lovely day in a Southern November, that I left the good people of Dover, and wended my way back, over the "gated road" to Mr. D.'s plantation. The sun was in a summer sky—

> "The loverock whistled from the cloud;
> The stream was lovely, though not loud;
> And many a Southern garden shed
> Its richest fragrance round my head."

A planter on a mule accompanied me part of the way. They are all loquacious and fond of company on the road, but few ask me my name or place of residence.

But one needs a Scotch impertinence in asking questions when traveling, if he would get the knowledge of a country;—I ask many of them their names, and many questions about this Southern clime.

One gets different ideas in different localities. In some places a teacher meets discouragement—loses "the scent on the track" of a school, and wanders about through the woods, from plantation to plantation, sad and dejected. In other places he strikes the track again, and spurs on his horse with animation and courage.

These two persons, like PAGANINI with his fiddle, and PAGANINI without his fiddle, are two very different things.

On leaving Dover we rode along Mr. B.'s plantation; an almost boundless cotton field came up to the side of our path; a plain unshaded house stood off a distance from the road, and negro quarters a little beyond it. There was the appearance of more thrift in the field than in the immediate surroundings of the house.

Before reaching the main road, I passed the widow C.'s plantation.

The family house, though old and rude, is really in a a nest of trees and vines; and children and hounds were playing about in its door-yard and garden. A spacious lawn, shaded by lordly oaks, lay before its door—a cluster of negro cabins was some distance from the house, beneath the shade of the China trees, in which negro boys and girls were frolicking about. Horses were grazing in a pasture of Bermuda grass; carriages were in their houses; everything had the air of an undisturbed old English manorial life.

This was the Southern residence of my friend—Miss E. M. P., who had lately been governess in Mrs. C.'s family. Life here, surely had enough attraction and romance about it to make the teacher's vocation a pleasant one.

From this plantation I went out into the main road and was, just as night-fall fell across my path, at the residence of Mr. D.'s, where I had stayed the night before, and beneath whose hospitable roof I remained another night.

In the morning I rode back to Mechanicsburgh, where I consulted with several of its leading men, whose names Mr. H. had given me, about their school.

They thought the present teacher would leave soon; that I had better bide my time, and they would pledge me the school on the event that he did leave.

Mr. H. of this place, whose acquaintance and his brother's I afterwards formed, and esteemed much, was the *frankest* Southron I had yet met.

He said the only objection—which he courteously waved —he had to my teaching their school, was, "I came from Michigan—*that bitter abolition State!*"

He was more frank than severe. I liked his honesty.

On reaching Major W.'s I was a tired cavalier—had been in the saddle two days—a longer and more prolix sitting than that of the "Rump Parliament," to me—besides, I had traveled over a route, rough, obscure and lonely.

I met Mrs. Dr. J. at the "Ridge House."

She was so pretty, and seemed so much like a Northern lady, that I felt as if I had met an old friend.

To her I presented my letter of introduction. And in the evening I gave the family this story of my first adventures in the South, in search of a school.

---

## CHAPTER VII.

> "While far from home, my narrower ken
> Somewhat of manners saw, and men."

Major W. came home soon after my return. He is one of South Carolina's chivalrous sons; a courteous gentleman, of fine intellect, much reading, and good literary taste.

He is six feet high, though not a heavy man, has light brown hair, bluish grey eyes, and, were it not for the browning of this clime, would have a fair complexion.

His plantation, as I before noticed, is in the valley. He has selected this spot among the hills, for his home, some two miles from it, on account of its healthier locality.

From the "sunny memories" of my sojourn in this pleasant land, that cluster about the Ridge House,—my first home in the South—it deserves a description in these Jottings.

It is about mid-way, on the "Big Road" between Vicksburgh and Yazoo City. The house, though it is now being finished inside and out, like a frame building, is built of oak logs hewn square. It is some thirty feet wide by sixty feet long, and a story-and-a-half high, while the roof extending out, like a planter's broad rimmed hat, over its sides, and, resting on posts, forms wide porches, a cool and pleasant shade in the warm summer weather. An open hall connects these two porches.

It is situated on a gentle eminence that slopes down gradually to the road. You approach it, in front, through a carriage gate that opens from the road into a broad lawn of several acres, graced with many a sylvan honor of the forest.

Riding across this lawn, you come to a little gate, in the palings of cypress boards that enclose the inner grounds about the house. To the left of the yard, running to the rear of the house, are three fine rows of locust trees; a tall hickory stands at the right, and a few others are standing in the rear-yard, while in the back-ground, the primeval forest rises up against the sky.

Major W. usually orders his horse in the morning, and rides along a fine, high, carriage road, that winds through an interval of beautiful wood-land, to his plantation, "down in the valley."

Here, from the porch of the old plantation-house, or riding out over the plantation, he can see how affairs are daily managed, over his whole domain.

Some thirty slaves, under command of his "field-marshal" work his large and beautiful prairie-farm; and the fruit of their labor is an "argosy" of cotton, which is annually shipped to New Orleans.

My first conversation with him, was about the panic among the Northern banks. He discoursed at some length on the banking system. Old JOHN LAW had, years a-gone, founded a bank, for the French people, on the El Dorado treasures of the Mississippi valley. His scheme had since been known as "The Mississippi bubble." This "bubble" burst, and its explosion was more fatal to the French than all the "infernal machines" in BONAPARTE'S time. But they had no more bubbles to burst, their banks were as enduring, as—

"These rich vales that feed the marts of the world."

He spoke of our Congress as if it were a chess-board, and he clearly understood the games that were being and had been played on it, by those men in Congress.

In speaking about their schools to him, he told me that there were good situations for teachers, but I must "bide my time," get better acquainted, and I would not have any trouble in securing a pleasant place. Schools among them, were mostly got up by individual effort. Of this, I had had a little experience.

To-night, the sky was all aglow with a roseate hue. Never did I see the stars shining out from so lovely a setting. Sand-hill cranes were flying South—an indication of cold weather.

The frost, that great chamberlain of old "Dame Earth," is now spreading her carpet throughout the wood-lands, before winter sets in.

But to another theme.

The main road running through Yazoo and Warren counties, is as crooked as an Indian trail, save where it is sometimes straightened, running between plantations, but as soon as it leaves them, off it goes again, as wild and wandering as ever; following the wayward freak of some ridge. A short rain makes the soil, of clay loam, as tenacious as tar to the foot or carriage wheel. But you find no stone, not even the slightest indications of gravel in the country.

A telegraph line, between Vicksburgh and Yazoo city, once followed the windings of this road, the wires being attached to trees, instead of posts. But it was so often broken by the falling of trees across it, that it was soon abandoned.

One meets, in traveling here on the road, throughout the country, the negro, driving fine carriages or costly coaches, with his beautiful "*proteges*" in them—the planter's wife and her daughters; also ladies on their palfreys galloping through the woods; the planter and his sons, ever on horse-back, with a large portmanteau swung across their saddles, for carrying sundries; or, if he is on the hunt, he is equipped for it, followed by his hounds; and, if returning from the chase, the most of them will have a deer swung across their horses, behind the saddle, and negroes mounted, carrying others. Or you may meet this sable cavalier, and his dulcena, riding their favorite steed, the mule; or perhaps you may find the solitary gin-stand agent, or traveler, wending his way, a-horse-back, through the State; or now and then, a German-Jew peddler, seated on his well-filled box, making his transit across the country, attended by his black satellite as a "whip;" and lastly, especially in the ditching season, wandering "Exiles of Erin," straggling along the road.

This is about all the travel you see. The stranger finds no welcome sign-post, an index to a "Way-side Inn," where he can pause and refresh himself and his weary beast. Neither does the thirsty traveler hail, near the road-side, by the planter's home, the accustomed well-sweep, so common in the country North, poised like an angler's rod, with its line suspending a bucket ready to dip into the fountain below, and bring up the cooling beverage. The planter seldom digs a well; its waters are too often affected by the mineral impurities of the earth. He uses cistern water.

Neither do you see any barns in the country; the green-cane pasture of the woods, the year round, saves him from stowing away fodder for his cattle, and the mildness of the climate precludes the use of them for shelter.

All the buildings you see, are, the plantation-house, a lonely church, a solitary school-house, standing off from the road-side, telling where some northern teacher has been; the gin-house, where the cotton is separated from the seed; here and there a stray rick for corn, or corn-leaves for fodder; and, occasionally, a roof over an open stall for horses. These are all the buildings one sees in the country, and they are all built of logs, save very rarely a planter's house.

There are no grist-mills, in town or country. All the corn they use is ground by one-horse-power mills, in the gin-house. The saw-mill is more of a *sine qua non;* but still you see but very few of them, the country is too ridgy for water-mills. Neither have I seen any bridges over the rivers—they are all crossed in ferry-boats.

Life is surely rather primitive here. There is more nature and less art than at the North, more forest and uncultivated land, less husbandry and good tillage. Houses are built more from want and convenience, and less from pride and for sale. They are homes for life, and are never placarded with notices "to sell or rent," like Northern farms and farm-houses. Their best houses are not costly. What man does for comfort and convenience costs him but little. But let him build to suit his pride, and his house rivals the "Taj of India."

I have noticed many traits of old English life in the South. The plantation-house, like the old English manor-house, has its broad grounds, but without the carpet of green, between its shady retreat and the road. The beauties of the landscape, about his rural seclusion, have not been violated. The planter also, may be considered a lord in possession of a large estate, and his slaves are his vassals. And, like your English gentleman of landed possessions, he loves the chase, keeps a parliament of hounds, and the requisites for the hunt. His horse is ordered at early dawn, when from his porch you can hear the winding of his horn, and instantly

> "Tray, Blanche, and Sweetheart all,"

are frolicking about him. He soon dashes off into the woods with them, and you may not see him again till nightfall.

The following, is a wild boar hunt, as narrated to me by Major W.'s oldest son. Some of these hunts are as fierce as those of Ceylon.

This animal, the bear, the wolf, catamount, and deer, are denizens of the Mississippi forest.

News came to him, he said, last evening, while at the plantation-house, that one of the horses had been badly gashed, his favorite dog killed, and the party driven out of the swamp by a ferocious wild boar.

He instantly ordered his horse, wound his horn to summon his hounds, seized his gun, and vaulting into the saddle, was soon at the edge of the cypress-brake, where the party were—

> "With horse, and gun, and horn, and hound;
> You might see the youth intent
> Guard every pass with cross-bow bent;
> * * * * * *

Lead in the leash the gaze-hounds grim,
Attentive, as the bratchet's bay
From the dark covert drove the prey,
To slip them as he broke away."

Having ascertained the position of the enemy, he dashed into the swamp to attack him with his dogs. They were soon upon him. He had chosen, like a true warrior, a vantage ground. And there he stood, bristled, with mouth foaming, and fanged for the onset. Near by him lay the faithful hound he had just killed, and as the others were tarried on, he attacked them with such a wild ferocity, that they fled, and could only summon courage enough to bay him from a distance.

After being foiled for some time, in getting a chance to shoot at him, a lucky shot disabled him, and one or two more brought him down. He was a terrible foe, and had fought many battles with the hounds, generally coming off victorious from both them and the hunters.

An overseer on one of the plantations, during the fall, had killed fourteen bears. He told many thrilling stories of the "hair-breadth 'scapes" he had made while hunting them.

But, to resume, our subject, there is much provincialism in the habits and customs of the South. And finally, should an Englishman seek the hospitality of the planter's roof, he could repose on a mattress spread on an old English bed-stead, the same lofty and rich posts, and richly ornamented canopy, with curtains, that once graced the royal bed-chamber of "Good Old Queen Bess."

The planter's fare is simple, and the chase supplies his table with much of its meat. I am not only pleased with this simple fare of the planter's board, but with their manner of sitting at table.

Their tables are usually long, and remain stationary in

the dining-room. This is sometimes a little log building separate from the house.

The father, at meals, takes seat at one end of the table, his eldest son at his right, then the next younger, and so on, down to the "wee bairn" that can "toddle" to his seat.

The mother is seated at the other end of the table, and her eldest daughter at her right, the sister next in age succeeding, down to the youngest. The guests, if gentlemen, are seated at the planter's left hand; if ladies, at his wife's left. If the father is a member of the church, a blessing is asked. I have known those, who did not profess to be Christians, ask blessings at their tables.

The boiled ham, cooked whole always, and which, on extra occasions, is tricked off with cloves, green leaves, and various-colored dainty bits, in a tasteful manner, is placed before the planter; his wife has the tea, coffee, and the delicacies before her. By the aid of servants every one at table is served.

In no place, not even in the most back-woods part of the country, have I ever heard what one often hears in the country, especially at the North, immediately after being seated at table, "Now take hold and help yourself."

The civilities of life generally "roughen" as you go from city into the country. Whether the South claims it as a part of her chivalry or not, is a matter of indifference to me, but, I certainly have not found the politeness and civilities of her town-life changed to boorishness, among the most back-woods planters of her country.

But again. The planter takes his time in eating—don't "bolt it down," as the Yankees do. Leisure and ease are inmates of his roof. He takes no note of time. Your Yankee will take time by the fore-lock, and push business through. But a Southron, never heard of the "old man with the scythe."

A friend of mine from Dowagiac, Michigan, making a trip to the South, stopped with me a few days; he, being a practical Yankee lawyer, was suprised at the air of indifference with which the planter spoke of time. He was not aware that time here,

> "Had lost his glass and was asleep on flowers."

A clock, almanac, and a good fire, are hard things to find in a planter's house. The only chronometer he has, is the cotton-plant, and that "ticks" but once a year. The word, haste, is not in a Southron's vocabulary. He has reversed the old adage, and never does that to-day which can be done to-morrow.

While waiting, a few days, at the Ridge House, for a letter in regard to a school from Dover, ere venturing out again in a new direction, I took a pleasant ride to Satartia. The day was fine, and, in an easy carriage, accompanied by a Southern lady, we rode alternately through beautiful wood-lands, and by fine cotton-plantations.

On coming out of the uplands to the bluffs that wall up a wide border of valley, on both sides of the river, and from which you descend into it, I had one of the most picturesque landscape views, I had yet enjoyed any where in the country.

The long winding strip of valley, that lay spread out below me, looked like a broad strip of variegated green carpet; the village of Satartia, and the planters' houses, five or six in sight, with their little negro villas about them, looked like beautiful raised figures on it; the fences looked like leaden-colored vines traced across it; while the Yazoo river looked like a winding strip of blue water-colored ribbon, running through the middle of it between green fingers.

From the bluffs we descended, by two gradual sweeps in the road, to the valley. A mile or so brought us to the town. In Satartia I saw some of the yeomanry of Mississippi. A knot of them in their dress and general appearance might be mistaken for a group of our wealthy Michigan farmers. But one would notice more than a usual number of riding-whips, or "raw-hides," on their hands, and the same undue proportion of spurs in the heel of the right boot. And in their conversation he would hear nothing of the farm and its products, but of the plantation and cotton. The Southron does not have such a variety of topics about his affairs in his conversation. They are fewer than with the Northerner. Neither do the business, cares, and toils of this life worry and torment his mind.

He talks about the weather as it is pleasant, or disagreeable to his own feelings, not as it affects his crop, or his business. If a "freshet" should have inundated and ruined half his cotton crop, or even the whole of it, he would talk about it with the non chalance of a TALLEYRAND. One listening to the range, spirit and humor of their conversation could tell them from Northerners.

And furthermore, the peculiar words and phrases—"I reckon," "right smart," "a-heap," and others that they used, would be a sure indication that they were Southrons. But, aside from all this, were I as blind as BARTIMEUS, and ignorant that I was in the South, I could, on riding up to the planter's gate, after having given the halloo, tell where I was, and who was addressing me, from the very words that I heard.

I defy a Northerner—even a Yankee, with all his natural adaptation of character, to address you and invite you in, like a true Southron. He invites you, in a way that no one else does. He answers your halloo, by meeting you at the gate, and in the kindliest manner extends you his hand, with his warm and friendly, "How do you do, sir? Won't you alight, come in, take a seat, and sit a while?"

In the first place, he addresses you in a gentlemanly manner, using the old Norman or knightly "sir." But let us remark here, that many words, phrases, and much of the manner and bearing of a Southron, are true remnants of the days of chivalry. Besides the use of the word "sir," we have mentioned, notice the word, "alight," or the expression, "get down from your horse," both of which they use, and both are words or phrases found, used in like manner, as characteristic of the feudal days. And the next sentence—"come in, take a *seat*, and *sit* awhile," expresses the true hospitality of the gentleman or knight in those hospitable days. Or, it is, with the other two terms mentioned, "part of the loyalty to the honorable and chivalric, which forms the subsoil" of a Southron's nature.

Now, your Yankee would, on hearing the halloo at his gate, eye you a moment, by way of "guessing" who you were, and then answer your salutation with his laconic "how-d'-ye-do." Would he go out to the gate to meet you? What *for?* He would, if he thought "'twould pay," or if he wished to—— ——"*dun you.*" And if he invited you in, it would be, "Won't ye hitch and come in?"

We saw nothing in the streets of Satartia to indicate that it was not a Southern town. The number of horses, saddled and hitched to posts, appeared to tally with the "riding-whips" and "spurs" we have before mentioned.

We saw but a carriage or two in the streets, hence few ladies were in town. But those few did, no doubt, as much trading as five times the number of Northern ladies would have done. A little incident, over which we were much amused, occurred in a town near this place, that will illustrate what we have said about their shopping.

The planter came into the store, where his wife was trading, and inquired about some bills of purchase that several merchants had presented him. He did not know that he owed these men a farthing. His wife glanced over them and smiled as she said, "Why, that bill of eighty-five dollars is the amount of FANNIE'S shopping at Mr. F.'s store. The one of one hundred dollars is mine. I could not get here half the articles I wanted, and so I traded a little at Mr. G.'s. And these other bills, (that amounted in all to over one hundred and fifty dollars,) why, you know CARRIE'S going off to school, of course she must have her 'outfit,' these are hers."

The planter appeared to be satisfied with this story; paid the amount of the different bills, his wife and daughters stepped into their fine carriage, the negro driver mounted to his seat, and drove off to their plantation-home; and he, mounting his horse, rode on after them, as if he was the mere "attache," or "purser," belonging to this lady and her splendid equipage.

There are but two stores in Satartia, yet each trades to the amount of sixty thousand dollars annually. The one is owned by Mr. H., a gentleman from Germany, who has amassed a fortune here among Southern planters; the other, by Mr. W., who, like very many other Northerners, left his home in search of the "golden fleece" South, and luckily has found it.

A Southern town, or road, never lacks one unmistakable sign of its being in the South. Though it moves along the streets and the road as slow and monotonous as the hour-hand on the dial-plate, yet it just as truly arrives at its point of destination; it is the negro with his prolix mule-team, before his lumbering cotton-wagon. You can follow him anywhere through the woods, by the crack of his long-lashed ox-whip, which he appears to execute, ever and anon, with a flourish about the heads of his mules, for the ostensible purpose of keeping them in motion. It is as good as a bell.

Our ride, both to Satartia and home again, we enjoyed very much. The road was very dry and smooth, and although it was near winter—the very last of November, it seemed to me, so recently from the cold Northern regions, "that the winter was past, the rain over and gone; for the flowers appeared on the earth; the time of the singing of birds was come, and the voice of the turtle was heard in the land."

Arriving at the gate, a servant was called, we alighted from the carriage, and walked into the hospitable mansion of our friend Major W.

And here let me describe the belongings, the moveables—what one would notice about a plantation-house.

Sitting on a board-shelf, resting on pegs driven into the logs, either on the side of the logs within the hall, or in front under the porch, you invariably find a water-pail, with the long handle of a cocoa-nut dipper sticking out of it. Also, in the porch, you see several long pegs driven into the logs, some four or five feet from the floor; these are for hanging the saddles, bridles, and that sort of things upon. But very often you see the vacant pegs, and the saddles and bridles lying on the floor beneath them.

> "And o'er the chimney rests the gun,
> And hang in idle trophy, near,
> The powder-pouch, fishing-rod and spear."

Between the logs, which are seldom "chinked," you will notice newspapers sticking out, and books or various things that have been casually placed there. You also usually find several vacant chairs in the porch, placed just as the last group who were seated in them, left them. Perhaps sprinkles of ashes from their pipes scattered on the floor near each chair, and the pipes themselves, lying between the logs hard by. Or you may catch the party there, seated in their chairs, chatting on the various things incident to such a group, and all smoking the accustomed cane-stemmed, thick, clay pipe with a man's head on it. If one of the group knows you, you are politely introduced to the rest. And whatever luxury they are enjoying, you are offered a share of it. If smoking, a pipe is handed you; or, if chatting, and you have no errand, you are supposed to be a participant in it. You are entitled to, or they seem to consider you as deserving their attention and hospitality. And, what is so common to man, "couchant or levant," in the old or new world, should that

"Real, old, particular, friendly, punchy feeling"

seize them, you are invited to drink with them, whatever you choose; many of the planters keep the various wines and choice drinks. Or, should dinner be ready, you are invited in to dine with them. You find the planter a most agreeable, courteous and hospitable man; and that his guest is the best entertained man in the world.

This is of a log plantation-house in the uplands, in the valley you find better buildings, everything else the same.

We had forgotten to notice the hounds; they are "belongings," and "*moveables*" that one would be apt to notice, from the fact that they are so much inclined to notice you. They are principally the terrier, and a hound between the blood and the greyhound. You will find them baying at you, at the gate, or lounging about the porch, or under it, or about the grounds, while whole tribes of

Shanghaes, troops of Turkeys, convoys of Ducks, and bevies of Guinea Hens, in vast numbers, are about the ground in the rear-yard.

---

## CHAPTER VIII.

"Early they took Dun-Edin's road,
And I could trace each step they trode;
Hill, nor brook, nor rock, nor stone,
Laid in the path to me unknown.
But a forest-land, which varying still
With ridge, ravine, like dalè and hill;"
'And where the broad plantation lay,
With its fields of cotton hedge-rows, gay.'

SCOTT.

Once more we were to go out in search of a school. Once more. But we were relieved this morning from taking another horse-back ride of some sixteen miles; Mrs. W. offered us a seat in her carriage, which we gladly accepted, and had the pleasure of riding with her and a young lady-cousin, to "Rose Hill," Colonel R.'s plantation.

In the balmy air of a lovely morning, in the last of November, we rode through a beautiful wood-land country, undulating with swells that swept down and away again, ere they rose to the prominence of hills. But the beauty of our landscape was marred by the high backs of ridges, that wound along and across it, like huge serpents, forming deep gullies, and yawning ravines between their intricate folds.

We passed several plantations with rather poor houses, and poorer fences around them. Looking like a thing utterly forsaken, and very much dilapidated, we saw a log school-house, standing off in the woods, some distance from the road. There was no house within two miles of it. It seemed too forlorn a place for any person. Yet the romance of teaching here had induced several teachers to leave their homes two thousand miles away in the North, to become tenants of this hermit abode.

We thought, as we passed by it, that perhaps "the romance of the thing" had led some one of our Northern young ladies here, and who, after being the occupant of this lonely abode for several weeks, had found the romantic mood somewhat changed. We imagined her sighing, as she urged some little Southern loiterer along the *flowery* path of knowledge—

> "What else, alas! could there betide
> With 'naught but romance' for my guide?
> Better had I through mire and bush
> Been lantern-led by friar RUSH."

We also noticed a plantation, just beginning in the woods. A house was half erected, and some fifty acres of the timber "deadened." Some planter, we were informed, was starting alone, without slaves.

A portion of the old forest, standing girdled and dead in the deep green-wood, always appeared to me one of Nature's burial-grounds.

On coming up to "Rose Hill" plantation, we seemed to be approaching "old Drummond Castle, of Hawthornden," or some other old English Castle, seated on a fine eminence, commanding a view of its rough, widely-extended and broken domain. It is a princely mansion, looking out from its elevated position through a wealth of evergreen-trees and shrubs; and many a lordly oak throws its shade over its sloping lawns.

We passed through several gates and yards before we were ushered, by a servant that had met us at the first gate, into the inner grounds about the "Castle." Here we found a rich profusion of ornamental trees, among them the magnolia, the holly, and all the evergreens—even the mistletoe, on a large shade-tree, was pointed out to us. There was neatness, taste and beauty displayed in laying out and adorning these grounds.

The residence is a two-story building, the second plantation-house we had seen in the uplands not built of logs. It has three dormer windows in front, and a fine porch with a railing running around it, and a little lattice-gate in its center, to which you ascend by four steps, and over which Colonel R.'s hand was extended, ever ready to receive and welcome his guests.

He is a Tenneseean, and received the title he bears under JACKSON, in the last war. He is a well informed man, of polite manners, and delights in the chase, for which he has ever ready trained horses and hounds.

For the sake of the education of a little grand-daughter whom he has adopted, he has erected a pretty little school-house, finely finished inside and out. He also allows a few other children to attend, as playmates for his little "*protege.*" This *petit* academy is, on Sunday, a little chapel for his family, a neighbor or two, and his tenants. Miss T., of Ohio, is his very excellent teacher. She has since died, while teaching here in this delightful abode.

We have been more particular in noticing Colonel R.'s plantation, on account of its rough, and apparently untillable domain of some six thousand acres, which nature seems to have formed more in a romantic than a utilitarian mood. And it is not a cotton-plantation. He only makes one hundred bales of cotton yearly. His attention is chiefly given to raising cattle and sheep. He informed me that he usually "marked" four or five hundred calves every spring. Planters generally have said that sheep could not be made profitable here. They have no pastures for them. Colonel R. contradicts this. He had just received a letter from Colonel WARE, of Tennesee, a celebrated "wool grower," pricing his sheep—the Cotswold breed. The wool was six inches long, and the finest and richest I ever saw. Will not the mildness of the Southern winter cause the wool to grow, during this season, instead of retarding its growth, as our cold Northern ones do?

After supper, at which we found a greater variety of the luxuries of life than we had usually done at planters' tables, and after we had had a chat with Colonel R., just before retiring for the night, he invited us all to attend family prayer with him. He did not forget to thank his God for the blessings of life he was enjoying. We were then shown to our room by him, a servant also attending us, who took our boots and blacked them. The room was finely furnished, and graced by a rich old ELIZABETHAN bed-stead. But as we

"Wrapped the drapery of our couch about us,
And lay down to pleasant dreams,

we should surely have preferred the thick "bossy shield of ACHILLES," to this hard bed. The mattress had been taken out from beneath the light feather bed, and, by accident, had not been replaced.

"The child will weep a bramble's smart,
A maid to see her sparrow part,
A stripling for a woman's heart;
But when o'er the trav'ler's weary bed,
Doth sleep, in vain, her poppies shed,
Then list the grief—the groans—the sighs
That flood with manly tears his eyes."

We deserve the pillory for having mentioned this, because not an unpleasant reflection should arise with the remembrance of the princely hospitality we ever met with at Rose Hill, from Colonel R. and his estimable lady. It was only the prick of the thorn we felt from sleeping on roses. Probably the thing would not occur again to a guest at this mansion, in a score of Olympiads.

In the morning we took the carriage, and drove to Oak Ridge, near which Esquire W. lived, another planter, to whom we had been referred, who wished "to get up a school."

"To get up a school," a phrase used here, often implies more than merely "hiring a teacher." It has a sort of "squatter sovereignty" significance; a log house is erected in the woods, and the teacher thus makes, or takes possession of his "claim." And the commencing of his term is called, "taking in school."

We, in our ride this morning, passed by another of these solitary habitations, or one that had once been inhabited, but was now, like an old bird's-nest, deserted of its dam and brood. It stood crowning a knoll in the woods.

"There was nothing left to fancy's guess,
You saw that all was loneliness."

Perhaps some Ichabod Crane of the North had here, between the hours given to

"Slates, books and boys,"

courted some Southern KATARINA VAN TASSEL, and won her successfully.

Our directions we remember to have been this, from Rose Hill to Esquire W.'s:

"Follow the ridge around the deep gulley, go through Mrs. J.'s plantation—a relation of Colonel RICHARD M. JOHNSON, and turn to the right by the Cherokee rose, and in a mile or two you will come to a garden on the left hand side of the road from the house; turn to the left around this garden, and you will soon be at Esquire W.'s."

We did so, and soon found ourself there.

This planter wished a school, and would be willing, with two or three others, to pay nearly fifty dollars per month. But *he* could not hire. They had trustees here, whom if I would come and see in a few days, they would decide about the school. We had only to rein our horses about and go back to Rose Hill—merely that and nothing more.

> "Look not sadly on the past,
> Faith and love are growing stronger;
> Buds of hope are swelling fast,
> Wait a little longer."

On our return to the Ridge House, we had been interrupted both going and coming, by driving around trees that had fallen across the road, Mrs. W. pointed out to us, the tree that had lately fallen upon a planter's carriage and killed a daughter, sitting by the side of her mother, while her mother, and a smaller sister in her arms, escaped unhurt.

The next day we visited Miss G.'s school, Bellevue Academy, that we have before described. The school consists of about fifteen scholars. Some come four or five miles, riding on horseback, attended by negro servants, and some come in carriages. The higher English branches, French, and music, were usually taught here. I think history is studied more at the South, than in our Northern schools.

It was a novel sight to see a school-room decked with boughs of the "rarest mistletoe," and branches from the evergreen holly. The following fragment of poetry occurred to us:

> "The mistletoe hung in the castle hall,
> And the holly-branch shone on the old oak wall."

Referring to them in old English mansions; but they seemed very appropriate here.

The school was under good discipline. It had been, generally, under the charge of Northern young ladies. The people here preferred them, not merely from their habit of getting school-teachers from abroad, but because they were fond of their society for themselves and their families. I have been prouder of Northern young ladies that I have met here as teachers, than of Northern young men in that vocation.

---

## CHAPTER IX.

> "Where the foot-path rustics plod,
> Where the breeze-bowed poplars nod,
> Where his pencil paints the sod,
> Where the old woods worship God."
>
> ELLIOTT.

The heavy dews of last night hung in drops from every leaf and bough in the forest, and when morning came, in her fresh radiance, she converted them all into jewels.

This is a tribute of splendor she pays to the day. Though she may do this at other times, on every fair morning, yet this is the Sabbath morning, and a peculiar robe of richness clothes everything. Nothing appears to be attractive in the house, for

"God and beauty are out of doors."

We are to go to church this morning. The servant has already brought out the carriage to the gate, and sits in his seat holding the horses. My horse also stands saddled, and hitched to the post. Master HARRY W. is to accompany me on his little pony.

A pleasant ride of two miles, over a pleasant road, brought us to the church. The building is of cypress-wood, and though homely and unattractive in its appearance, yet the forest trees standing about it beautify the place of the sanctuary. It is the church we have before described.

We found that many people had already arrived. The planters and their sons came on horse-back. Their horses stood, here and there, under the trees, with the bridle thrown over a lower limb, or fastened to small trees and clumps of grape-vines. One of them will stand hitched to a little twig, all day long, as contentedly as if hitched to a post.

Carriages, silver-plated, flashing back the sun-beams from their burnished surfaces, with negro drivers in livery, sitting or lounging in their seats, each with the reins in his hands, holding a fine span of horses before them, are standing in various places about the church, in the shade of the trees; others come glittering and whirling up, in different directions from out the woods, pause a moment at the steps, while richly dressed ladies step out of them, and walk into the church. Other planters, and young men, with now and then a lady, on horse-back, continued to come, till enough men had assembled to constitute several groups, that stood conversing here and there about the church.

I was a stranger among them, and, from the novelty of it, an observer of this Sabbath scene, which, that no more appeared to come, I now supposed to be completed; when I saw, emerging from a bend in the road, a plain dressed getleman and lady, in a poor old buggy, drawn by a horse as poor.

This lonely vehicle, that came up and stopped before the church door, appeared very coarse and plebeian, when compared with the splendid patrician equipages that were glittering about it. This gentleman, who was middle aged, with his young looking wife, stepped out of the buggy; the latter went into the church, while the former went about from group to group among the planters, and shook hands in a very friendly manner with them all. They greeted him cordially and with much respect. It was parson A. who had formerly preached to this little church, and who was now on a visit to his old parishioners; he was to preach to them to-day. They all followed him into church—some rather slowly, for it was a day, when "the idside of the door was the wrong side of the house."

Seated with parson A. in the pulpit, was a younger parson, who had not yet received license to preach; he was in his "exhorting days." The young Methodist minister begins by first preaching to the negroes; then he is admitted to the conference, from which place he is sent out on his circuit.

The sermon was a common one. I was very much mistaken in the man. He had a high forehead, and a head that indicated large intellectual powers, with a physical development that a Senator would be proud of. The sermon was on the pitch of a roused BOANERGES. I lost the text in the *low* voice in which it was announced, and I lost most of the sermon in the *loud* voice in which it was delivered. The little snow-ball that started at the top of the hill, came down upon us, at the foot, in a perfect avalanche. I could not help thinking that this man had enough material in him to make two or three common ministers.

The people seemed very devotional. Almost every one knelt, during the prayers that were offered, and I was informed, afterwards, that more than two-thirds of the congregation of sixty people, were professed members of the church.

I believe that, for a warm shake of the hand, or true friendly greeting, either among themselves or with strangers, Southrons would be noticed. There was, at least, a warmth of feeling and friendship expressed by this Sabbath concourse, towards each other, as they met and parted at church. that I particularly noticed.

## CHAPTER X.

> "The best laid schemes o' *mice* and *men*,
> Gang aft a-gley."
>
> BURNS.

In a few days I mounted my horse again, not Rollo, whom I had heretofore rode; I had changed and got one safer; the former was too shy, often causing me to ride in fear. He would take alarm and start suddenly from the flight of a bird over my head, and whenever one of those great black, American vultures raised itself on its lazy, albatross wings, from the fence, where troops of them would sit all day long in the sun, after having gorged themselves like carrion crows, he would start so suddenly that I had the utmost difficulty in keeping my seat in the saddle. But the bay pony I now rode, and whom I claimed as mine, after I had found out his good qualities, nothing frightened him; he would pass through the most alarming scenes as undisturbed as a canal-boat.

It was his custom after I had raised the latch of the gate, to push it open with his head, and if it swung back too quickly against his haunches, ere he got through, he, instead of kicking at it, and running from it, as Rollo used to do, would turn around and push it back with his head. I have often given him the reins and let him manage the gate himself.

Instead of going immediately to Esquire W.'s, as I had promised to do, or intended, I rode on to Dr. H.'s, in Milldale, three miles further, as I was informed he wished a teacher, and that it was also a fine situation. Dr. H.'s residence was the best finished log plantation-house I had yet seen. The walk to it from the gate was avenued by fine rows of arbor vitæ trees. It was a beautiful rural home, with its humbler negro dwellings in their shady retreat back from the road. I found him a man of science, and fine reputation in his profession. Many of his old students were located in different parts of the country, in the practice of medicine.

He wished a teacher, but could not hire one until the new directors were elected. He would write and let me know, when that event transpired. Here was another bud of hope, encouraging me to—

"Wait a little longer."

I rode back to Esquire W.'s plantation, through a beautiful wood, where birds, with plumage in all the lovely, parti-colored hues of its foliage, were singing. His domain was rough and broken. His house—a rude, log structure, the palings about it, old and wretched. Three or four arbor vitæ trees, with two of their tops broken off, alone adorned the door-yard.

The family consisted of himself and son, three buxom, healthy daughters, the oldest of whom had just married a young Missourian, who was overseeing for his father-in-law. Besides these, there were several small children, with two or three relatives, living in the family.

At supper I met them all. They were seated at the table as I have before stated;—the father was at the head, like the old patriarchal wood on the banks of the Mississippi; the oldest son was the growth below, and so they went lowering down by regular grades to the youngest stripling. While on the other side, the youngest daughter commenced like the young cotton-wood tree, and from her they rose up in successive gradations to the parent-wood, which was here gone—the mother had died. The eldest daughter took her place.

The father asked a blessing, and then proceeded to serve us, by the aid of a servant, to the plain fare before us. I have seldom seen the boiled ham missing before the planter, at his table; fresh pork supplied its place here. This was occasioned by the fact, that the "Ides of November" had just passed among the herd of swine on this plantation.

During the evening Esquire W. gave me his history. He was, he said, in religious parlance, what was denominated a "hard shell Baptist." But there was not much in a name. A "hard shell Baptist," he thought, was a misnomer. At least, their shells were as soft as *any body else's.*" He told me that this anti-mission sect of Baptists were numerous in the "piny-woods" part of Mississippi.

He began life for himself, as an overseer on Mrs. Judge SHIELD'S plantation. He was there in that capacity, when a "raw Yankee boy," from Maine, came there to teach in her family, who afterwards was so widely known as the eloquent S. S. PRENTISS. And he had the honor to have given him the first fees he ever won in a law-suit.

In the morning I met the trustees,

> "Now by two-headed JANUS,
> Nature hath framed strange fellows in her time."

I did not like their looks—the way they talked about their school—the wages they offered me—some forty dollars per month and board myself—nor their school-house—nor the idea of walking so far to a boarding-place.

They told hard stories about their neighbors—the old trustees using the public money, and then refusing to pay the district the amount expended. They were hard cases, and it could not be collected of them.

Considering all things I concluded not to teach this school. Before I left, Esquire W. made me an offer to teach as private tutor in his family, with a salary of some five hundred dollars per year, and a home. I kept this as a "forlorn hope" for a week or so, but abandoned it as soon as a brighter prospect dawned upon my path.

A few hours' ride brought me to Rose Hill, where I stayed all night, and the next day went home.

During this week S. and I took a horse-back ride of six miles. We went to call on a rich planter's daughter. At the North it would be going to see a young lady in the country. Here ——— ——— we'll see.

I don't know what horse Chevalier BAYARD rode on such trips, but ours were pacers—both S.'s and mine. And, by the way, all these horses are pacers, which is a fortunate thing for this equestrian people, for the gait is as easy as a carrriage.

The morning had been rainy, which with yesterday's deluge had made the roads very muddy. I feared my horse would slip and break his neck, or mine, or both, all the way there. I know our Northern horses, unshod like these, would have slipped down twenty times going this distance.

We reached Mr. M.'s plantation just in time to lose our dinners. He has a fine residence; the walk from the front gate to it is shaded by beautiful arbor vitæs, and the entire grounds about the house are adorned by fine ornamental trees. A tall "Spanish Dagger" stood leaning its crested head against the veranda, and various clumps of shrubs and flowers studded the yard.

We found Mr. M. an intelligent gentleman, with whom we conversed quite a while about a Northern land—lying somewhere between the great lakes and the matchless Ohio. He is a richly possessed Southron; and with hi family usually spends the summer in traveling.

Miss CARRIE, his daughter, the young lady who was honored with our call, was as naive as a "NINA"—as full of chit-chat as a Bob-o-link is of song, and as playful and frolic as "gentle ELIA." From a hint in her conversation I concluded that she had visited the North, which led me to ask her if she had.

"O yes," she replied, "Ma and Pa, sister and brother and I made a tour of the North last summer." And then changing the subject with an air of indifference that vexed you, she seemed to say,

"Don't ask any more questions, Mr. Northerner, I

have seen your Hurons and Eries, your Niagaras and Trentons, your Avons and Saratogas," as if they had been little "stations" she had passed by along the rail-road.

While conversing with her father, she and S. left us. In a short time I heard the strains of music from another room. Mr. M. arose and invited me into the drawing-room, where we found Miss CARRIE entertaining S. by playing some lightsome tune on a magnificent piano. She then played for us, uniting her voice with the rich tones of the instrument, which we enjoyed very much. We were in that mood when association enhances the enjoyment of music so much, and sets one a-dreaming. The music got the start of us, we know, and it puzzled us to tell how well Miss CARRIE did play.

The room was ornamented with large paintings of the family; books magnificently bound laid on a rich center-table, and a little cabinet of many curious and rare things brought home from travel, with fine daguerreotypes of the family, of a daughter away to the North at school, of a Miss W. of Vermont, late governess in the family, and whom Miss CARRIE said she "loved most dearly."

Although I remember this visit to Mr. M.'s plantation, as a most pleasant and agreeable one, yet as WILLIS would say, it was "sandwiched" between two slippery horse-back rides. I remember one hill was so steep that my horse, going down it, slid on all fours, a rod at a time, while I feared that I should perform one of those "circus-evolutions" over his head.

After waiting a few days I heard that the new trustees in Milldale had been elected, and I started out the third time for that place. It was sixteen miles distant on the Ridge road towards Vicksburgh. I am one of three competitors for the school. This, aside from the doubt of my getting the school at all, makes my chance two thirds less.

And my competitors have both the advantage of me; one is a Mississippian—an old teacher, well known to the people. The other is a Missourian, residing with a relative who is one of the patrons of the school.

I had gone to Milldale the day previous to the trial, for we understood that we were to be examined by a graduate from college, and the one that passed best was to be selected as their teacher.

It was 10 o'clock in the morning of a beautiful day—one of those days in which "nature is glad all over from flower to star," as I reined my horse up to the blacksmith's shop, about which the people had assembled, ere going over to the school-house, to witness the examination. The whole neighboring country had turned out, as if it had been training-day.

Colonel R.'s son riding by in his carriage, seeing me, a stranger—Dr. H. could not be present—stopped his carriage and introduced me to five or six of the gentlemen present. It was one of the many kind and gentlemanly acts that it had been my lot to experience South, but this was of a nature deserving one's warm and sincerest thanks.

At the appointed time we all went over to the school-house. It was a frame building, and the finest one I had seen of the kind, situated on a pleasant knoll, back from the road in a fine grove of trees.

The Missourian told me, on the way there, that although he had taught school once, he had been training horses lately, and was rather rusty in his knowledge. He was an athlete—stout and robust, fitter for any other arena, I thought, than that of the school-room.

The trustees were men of sober judgment, and possessed of intelligence sufficient, at least, to perform the functions of the highest official duties in the county. Mr. H., the collegian, and the gentleman who was to examine us, appeared to be a man of sound intelligence and good attainments.

After an hour's attention to other matters, the officers came to the affair on hand. The Mississippian was well known, he "rested his case with the people." Not so with the Missourian and myself. We were called on, lawyer-like, to make the "points in our case," that they might get some clue to our character and standing. The Missourian took the floor first. I have no intention to disparage the fellow, because he was a rival for the school; I certainly feared the Mississippian the most in the trial; but I could not help thinking, while he was relating his experience in teaching, which was not very interesting, that he, like TONY LUMPKINS, in GOLDSMITH'S play, had never

> "——puzzled his brains
> With grammar, and nonsense, and learning."

After he had got through, they called for a letter of recommendation. He had none. But his relative—one of the patrons of the school—would inform them, should they wish to know anything more about him.

I had the advantage of the closing plea. What I had to say "was summed up in brief." They then called for a letter of recommendation. This was a "bar" to my plea. I was worse off than the Missourian; I had given away all my letters of recommendation, and had no friend to vouch for me. At this juncture, I chanced to think that I had two letters that Professor H., of Detroit, Michigan, had given me, and although they were not addressed to gentlemen whom they knew, I presented them as my *dernier resort.* It was a timely hit; from the fact that they were addressed to Southrons, they carried much weight with them. Having read them, they appeared to be satisfied.

But yet, the real combat was to come. We, as champions, had entered the "list," by merely "touching the refrain of our spears to the shield." We were now to enter the arena by "touching their points against it." A critical examination was to ensue. But, at this crisis in our trial, the trustees held a short conference by themselves, after which they deliberately told us, that all they could now do for us, was to give us the chance of getting the school by drawing up a subscription, which we could have the privilege of circulating among the patrons of the school, and the one that got the most signers, Mr. H. would examine, by way of installing him into his office. This was a poser—a poser.

I concluded to parley no more about the matter. But, before I left Milldale, through the solicitation of Dr. H., I drew up a writing in regard to my teaching the school, which, he assured me, he would have circulated, and let me know the result. The other applicants, of course, would do the same.

I stayed all night with him, at his fine home, and very much enjoyed his society, and that of his lady and their two pretty daughters, who had lately been attending boarding-school in Vicksburgh. Mrs. H.'s brother, Mr. FRANK J., an intelligent and worthy young gentleman, was residing in their family. He had been their late teacher.

The next morning I started for home. Giving the loose reins to my horse, I rode along enjoying the lovely weather of a tropical December—the Southern woods, in their long spanish beards, though faded and partly leafless, yet beautiful with their ridges crowned with oak and unknown trees; with their evergreens—their clambering and tangled vine-work; with their dells "choked up" with the green, luxuriant cane; with their bird-songs, and soft gushes of rustling leaf-music.

Tired of sitting so long in the saddle, I got down from it at the gate of the Ridge House, past mid-afternoon. But much to my disappointment, I found no letters from home—none from anywhere else.

This, with all of my fruitless adventures in search of a school, made me feel rather melancholy. I don't believe that disappointment has any new springs that she has not lately touched to surprise me.

I never was a favorite of Dame FORTUNE; I believe, instead of recognizing me as one of her children, she has played the cruel step-mother to me; and, considering me a little truant, has laid the rod on unsparingly. If, in a ramble in the woods, with my play-fellows, I cut my name on a tree, visiting the spot again, I was sure to find it effaced, while those of my mates remained untouched, as if guarded by her. I really believe she, from the first, intended to thwart my schemes—cross my luck, and disinherit me from my share of enjoyment in this life, that her favorite children might have it all. If there was a shadow, she has thrown it across *my* path, and often, with more cruelty, across my heart. And, in fine, if I am to judge of her, from the rigid lessons she has given me through life, she has considered me her little HERCULES; for my tasks have always been the hardest, and most severely imposed.

"Dame LIFE, though fiction out may trick her,
And in paste gems and frippery deck her;
Oh! flickering feeble and unsicker,
I've found her still,
On wavering like the willow wicker
'Tween good and ill."

Reader! don't consider this a *do-lo-rous* lament, just on the eve of a *felo-de-se*. No; It is merely what, in friendly parlance, is termed—"unbosoming" one's self of troubles, to some "bosomed-friend;" or, I felt a little of the "woful agony" of the "ancient mariner,"

"Till my ghastly tale was told,
And then it left me free."

But I sometimes fear that my pedagoguic "laurels" here, will turn to Southern willows; or, that I shall have to twine my wreath of magnolias, hollies, Cherokee roses, that I shall earn in trying to find a school, and go home.

But we are to have the holidays next week; we shall enjoy them and tell you something about them among this feudal people.

---

## CHAPTER XI.

"Lo, now is come our joyfulest feast!
Let every man be jolly,
Eache roome with yvie leaves is drest,
And every post with holly.
Now all our neighbors' chimneys smoke,
And Christmas blocks are burning;
Their ovens they with bak't meats choke,
And all their spits are turning.
Without the door let sorrow lie,
And if from cold, it hap to die,
We'll bury 't in a Christmas pie
And evermore be merry."

*Sketch-Book.*

"And is old, old, good old Christmas gone? Nothing but the hair of his good old gray head and beard left? Well, I will have that, seeing I cannot have more of him."

No, good old Christmas is not gone. Though he is not so often seen in his jolly, merry humor at the North, as in the good old time agone;

> "Still linger in our Northern clime
> Some remnants of the good old time."

Yet this morning I thought the old fellow had really come, for, ere I was up, just as the day was coming in from the East, the negro servant came into my room to build a fire, and he had scarcely opened the door, ere he shouted —"*Christmas gift*, Mr. VAN BUREN! *Christmas gift*, Mr. VAN BUREN!" and ere he had shouted twice, another came in, and yet another, till the room was filled with a joyous, merry chime, of negro voices, shouting, "Christmas gifts," to me.

But it was not only in my room; I heard them shouting it to every one about the house. The cry sounded from every room,—"Christmas gift, massa!"—"Christmas gift, missus!" "Christmas gift!" to every one they met.

After the family had arisen, there was a merry peal of "Christmas gifts," as they met each other, Miss G., or myself. I returned their greeting as I had that of the negroes, by wishing them a "merry Christmas," but it was lost amid a shower of theirs. I became discouraged—changed, and shouted "Christmas gifts" with them.

As soon as this greeting was over, and we had all assembled in the sitting-room, servants came in with foaming cups of egg nogg, on servers. There was no use talking temperance now. They urged the cups to our lips, if we did no more than sip a bubble on the beaker's brim, we must do it by way of drinking health to good old Christmas. We had scarcely done this, ere Miss G. came in, and detected us in replacing the cups on the server.

She hinted something about temperance, and reporting us to our Northern friends.

We replied, that we would leave it to the hand that penned such a note, whether it was not telling its own story; that it had held, this morning, a foaming goblet of egg nogg, to her own lips.

We were soon summoned to breakfast. Our repast was truly a sumptuous one. Barrels of apples, oranges, oysters, large quantities of wine, and all the cheer for the holidays had been received from New Orleans.

We had a chat, at table, about the Southron custom of greeting one with a "Christmas gift," instead of wishing you a "merry Christmas," as we of the North did. They knew nothing about the origin of their custom, it had been with them time immemorial.

I noticed all the negroes were in high glee;—

"The negro is a merry negro, when
Old Christmas brings his sports again,
'Twas Christmas broached the migh'est ale;
'Twas Christmas told the merriest tale;
'Twas Christmas' gambols oft could cheer
The negro's heart through half the year."

Besides, he announced to them that cotton-picking was over and gone, and that they could revel in fun and frolic for a whole week.

I can give no better idea of the manner of spending the holidays in the South, than by quoting from a writer who thus describes them in "Merry England:"

"In large houses are large parties, music and feasting, dancing and cards. Beautiful faces, and noble forms, the most fair and accomplished of England's sons and daughters, beautify the ample firesides of aristocratic halls. Senators and judges, lawyers and clergymen, poets and philosophers, there meet in cheerful, and even sportive ease amid the elegancies of polished life. In old-fashioned, but aristocratic country abodes, old-fashioned hilarity prevails. In all the families, hearty spirits are met, and here are dancing and feasting, too."

Sir WALTER SCOTT, in giving a description of Christmas in "auld Scotia," thus merely repeats the above in his beautiful verse:

"Then opened wide the baron's hall
To vassal, tenant, serf, and all;
Power laid his rod of rule aside,
And ceremony doffed her pride.
The heir with roses in his shoes,
That night might village partner choose;
The lord, underrogating, share
The vulgar game of 'post and pair.'
All hailed with uncontrolled delight,
And general voice the happy night,
That to the cottage as the crown,
Brought tidings of salvation down."

This is literally true of the South. Throughout the country, on every plantation, there is a merry time—a joyous leisure from all work; merry Christmas is with them all. The negroes, whole troops of them mounted on mules, male and female, laughing and singing, go from one plantation to another; thus gathering in jolly groups they feast and frolic and dance the time away.

They are all dressed in their best, many of them in broadcloth. They have their nice white dickies on, their boots are blacked, and a white or silk handkerchief is sure to display itself from some one of their pockets, or from their hand. A negro is your true frolicker. His sable periphery will hold more merriment, fun and pent up animal spirit, than any other human being's.

To see a group of them on the floor, or on the lawn, beneath the shade of the China-trees, when

> "Hornpipes, jigs, strathspeys and reels
> Put life and mettle in their heels;"

whirling in the giddy mazes of the dance with their buxom dulcenas, each seeming to vie with the other in dancing the most; it is one of the finest specimens of animated nature I ever gazed upon.

No restraint of the ettiquettish ball-room, to fetter their actions and motions, but, charged like galvanic batteries, full of music, they dance with a vigorous *vim.*

Restraint! whew! they'd burst like steamers. No. They must dance untrammeled; the action must be suited to the spirit, the spirit to the action—perfect *lusus naturaes!* What luxury of motion, what looks—breathing and sighs! what oglings, exclamations and enjoyment!

This is *dancing.* It knocks the spangles off your light fantastic tripping, and sends it whirling out of the ball-room.

Dancing is not confined to the negroes alone, the planter's whole household is entirely given up to merry-making during the holidays.

The dance and festival is first held at one planter's house, and then at another's; two or three often assembling in one place, where they have what is termed a "storming."

I spent the holidays at the Ridge House. We had, beside our own family, two cousins with us, and several of the young ladies from adjacent plantations. One of the cousins, who was rather conspicuous in merry-making, was called cousin JERRY, or, more commonly, JERRY.

His form was in a very slight degree inclined to the circumflex. But when standing erect, he was considerably above the medium height. He had light brown hair, and eyes of a dull, dark, hazy color. His beard, usually, at the latter part of the week, showed like stubble-land at harvest-home. He was dressed rather plain, and was not particular about his collar and dicky, if they did not retain the whiteness of "JULIET'S hand," he would wear them after they were a little soiled. JERRY had one of those kind of minds that retain its originality, despite all the pumice and polish of education; nothing seemed to embellish it. He had been at an academy—studied hard, and taught school; yet his mind was unimbued by a single thought from study or books. He had nearly finished the forenoon of life a—bachelor; and but one thing hindered him from traveling life's dull round without trouble; and that was—woman. She had affected his heart with a spell of her prettiness and love. She was a beautiful Will-o'-the-Wisp that was ever flitting across his path, luring and bewitching him.

Amid the revelry of the evening he was the Don QUIXOTE. His body a little inclined moved down the graceful sweeps and giddy mazes of the dance, without animation; his arms hung dangling at his side; the only motion that he made was a slight shuffling of his feet in heavy boots. His partner was Miss G.; she was indeed a pretty Will-o'-the-Wisp, leading him a dance. Her dark flowing curls, and fine sparkling black eyes entranced him. But, in the circumlocution of its sweeps, he would often lose her, when W., one of the revelers, would step in, intercepting him, and finish the figure with her. Then again, Miss MATTIE, or, as he called her—his "dangerous little cousin"—would, by the witchery of her pranks, get him so tangled up in the warp and woof of the dance, that he, unable to extricate himself, would dance at random, to the amusement of all. At another time, he, undertaking to go through one of the whirling evolutions with his partner, threw out his awkward feet, she stumbled over them, and fell superbly prostrate on the floor; while he stood, astonished and sorrowful, looking down upon her with a wondering stare.

During the evening I was also much amused with young Dr. Y., a wealthy planter's son. He had got rather merry with the dance and wine, and called upon the old negro, who was fiddling for the party, to play a favorite tune of his, for *that* dance. And after it had been played for him repeatedly, he called for it again; throwing down, as usual, a half-dollar at his feet.

The old negro replied, "Why massa, I jus done play that tune, for you, five or six time."

"Play away, I tell you," cried the Dr., "there's your money," throwing down another half-dollar. This he repeated so often that we began to wish ourself in the place of the old negro, fiddling for such a shower of silver.

During the evening some of the young folk left, to attend a wedding among the negroes at the quarters. JERRY, rather anxious, of course, to know something about the nuptials, asked several questions concerning the wedding; and among the rest, he wished to know "whether the course of 'niggers' love' didn't run any smoother than white folks'?"

This was a pretext to rally him; which Major W. began by saying that he had observed that "JERRY was fond of lonely walks in the woods, gathering flowers and mistletoe boughs for the ladies—repeating poetry, and musing on the stars. These," he said, "were unfailing signs that he was sighing for some lady-love."

To all of which, JERRY, who had a droll humor, made many a shrewd reply.

But when the Major told of one of his lady-love's cheating him—getting married in his absence; and how that JERRY, not knowing this, had, on his return, approached the "nest," with silent and wary step, to secure the prize, but, lo! on grasping, he found the nest warm, but *the bird had flown!* to this JERRY replied, "That although he sorrowed much over the loss of the bird, he condoled much more over her fate, being caught—referring to her husband—in the "fowler's snare."

"And more than this," said he, tauntingly, "the poor bird will soon be a starveling; for the old man didn't give the poor drone anything with her, and he hasn't industry enough to keep a chicken alive."

JERRY'S love had a golden element in it. It

> "Was no flickering flame that dies,
> Unless when fanned by looks and sighs,
> And lighted oft by ladies' eyes;
> He longed to stretch his wide command
> O'er heiress CLARA'S ample land."

The hospitality of the Ridge House was extended to many a guest for the night. Our room was supplied with couches for several. We had JERRY with us.

After the sound of revelry had ceased, the last taper been extinguished, and the revelers were all asleep, or in the realms of dream land, the loud and repeated "halloo" was heard sounding out from the gate, on the still air of night.

A servant answered it, and soon ushered in young Mr. H., a neighboring planter's son, who came with news that soon aroused the whole household.

The negroes, in the east part of the county, had banded themselves, in a fierce and furious band, against the whites, and were coming into our neighborhood, murdering every family in their approach.

Major W. read the letter the young man brought, containing the awful news, then calmly told his family and guests that they might get out their guns and make every necessary preparation for defense. But they would please excuse him, as he had been up late and needed rest, he would retire again. But he would thank them to let him know when they came, and he would get up—marshal all his forces and defend his "Castle."

At this, feeling safe, in the coolness with which Major W. treated this report, we all retired to rest again, and soon forgot the cause of our alarm. It was not so with JERRY. Visions of muskets, bowie-knives, pitch-forks, scythes, and the coming of the vengeful foe, floated before his half-shut eyes. At every sound he heard, the remainder of the night, he would start up, grasp the Jew-peddler, with whom he slept, and cry out, "There! the niggers are coming!"

And out of bed he would spring, to awaken Major W. But some one would call him back and quiet his fears. Others would tell him that they did not fear the niggers, as long as he was about the house, like a ghost, in his night habiliments. The negroes never came.

The wedding, above mentioned, took place at the plantation-house, on New Year's eve. Two of Major W.'s slaves were there united in marriage. Many of the young folk, and very many of the blacks, were present on this occasion. Everything being ready, the two stepped forward to be married. The blooming bride, showily dressed, came forward in all her sable beauty, with eyes of sparkling blackness, and—

"Mouth with pearl and ruby glowing,"

and gave herself, as a New Year's gift, to a robust negro.

The twain were pronounced—a sable unit, by a minister residing in the neighborhood.

New Year's morning we had for the accustomed—"I wish you a happy New Year," that which I had been used to hear—the Southern one of—"A *New Year's gift.*" The festival went on during the day, and at night we had a "storming."

The next day, I was witness to a really affecting scene; one that remained very vividly impressed upon my mind. Major W. and his brother-in-law, Mr. H., had held, for many years, their slaves in conjunction; working them on the same plantation. To-day, Mr. H. was to take his slaves to a plantation he had recently purchased, in another part of the State. Major W., his lady and family, went out, as the negroes stopped at the gate, to bid them good-bye. They shook hands with them one by one, as they passed on, and cried as if their own children, brothers and sisters, were leaving home. The family, negroes and all, were in tears. But poor old EASTERN—uncle EASTERN, as the children always call him—he too was to go. He had been the faithful servant in the W. family for many, very many years. But he had built their fires for the last time. And all the kind acts and offices he had performed for the family, which had bound him to them during a service going back to the earliest childhood of the oldest of the household, were now to cease.

This faithful old EUMÆUS, shook hands and bade his master and mistress, and all the children, good-bye, with eyes suffused with tears, and voice too full for utterance. They all wept. He was truly the fitting one to close so affecting a scene.

## CHAPTER XII.

"Inveni portum. Spes et fortuna, valete.
Sat me lusisti: ludite uunc alios."
"My port is gained, farewell to the freaks of chance,
The dance they led me, now let others dance."

LE SAGE.

After a respite of the holidays, I got into the saddle once more, to make another adventure. My route was along the Yazoo valley. Major W., and Dr. Y.'s son, who resided there, assured me that I could get a good school in that region.

Two incidents, in this trip, left themselves traced upon my mind. At the foot of the slope, in descending from the bluffs into the valley, at Satartia, during the rainy season, there is a slough of clay mire—a "terrible pass." Your horse literally wades and plunges through it.

As I came to the brow of the hill, I saw two horsemen, down below on the other side of the pass. They had brought their steeds to a halt, and were apparently considering whether they had better venture through. One was the Irish teacher, whom I have noticed a-back. He seemed to be "telling his rosary," ere he made so formidable a risk. I sat on my horse and watched their progress, till their horses struggled and floundered through.

Next came my trial. I never rode in so much fear in my life. My horse's feet sunk so deep in the mire, and he struggled so hard to extricate them, that I thought, at times, he would pull his legs off, in endeavoring to pull them out of it. I rejoiced after he had pitched and floundered through, and was once more on *terra firma.*

There was one more pass—crossing the Yazoo in a ferry-boat. The river was high, and the wind was blowing at a furious rate, tumbling its waters into surging swells. I had hallooed a long time, and waited for the negro ferry-man to come and row me across. He came at last. I upbraided him for his delay. He replied, " 'Twasn't no reglar ferry; he needn't come less he was a mine to. There wasn't travel 'nuf to make it pay. His massa had wished the ole boat sunk, many time."

I told him, if he was ferry-man at all, he should be prompt, and not keep people waiting so long. A man's friend might be dying, while he was waiting his slow motion.

"He couldn't help it; his friend would have to wait, sar; 'twas all mere 'commodation in him, he needn't come less he was a mine to."

I told him to stop his blarney or I would throw him into the river as food for the alligators.

Our next trouble was to get the horse on board. The negro took hold of the bridle and tried to pull him on the boat, and the horse endeavored to pull the negro off; while I was on shore, making sundry evolutions and applications, about the horse's haunches, in favor of the negro's getting him aboard. We finally gained the day and got him loaded. The negro then pushed off from the shore and commenced rowing, I standing in the middle of the boat, holding my horse by the bridle. The current was strong, and despite the lusty arms of the oarsman, who plied with all his might, the boat was a mere plaything, and we elfin folk upon it, tossed about by the wild pranks of the wave. We were going down stream very fast, but I saw we were nearing the shore, which we finally reached after a long struggle.

I led my horse up the bank—paid the negro his two bits, which he thrice and four times earned—got into the saddle and rode off, looking back at the ferry-man struggling with the current's fury in re-crossing.

After riding along on the banks of the river half a mile, I came to Mr. G.'s plantation. He is very wealthy; the broad and beautiful valley here, is owned on both sides of the stream, for some distance, by this gentleman and his sons. Here I saw the first steam saw-mill, and the first cotton-gin, driven by steam.

Major W. had referred me to his friend Mr. W., with whom he advised me, as I could not reach my point of destination by dark, to stay all night.

A solitary horseman, wending his way along on the banks of the gentle Yazoo, might have been heard, on a pleasant day in December, hallooing at the gate of a Southern planter's residence, as DAN PHŒBUS drew up the reins of his steeds and halted at the evening station.

A smallish sized gentleman, in answer to his halloo, came to the gate—invited him to "get down from his horse and walk in."

His house was on the river's brim. It was one of the smaller log plantation-houses. I thought of POPE'S cottage when I saw it and its owner.

"A little cot with trees a'row,
And like its master, very low."

I alighted—my horse was taken care of—and walked into a room, in one corner of which was a large old English bedstead; a wash-stand with its bowl stood in another. These, with a few chairs, constituted its principal furniture. But a good warm fire, blazing in a broad, old-fashioned fire-place, gave an air of comfort and cheerfulness to the room.

I have, in traveling here, gone back, not in fancy, half a century, and really enjoy the pleasure of occasionally dropping into the old-fashioned homes, and taking a seat by the social, enlivening fire-side of the "Old Folks at Home," fifty years ago, ere the dull and cheerless stove was thought of, spend an evening in delightful conversation around the "old hearth-stone"—the sparkling ingle, rendered sacred by the memory of those who "have long gone before."

We found Mr. W. an intelligent gentleman. We discussed the politics of the day, and talked about some of the leading politicians North. I really think a Southern gentleman is endowed with those qualities that are requisite in entertaining a guest. The North has not got the time, or she does not take it, that is requisite in bestowing upon one all those kind acts, and variety of attention, that true hospitality is so fond of giving.

Mr. W. is from Tennessee. He has three hundred acres of cultivated valley-land, and some twenty-five or thirty slaves. His crop of cotton this year, which was a good one, brought him sixty dollars per bale. This is like Northern farmers getting fourteen shillings or two dollars per bushel for their wheat.

At table I met Mrs. W., an amiable and pretty lady, and a Miss A., the first native teacher I had met in Mississippi. She is governess in Mr. W.'s family.

After supper, Mr. W. and I retired to our room and continued our chat till long past "curfew time." The ladies kept in their room. It is not really "caste," but the feminine ingredient here, does not remain so long, or unite so often, as an article of the household compound, as with us at the North.

On retiring to rest, I found the usual bed, broad enough

to "sleep" JOHN RODGERS in, with his whole family and the little one at the breast.

Here one can easily follow Dr. FRANKLIN'S healthy advice, in having a "spare bed" for the last half of the night. All that you have to do, after sleeping the hygienic time in one part of it, is, to take a couple of turns, and you are in the "spare bed."

Here I fall asleep listening to the murmurs of the gentle Yazoo, while steamboats, illuminated as on some festive trip, are passing up, or dropping down the current.

The next morning I continued my route along on the banks of the Yazoo. About half a mile from Mr. W.'s I came to a turn in the road, and doubted whether to take it, or continue on in the straight road. I remember that a little negro, a few days ago, while I, at an angle in the road, far away in the woods, was pondering which of two directions to take, met me, somewhat in the manner, I thought, that old TIFF'S dinner did him, and who saved me from going some twenty miles out of my way. I felt very grateful to the little fellow and thanked him very much for his timely hint. Here a black milk-maid came up, with a pail in her hand, as I was about to take the turn, and cried out, at a little distance, on the run—"No, no, sir, you mus not take that road; you never reach Yazoo city by taking that road; that will take you off into the swamp."

In some two miles I came to Mr. W.'s younger brother's plantation. He has a neat, little unadorned cottage, with some pretty shade-trees around it. I afterwards became acquainted with these two brothers, and their families, and have spent many a pleasant hour in their society. "There are those among our friends whom we'd ever remember as kith and kin"—these are of them.

Young Dr. W.'s plantation was next on this road. He also is a Tennesseean; in which State he spends his summers—his winters in the Yazoo valley. We afterwards became acquainted with him, and found him one of the most sterling young men we had met in the South. He is in possession of a fine fortune. He has lately erected a pretty cottage on some picturesque locality of his plantation, and invited one of Tennessee's fair daughters to become mistress of it. They tell me—

> "She is bonnie; all the Highlands round
> Was there a rival to my JENNIE found?"

This poetic allusion is merely the sentiment of a Southern friend's letter, lately informing me of Dr. Y.'s possessing a "bonnie bride" with the command of a "pretty cottage."

I soon came to Mr. B.'s, one of the gentlemen to whom I had been referred, who wished a teacher. I stopped and took dinner here; mentioned my errand. I was opportune; and from the manner of the gentleman I knew that I was dealing with one in whom I could repose confidence and trust.

After dinner Mr. B. mounted his horse, and we rode a mile and a half to his neighbor, Mr. P.'s, plantation. This planter, also wishing a teacher, ordered his horse, and we three rode still another mile, to Dr. Y.'s residence, where in a very short time, these three wealthy planters secured my services as teacher, giving me a salary of five hundred dollars per year, and a home, besides allowing me all I could make out of extra scholars. Thus closed my adventures in pursuit of a school in this Southern land.

After two months' search I had found the prize. Disappointment had lurked in every one but the last, and, in that I found a three-fold reward.

The next day I returned to the Ridge House. The following morning Mrs. W. came into my room, and asked me if I did not wish to take a "drive" with the young ladies. They were going to make some "calls." The carriage was brought out, and, in

"The breezy call of incense-breathing morn,"

we enjoyed a fine ride through the beautiful woods, and along the pleasant valley to Mr. J.'s plantation. He is cousin to Colonel RICHARD M. JOHNSON; has a fine estate in Tennessee, where he spends his summers with his family, and his winters in this beautiful vale. Young Mr. W. C. H., who was here, uncle to Miss MATTIE W., one of our party, introduced me to Mrs. J., and her daughter, as Mr. BUCHANAN. Being about to correct his mistake, we told him it was just as well, passing *nom de plume* now-a-days was fashionable, it might bring us into celebrity.

Mrs. J. is a graduate of the famous Troy school, New York. We had a chat with her daughter, a very pretty young lady of cultivated manners. She has a brother in the Virginia University. She played on the piano and sang a love-ditty for us very prettily.

We had a chat afterwards on the mosses. Nature, we thought, had done some strange things in her time, and among them, was the freak of hanging the mosses on the tops of the trees.

But, some one replied, it was a pretty freak.

Yes, nature, like the beautiful OPHELIA, wandering in a mournful mood, about the woods, and along the streams, had hung her "fantastic garlands," and "coronets" of mosses, on the tops and "pendent boughs" of the trees.

Or was it in this region that PROSERPINE was gathering flowers, when PLUTO—the old gallant—stole her? and that FLORA, grieving her loss, had draped these woods in this streaming moss, as a badge of mourning for her.

What pleasant memories one has of visiting pleasant persons and places. The memory of that call, to-day, as we are transferring it from our journal to these pages, has all the freshness of the beezy morning in it;—we hear the sound of the voices of those Southern ladies, in that chat, the tones of the piano, responsive to the touch of Miss J.'s fingers, and the singing of that love-ditty, now as then, just as soft and musically.

But it was not so then, and we presume it is not so now, with our young ladies. Memory does not—

> "Restore every rose or secrete its thorn."

If she does, there is a rose-leaf that lies "doubled up" under the little Sybarite; for in their conversation, on our return, which was in half whisper, I heard them say, with countenances sorrowful as NIOBE'S weeping her children—that they —— —— "did not enjoy their call a *bit;*"—they had made one—"*a little too long!*"

Oh, the exquisite Sybarites—lovely PERIES, shut out of paradise because one of their morning "calls was made—*five minutes too long.*

Before going to my school in the valley, I received the following note, while at Major W.'s:

---

OAK RIDGE, Jan. 9th, 1858.

MR. A. D. P. VAN BUREN,

DEAR SIR:—I have the pleasure to inform you of your election to teach the school at Milldale, during the present year, if found compotent, and I am appointed by the Board to certify to that fact. At your earliest convenience I will confer with you for that purpose.

Yours respectfully,

JAS. T. HICKS.

It was gratifying to me to receive this letter, although it came too late to secure my services as teacher; yet after the efforts I had made—for fast and far had I ridden, to secure the school, and had even entered the list with two other champions, in a contest for it—it was the victor's wreath, although I did not wish the prize I had won.

I also heard a few days later, that the Mechanicsburgh school had closed. This was the school I first had in view; but although the news that I could have it now, came like CHESTERFIELD'S letter to Dr. JOHNSON, too late to be useful, yet it brought to me this incentive—courage for the trying scenes in the future.

In a few days I left my home at the Ridge House for one in the valley.

I had sojourned in Major W.'s family over two months, and had, during that time, not only received the kindest hospitality from him and his family, but had had a servant to wait on me, and a horse and saddle at my command. And when I asked him what I had to pay for all this, he replied—"*Not one cent, sir.*"

The manner in which he said it, evinced the truest generosity that it was ever my lot to receive. And as I bid them good-bye, and mounted my horse to leave this pleasant home, where I had spent so many pleasant days, and experienced so much kindness, it occurred to me that the memory of many, very many other treasured things in this life, would grow old, fade away, and be lost, long, *long*, ere I should forget the WILDIES.

"The bridegroom may forget the bride,
Was made his wedded wife, yestreen;
The monarch may forget the crown,
That on his head an hour has been;
The mother may forget the child,
That smiled so sweetly on her knee;
But I'll remember thee, GLENCAIRN,
And a' that thou hast done for me."

## CHAPTER XIII.

"Pretty rural homes they were,
Down in a dale, hard by a river's-side,
Near to resort of people that did pass
In travel to and fro." SPENSER.

### OAK VALLEY.

Mr. B. is a Tennesseean—an intellectual, reading, energetic, reliable man. He is a true Southern gentleman; urbane, chivalrous, and dresses with taste. Were I to draw a portrait of a real Southron, I should ask him to sit for it. He is of a fine family; has himself been elected to a seat in the Mississippi Legislature; was a delegate to the Cincinnati Convention and helped nominate Mr. BUCHANAN. One of his brothers is the editor of the "Mississippian," the first paper in the State; and another is a member of the Lower House of Congress.

He has a fine plantation of four hundred acres of arable valley-land, worked by forty or fifty slaves. His negro quarters are a little village amid sheltering trees.

His residence is a neat and tasty edifice, embowered in a profusion of shade.

In the front ground, you see several magnificent China-trees, with their umbrageous tops all a-bloom with lilac blossoms.

Tho orango myrtlc, with its glossy green foliage, trimmed in the shape of a huge strawberry; the crape myrtle with its top hanging thick with long cone-shaped flowers of a peach-blow color; the cape jasmine, with its rich polished foliage spangled all over with white starry blossoms;

the laurea mundi—that emblem of the peach-tree in evergreen; and that richest and sweetest blossomed of tropical shrubs—the japonica—that never blossoms only in the winter.

Besides these, there are rows of cedar trees, the trimmed arbor vitæs, and other perennial shrubs, in clumps about the grounds, with the holly and that pride of FLORA'S—the rich glossy-leafed, and snowy-blossomed magnolia.

Adjoining the front grounds is a garden, abounding in every variety of esculent vegetables, choice fruit-trees, and luscious grapes. It is also radiant with flowers and roses. How appropriate here the following beautiful lines of VIRGIL.

"——'et ubi mollis amaracus illum
Floribus et dulci adspirans complectitur umbra."*

Opposite the residence across the river the banks are crowned with over-hanging trees, presenting to view—a most richly picturesque, foliage scenery.

The house is expensively furnished inside.

Mrs. B. is a very amiable lady. They have an interesting family of children, whom they intend shall have the benefit of a fine education.

My home, for the last six weeks of my sojourn on the banks of the Yazoo, was in this delightful abode at Oak Valley.

## WILLOW DALE.

Mr. P., another of the patrons of our little academy, is a North Carolinian. He is an intelligent, worthy planter of convenient politics. He has read many a quaint and

*"And where the soft mojorum, breathing upon, embraces you with its flowers and shades."

rare old volume; and is a very good naturalist—the best I have met anywhere in this region. To him, and his young and accomplished lady, I am indebted for much of the enjoyment of my life South. At their noble mansion, in Willow Dale, I became acquainted with many fine Southern gentlemen and ladies.

His very large, fine residence is half hid in the luxuriant shade of many beautiful and rare trees. There is the umbrageous China-tree, in all its rich, feathery foliage; the deep-green, and the dingy, broad-leafed mulberry; the Lombardy poplar, with its top shooting up in tall, nodding plumes; the aspen, with its leaden-hued leaves lined with silver; the box-elder, the golden willow, the lovely althea, the sensitive mimosa, and all the evergreen trees, shrubs and vines, with a wild profusion of flowers and roses.

The honeysuckle clambers over a lattice-work well-house to the left of the residence, while in front, on each side of the gate within the palings, is a trellis-frame; the wood bine has climbed over and hung thick with festoons the one, and the white jasmine the other. Then, there stands on the open lawn before the house, the beautiful Spanish and willow oak, with the noble elm, and many a lofty pecan, in all their forest grandeur.

The grounds about the house, besides being thus ornamented with trees, shrubs and flowers, and finely laid out with walks, are always kept in neat order—the grass is mown down when it gets too high, and the walks are cleanly swept.

## ROUGH AND READY.

Dr. Y., (since dead,) the other patron, was a taciturn gentleman, a man of intelligence, but of stern bearing. He would have made a brave officer—one of your men that would have faced the assailants, or led a "forlorn hope" at Stony Point.

He had dark hair, dark eyes, and rather dark complexion. He was a Virginian by birth—had formerly practised in his profession, but had grown rich as a planter, and lived at his ease. His estate consists of two valuable plantations, one each side of the Yazoo; they are nearly opposite each other. Two overseers, with forty or fifty slaves each, work them.

His residence is just such an one as such a man would choose—plebian, like himself. It is a pleasant-porched, log building, and appropriately named, "Rough and Ready." One would imagine such an abode, the home of the hero of Buena Vista. It is a rude gem in a setting of China-trees, "chased" over, in front, with honeysuckle and woodbine.

The house, though of logs, has a drawing-room richly furnished. His daughter, an accomplished and beautiful lady, has a choice library in it, of many a rich and rare volume.

The first evening I passed in the valley, was at a party given at "Rough and Ready."

Here I met some of the chivalry and beauty of the South, its

"Belted knight and lady fair."

Dr. Y.'s daughter was truly the DIE VERNON of the evening; although more accustomed to refined society and the elegancies of life. Yet she resembled, in her beauty and carriage, the "heath bell of Chiveot."

Her party was composed of young ladies and gentlemen; some from Yazoo City, and some were wealthy planters' sons and daughters.

A Miss W., friend and relation of Dr. Y., was one of

the number. She was, I should think, one of the fairest of Southern ladies; of rather a voluptuous form, refined manners, and moved admirably. I had almost called her a fresh, rosy blonde.

> "Her cheeks were like the Jersey peach,
> Her eyes were blue and clear;
> Her lips were like the sumac,
> In the autumn of the year."

She was a graduate of the celebrated Troy School, New York. There was something in her manner—it was not hauteur, but something that education from abroad, and the elegancies of Southern life give. And there was something in her accent, when talking, not—a *belle* lisping, but something that assured you that she would have been a proud rival to IDA MAY—a Southern "MABELLE."

Reader, did you ever think that all eloquence was not forensic—only heard from the rostrum and the hustings; that there was eloquence and music in the human voice, when talking?

That sweet songstress of the South—AMELIA—might have included the pleasures of conversation, in the following beautiful lines of hers:

> "There's a charm in delivery—a magical art,
> That goes like a kiss from the lips to the heart."

In this pleasant land, where conversation is so much a source of enjoyment, there are many charming talkers. Miss W. was one. In our evening chit-chat, as she lisped the words with a fine accent, they became a tissue of gems. She would repeat POE'S Raven with the effect of a FANNY KEMBLE, or a SIDDONS.

During the evening she played on the guitar and sung for us,

"Woodman, spare that tree."

Had the rude forester, though a Vandal, with his axe raised to cut it down, caught her tones, he would have desisted, and spared the tree—subdued by the touching effect and "concord of sweet sounds." Our party, the first part of the evening, was in little groups, each having a theme of its own.

We remember ourself to have been seated by the side of a very pretty and attractive young lady, of elegant manners, a fine conversationalist, and whom we had noticed to have received the attention and admiration of all; so much so, that we considered her the "JESSAMY Bride" of the party.

We had studied the countenance of a younger sister of hers, at intervals, who was seated a little way from us, chatting with a young lawyer from Yazoo City; and it paid us well for the perusal.

I could see, in the young gentleman, that Southern politeness and gallantry to the ladies, that is so much a part of chivalry. Their language to them was correct; there was a reserve in their bearing towards them, and they looked upon them with more admiration than a Northerner is accustomed to see given to the fair.

Then the theme of discourse was much about ladies—their beauty; gentlemen—their chivalry, and such like topics. Finally, one would notice much devotedness, on the part of the gentlemen, to the fair of the South; and that the ladies received it with a politeness and *naivete*, as if it were an homage due them.

The latter were dressed splendidly—some of them wearing much jewelry.

The supper should have been noticed in its proper place. To tell the truth, we scarcely know how to notice it at all;

for our English, and a smattering of French, was run ashore by some of the dishes. It came, though, about the middle of the evening. A large cake, frosted and decked with various-colored leaves, shot up in the center of the table, amid the other luxuries, like a round-tower.

The different courses commenced with oysters. Fresh strawberries, oranges, and other rare fruits, and choice wines, were on the table.

After supper we retired to the drawing-room, where some spent the remainder of the evening playing whist, others chatting. But they were, at intervals, diverted from their amusements by a neatly dressed female servant, wearing a fine turban on her head—the servants in all planters' families wear these turbans of different colors, which make them look like Oriental domestics—who passed around among them wine, cake and fruit, on a server.

Late in the evening our dormitory was shown us by a negress. It was a small log structure, a few rods from the main residence; a servant also came in and took our boots, which we found in the morning as glossy as magnolia leaves.

The next day, in speaking about the party, some one of our friends rallied us about having such an interesting *tete-a-tete* with a rich young widow last night.

We, of course, were ignorant of the railery, and demanded an explanation. Our friend informed us that the young lady that we had been so interested in chatting with, last evening, was the young, attractive, and richly-possessed Mrs. M.

Most certainly we were not aware that we had been conversing with a lady dowered with such a Potosi of wealth.

Her plantation is adjoining Dr. Y.'s. Their residences are strikingly in contrast.

One, plebian and the other patrician. The one rustic, the other, suburban. The latter edifice is not costly, but a modest little cottage, nestled amid trees on a delightful parterre of greensward, tastefully meandered with fine bordered walks, and studded with clumps of shrubbery, "like flowers wrought elegantly on tapestry."

Near the residence is a natural mound, some twenty feet in diameter at the base, which lessens as it rises to the height of eight or ten feet, at which point the top is cut off, and on it has been reared a picturesque little lattice-work summer-house. This lovely abode reminds one of a *petit* "Iranistan."

"Low was our pretty cot; our tallest rose
Peeped at the chamber-window. We could hear,
At silent noon, and eve, and early morn,
The Yazoo's faint murmur. In the open air
Our myrtles blossomed; and across the porch
Thick jasmins twined; the little landscape round
Was green and woody, and refreshed the eye."

## CHAPTER XIV.

Habits and manners change, as people do, with climes,
"Tenets with books, and principles with times."

POPE & I.

Dr. JOHNSON once asked GOLDSMITH if he could love a friend where he disagreed with him on any subject, as well as if he did not.

GOLDSMITH thought he could not. The Dr. said *he* could.

Taking the last view of the subject, one can easily waive the political discrepancy between the North and South, and have nothing to mar true friendship between them. This makes it far pleasanter for those who are sojourning here from the North.

So much had been said about a *Northerner's* coming South, to me, last fall, that the Southrons looked upon them all with suspicion; that one must "overhaul" his politics, and leave at home all that was not convenient; and then, unless he could give the true Democratic "shibboleth," there was danger in crossing "MASON and DIXON'S line;" that I felt, on coming here, like a THEMISTOCLES throwing myself upon the clemency of the people.

But in this I was disappointed. I found that the South that one reads and hears of, is altogether different from the one that one *sees* and becomes acquainted with.

Sir WALTER SCOTT never met his friend IRVING, at his gate, with a more friendly—"Ye are welcome," than I have received wherever I have been in this "sunny land."

And I have sat by the planter's fire-side, and conversed with him on that hateful subject, which those "boys" in Congress have quarreled about and fought over so long—talked about the Union—the North and the South—children of the same parents—the

> "Twa that hae paidl't i' the burn
> Frae morning sun till dine,"

till they fell out on the slavery question; and but one Southron yet has asked me my politics.

But then it might not have been so a year ago, before the Presidential election.

A few evenings since, in conversation with some one at Willow Dale, we took up the subject of "Bleeding Kansas" —that has "bled" as that "old Democratic war Chief" of the North, DANIEL S. DICKINSON, says, "till there is no more blood in her than there is in a white turnip."

The point in dispute was whether she ought to come into the Union as a Free State or not. After having discussed the subject at some length, some one proposed that we should decide it, by playing a game of chess; and, as the North was the "Lady-love" whose gage I professed to wear, that I should represent her.

I told them to select a champion from their side, and we would come to "a passage at arms," and decide this important question.

To my surprise a young *lady* stepped forward, to represent the chivalry of the South. This was something really of the

> "Days of belted knight and Lady fair."

But where did a knight ever in

> "The fair fields of old romance,
> Essay to break with a *lady* a lance."

The whole game was watched with much interest by the party present; for it was the Saxon North, against the Norman South. The issue of the game was for quite a long time doubtful, each losing a few men, till I took my fair foe's queen, and then her knights, when she exclaimed—"There goes my chivalry!"

I soon after check-mated her king, when she cried out—"Kansas is a Free State!"

One of the ladies present remarked, that had it been her, she would have played three years, as long as JEFFERSON did with the Frenchman, before she would have given up.

The topic of conversation following this was about the North and the South.

The North was Saxon, and eminently practical. The South, Norman, and from the "utile et dulcis" of life, she, enjoying her abundance and ease, takes the "dulcis." If the South is not as practical, neither is she as professional as the North; although her titles, degrees, and diplomas are plentifully bestowed upon her sons, by her own schools and ours, yet they merely consider them, as the old Romans did oratory, necessary to the gentleman.

Hence you find scores of doctors, lawyers, school-teachers, and those practising the various professions here from the North.

The South has been in the habit of giving her schools, and much of her professional practice to Northern young men, to induce them to become her citizens. At one time there were more than forty members of Congress from the South who claimed New England for their birth-place.

The intellect of the South is not called out by such incentives as at the North. Northern young men are not born with gold spoons in their mouths—inheriting fortunes. But the old Latin maxim applies to one and all—

"*Quisque suæ fortunæ faber.*" Every man is the architect of his own fortune.

And their road to it is through the various pursuits in life; and the chief means of rendering them successful is a good education. This is the philosopher's stone, that converts their labor into gold.

Had the North as genial a clime, and as luxuriant a soil as the South, she would not have an intellectual New England, that stands like SAUL among the prophets, head and shoulders above every other part of the Union; she would not have the "spur that she now has to prick the side of her intent."

Man is naturally indolent, and were not appetite, self-love and passion strong, he would die out, body and soul.

He would prefer the life of Tom Moore–

> "Lying in the bowers of ease, smiling a fame."

Or dream away life, with Thompson, in his "Castle of Indolence," who, although he sung man so 'falsely luxurious" probably never saw the sun rise five times in his life, or ever really

> "Enjoyed the cool, the fresh, the fragrant hour,
> To meditation due, and sacred song;"

but was so "luxurious" that he has been seen, standing with his hands in his pockets, eating a peach from the tree.

Where nature has failed to yield man wealth from the soil, he has added science to make the glebe more productive, or failing in this, he has sought some useful trade, or husbanding his own intellectual resources, has relied upon his talent to secure him a competency for life.

Hence the adverse soil of rude and rough New England has developed her science, and driven her sons to the intellectual pursuits of life.

It is not so South. Nature has been more lavish in her gifts, and man has not resorted to his genius to supply his wants. Hence the mind is unaroused by the stimuli of necessity. While you are making science, art, invention, all subserve to the daily uses of life, they would think it some like "carrying coal to Newcastle." All the science necessary here is to plant cotton, hoe cotton, gin cotton, ship cotton, and sell cotton.

They do not generally make their own implements of husbandry. They buy everything from a gin-stand down to an axe helve, of the North.

The usual hum of business one does not hear in these Southern towns; they are more quiet than ours. No whirling mills—no whining machinery—no clang of anvils—no ringing of factory bells—no din and bustle of the crowded mart. They have no wheat to grind, no manufacturing, and but little "smithing," to do; hence their trade and traffic have no strife and commotion. From the quiet appearance of their towns the stranger would think that the energies of trade were hushed—that business had gone into a pause, or was taking a siesta.

The North is set off finely by contrasting it with the South. One thinks more of it, after viewing it from a Southern stand-point. He sees its stirring business life, its thrift, industry and economy. He sees its thousand various pursuits, and trades, by which its citizens earn a livelihood, and secure a fortune—her churches and school-houses, manufactories and work-shops—those "Aladdin Caves," where, with labor for her "lamp," she constructs the innumerable works of her genius with such magic skill, or converts her forests into blooming fields, builds her towns, levels her mountains, constructs her railroads, and does all things.

From another point of view the South is set off by contrast with the North; it is from its half-tropical year.

---

## CHAPTER XV.

### WINTER.

"Then Winter's time-bleached locks did hoary show,
By Hospitality with cloudless brow."

BURNS.

If there is a character in the whole Northern land, that a Southron dislikes, one that he hates worse than GREELEY, it is "Old HIEMS." They can stand HORACE, and the thunder of his *Tribune*, better than the old icicled hero, with his cold, and wrath, and magazine of storms.

Their year is more monotonous; it has thrown the winter out of its calendar, and has taken only the disagreeable days of our fall and spring, and made a winter of them, that passes well enough in this clime. In truth, a Southern winter, is a gift to these two seasons, being cut into halves; one part is added to the spring, and the other lengthens out the fall. Spring is like summer, summer like autumn, and autumn so much like winter, that they may be said to have no winter at all.

Our winter is unlike any other season of the year—it is something new—a deep, earnest, sublime scene. It is the "Tragedy of Old HIEMS" on the year. There is no play or farce about it. It is another OTHELLO killing that lovely DESDAMONA—the goddess of autumn. I have watched the winter sky of this clime when it seemed

"Gathering its brows with gathering storm,"

and have anxiously waited to see the elements have their mad revel out. But, it was a broken-down tragedy. It was "RICHARD," when "RICHARD" was not himself. There was no "winter in his discontent," but summer-like,

"He capered nimbly by his lady's chamber,"

and did not act out the roused fury of the passion in him.

But they dread our winter, because they dislike to burrow up, five months in the year, as the Lapps and Finns do. Our ladies—pretty parlor annuals—lovely exotics, mewed up half of the year in air-tight rooms, heated by air-tight stoves—no wonder they die of the consumption. Did not our ancestors live longer and enjoy life better ere the stove was in use? Those stoves! "*Oh, tempora! Oh, mores! Quousque tandem abutere.*"

O, ye Goths and Vandals of the North! will neither the examples of our wise forefathers, nor the happiness of the present generation, keep you from invading their homes and robbing them of the health and enjoyment that were once their very penates?

Nothing can compensate for it; human progress has actually failed in introducing the stove. They use none in this clime, not even in cooking.

The old iron crane, fastened to the jambs, still swings to and fro over the fire, tricked off with its "big and little pot-hooks and links of chain," and the venerable old "bake-kettle" sits in the corner,

> "Just as they used to do—some fifty years ago."

## SPRING.

> "Next came the loveliest pair in all the ring,
> Sweet Female Beauty hand in hand with Spring."

This season does not come as at the North, with a sudden rebound from the thraldom of winter, in all its fresh and green glories. Her glad approach causes no streams to leap from their icy fetters; nor does she come with her bird-songs. They had long before heralded her coming in the forest. Neither with her

> "Buds and bells and blossoms,"

flushing all the fields with green, "enamelling the meadows with primroses, cowslips and daises." We had had many of the birds and flowers with us all winter; and then the hyacinth, the jonquil, the Japan or German rose, and

> "The daffodils that come before the swallow dares,
> And takes the winds of March with beauty,"

and all your "winking May-buds, that ope their pretty eyes" with early spring, appear here in February, so that spring does not give so much of a new floral edition, as the winter one revised, enlarged, and more fully illustrated.

May left the corn tasseling out, the negroes hoeing the cotton for the second time; the fig, the plum and the June apple getting ripe, the pea in the yellow leaf, and the rose and magnolia in full bloom.

## SUMMER.

> "Then, crowned with flow'ry hay, came rural Joy,
> And Summer, with his fervid-beaming eye."
>
> BURNS.

The epithet, "sunny," is appropriately applied to the South. There is much more sunshine in the day-light here than with you at the North. The thermometers may be alike in both places, yet it is sunnier here. The sky, though perhaps softer and flushed with more gorgeous hues, is not so dark and gloomy as at the North. And there is oftener

> "A wind to drive the clouds away,
> And open day-light's shutters."

I have seen the whole cloud-lined canopy of heaven resting on a most lovely sunset-painted base—a bright heavenly border circling the whole horizon, whose colors grew softer and fainter, as they reached upwards, till they died away in the blue arch overhead. The Southern world was most beautifully tented in.

During a storm I have often wondered where the rain could come from, and how it could rain so long and copiously from such thin clouds. Then the suddenness of the storm takes you by surprise. The coming event casts no shadow before.

> "A little stir among the clouds"—

and lake and river bubble.

There are no mountains nor hills here, hence no twilight. The sun goes down with a bounce. These beautiful lines of SCOTT are not true in this clime:

> "Here, too, are twilight nooks and dells;
> And oft, in such, the story tells,
> Of damsels kind, from danger freed,
> That grateful paid their champions' meed."

We only doubt their truth here in regard to *twilight*, remember. One can, in mountainous or hilly countries, read or write some time after the sun has gone down, by the lingering light; but here it is snatched from your book or paper, and the curtain is dropped.

June was not a very hot month. The thermometer ranged at no time above ninety in the shade. But July has been hotter by some two or three degrees. It is not, as at the North, an extremely hot day or two, then cool weather; but day after day nothing but sunshine—the same summer heat, interrupted only by frequent showers, which leave the air a little cooler. This affects a Northerner more than the fitful weather of his own summers, whose intermittent heat ranges from eighty to over one hundred degrees, Fahrenheit, but is followed by a relieving coolness. There is occasionally a relief here; the nights are often cooler. I have felt during the hot days in July and August like crying out—Oh! that night, or a thuder-storm, would come!

Many are affected, especially the white laboring class, by what is termed the "heat." It not only gives them an "itching palm," but it breaks out all over the body in little red pimples, and worries the whole man with a burning, itching sensation.

The people dress light. The vest is thrown off, and the rest of the clothing is thin. Yet you find the Southron enveloped these hot days, in his wrapper and drawers.

Their summer has a listless languor—amusements are abandoned, and every one seeks the shade.

The "accustomed fever" of the South, which generally attacks a Northerner the first season, by way of acclimating him, appeared some time past the middle of June. And it was thought by many physicians, considering the flood along the Mississippi and Yazoo, especially if it abated suddenly, that we would have a sickly season. But it was not, though many planters and their families had the fever, and many negroes on the various plantations were sick with it; still there were not many deaths. It is a more malignant type of a common Northern fever, but is dealt with in a much severer manner by the physicians, who usually prescribe quinine and calomel in abundance.

The yellow fever came later. This is confined to towns and cities on the Mississippi and its navigable branches. And although by quarantine great caution is taken, yet it is brought up from New Orleans by the steamers.

This dreadful disease has some singular features. It seldom attacks a negro, and never a white person but once; yet if they survive it, like an insidious and treacherous foe, that breaks its pledge of security given to a former captive when caught on other grounds, it attacks you more fatally the second time, if you are exposed to it in any other place than where you first had it.

Mr. P., of Willow Dale, who is very kind to his slaves, doing, when they are sick, all that he or medical aid can, for them, told me that no event was dreaded by him so much as sickness among his slaves. During epidemics—save the yellow fever—negroes are attacked more severely than the whites. It is hard to control their appetites. As soon as they are convalescent, and able to eat at all, they feed themselves without fear. The fatter the food the better. He further remarked:

> "When they live, they live like pigs in clover,
> And when they're sick, they're sick all over."

And here, in conclusion with this, let me introduce to you an important character—the planter's field-marshal—in common parlance, the *overseer;* who is, besides being in command of the *corps de Afrique*, their physician; has his "set of medicines," and, in case of sickness among them, is considered as good as half of the doctors. You often meet intelligent young men among them; and I have seen several wealthy planters that began by overseeing. What is generally termed a "slave-driver," is not an overseer. A "slave-driver" is a negro who acts as overseer. A faithful, trusty negro is often put in charge of the rest, when the overseer is absent, or in case of emergency. The overseer has his horse and saddle, and rides over the field, or changes and walks, as he sees fit. He is always distinguished by his "insignia" of office—his "baton"—the whip, which is ever in his hand. He has entire command of the slaves;—the correcting and punishing is all left to him. He decides on the most trivial, or weighty matters. The planter has nothing to do with them. The overseer is often the cause, especially if he is a hot-spur in temper, of much trouble among the slaves. His residence at the "quarters," though it may be like the rest, is a sort of a governor's-house among the negro cabins.

We have said the planter had nothing to do with the

governing of the slaves. He has not; yet there are cases, of course, in the jurisprudence of the plantation, in which the planter, as higher authority, is consulted.

The overseer, for his services, gets from four to fifteen hundred dollars per year.

## THE FLOOD ALONG THE YAZOO.

This flood continued till past mid-summer. The Yazoo, after overflowing its banks, and part of many plantations in the valley, in August, finally fell back into its proper channel. The losses sustained by planters along this stream, in cattle and crops, are laid at half a million of dollars. One of our neighbors has been damaged to the amount of thirty thousand dollars. Yet you hear no complaining or condoling over losses. These losses are, in regard to digestion—conviviality—accustomed enjoyment, and sleep, mere bagatelles to the planter.

The high water drove the cattle from their usual range, and confined them to such close quarters, that, for some time during the summer, they were fed on corn-stalks. The only hope the poor creatures had, after the loss of their accustomed summer-grazing, was in the new growth of grass that might yet spring up, on the flood's receding. Their cows give less milk than those that feed in the rich meadows of the North.

They never speak here of the good pasture their cows have, but of the "wide range" they have. This is in the woods, around the swamps, and everywhere, outside of the fields.

The planter usually keeps from fifteen to fifty, or more, cows. Including all his cattle, he may have an hundred head; many have more, with some twenty or thirty mules, and some five or six horses. In counting his cattle, as winter sets in, he often finds quite a number missing. The poorer people living in the back-woods, besides being lumbermen, are frequently "cow-boys," and steal the planters' cattle, which they kill and sell in market.

Corn ripened about the middle of July, and its leaves were all stripped from the stalks, bound into bundles, and put into stacks or ricks for winter fodder. And now, mid-August, the time for picking cotton, has come. There is no field that a negro enters, in which he loves to labor more than in this—certainly he labors in none more beautiful. I would give an impossibility, could I describe one of these cotton-fields stretching away along the valley till it loses itself in the distance, as it appears to me. The innumerable little cotton-trees, growing from six to eight feet high, standing close to each other, in interminable rows, a short distance apart, every weed and spear of grass hoed out, look like vast fields of neat, well-trimmed hedge-rows. The "bloom," which appears the last of May, or the first of June, resembles that of the morning-glory, and like it, opens white in the morning, but as the day departs it grows red and folds its leaves. It blooms first at the bottom; and there is where the bolls first begin to open, continuing as they form to open higher and higher, till the topmost one has "snowed" out its cotton-flakes. Were the bolls all to remain as they expand, from bottom to top, of these little "trees en-row," over the whole field, we should have presented to our admiring gaze those fields of "mimic snow" that the tourist has so often described. But the negro, determined that

"A thing of beauty *shall not* be a joy forever,"

as soon as the lower bolls have sufficiently expanded, arms himself with his cotton-sack strung around his shoulders, and commences picking this lower border of cotton, and continues as the bolls open to the top; at which time the field looks the snowiest. An industrious negro will pick ten bales, of five hundred pounds each, in a season. From early morn to night-fall—from mid-August to Christmas, he is a cotton-picker. All this time the high-boxed cotton-wagon is plying between the cotton-field and the gin-house, and the "gin" is continually going—separating the seed from the cotton. As fast as the planter wishes to ship it for New Orleans, it is thrown into the press and the bales are turned out.

Connected with the cotton-gin, the planter has a corn-mill, where he grinds all his corn into meal. Here, on his own premises, is the fountain, from which so much Southern wealth flows—from which all the "corn-dodgers" and "hoe-cakes" spring. And what is not a little singular, they always prefer the white meal, to make the bread for their tables. The yellow, surely, is the most nutritious and palatable. But although they eat so much corn-bread, they eat but little hasty-pudding and milk. This pudding is often on their tables, but it is usually eaten with sugar or sirup. Like many of the people in Michigan and the West, they call the New England Hasty Pudding—that luxury of a dish—*mush!* I very much dislike this name for it. It surely is not like "JULIET'S rose;" to me, with this other name, it certainly does not "smell as sweet."

> "The soft nations round the warm Levant
> *Polanta* call; the French of course *Polante;*
> E'en in my native regions how I blush
> To hear the Pennsylvanians call thee *Mush!*
> On Hudson's banks while men of Belgic spawn,
> Insult and eat thee by the name sup-pawn,
> Thy name is Hasty Pudding!"

But they have a much pleasanter name for what we call *loppered* milk—*bonny clabber.* This is often on their tables, which, sprinkled with sugar or nutmeg, and eaten with the latter name, I think relishes much better.

In the garden, both here and at Oak Valley, I find many things strangers to me, that I have grown fond of at the table. The Cabbage Pea, with its large broad pod, makes a fine soup ; and another one, the Asparagus Pea, with a small, round pod that grows from a foot to three feet in length, makes a choice dish at table. The Lima Bean is well known, but it has its relative here, the Butter Bean, which, besides being a most prolific bearer, is first, par excellence, when cooked. An Artichoke grows here, which, when prepared for the plate, is said to please the dainty epicure. The Egg Plant, the fruit of which hangs from its little, tender tree like great, elongated purple eggs, and when served at table, many are fond of, I must confess, to my palate, has no particular taste or relish. A vegetable bearing a cone-shaped pod, called Ochra, and which, when ready for eating, is very palatable, grows in their gardens. There are many other vegetables peculiar to this clime, I have not space to notice here. The whole family of Cabbages is inferior to ours. That of the Onion is much more numerous, and just as good.

The Irish Potatoe, though not a real Southron, forms a very acceptable connection here. It is large enough for eating when the yam and sweet potatoe begin to fail, in the spring, and it holds its place on the table till in the fall, when the more favorite ones, which ripen late, and are not eaten, unlike the Irish potatoe, until they are ripe, claim their accustomed place. It is then cooked only semi-occasionally.

The apples, save the June apple, and the Early Queen, are coarse, and inferior to ours. The Nectarine and Apricot are very fine. The Plum is not so good. The Peach that had been represented all along as much superior to ours, rivaling even the famed ones of Jersey, when I came to eat it, really fell short of my "sugared suppositions" of it. I find some of the richest variety of Pears here. The Bartlett I never saw larger and finer flavored. The Seckle, from Ohio, is rich and excellent. There are others just as worthy of notice. The Grapes are fine. The Scuppernong, from North Carolina, and from which, in that State, an excellent wine, in high repute here, is made, is a large, rich-flavored Grape. It is a russet when ripe. The Le Noir, an abundant bearer, is another fine Grape of a purple color. The Fig—the planter really sits and enjoys life beneath his own vine and fig-tree—is a large-leafed tree, with no main trunk, but shoots up in branches like the stalks in a wheat-stool, and is like the Tomato, also here, a great bearer. The first crop ripened and vanished by the middle of July —the second soon followed, and a third came after that.

The planter's wife has been busy since fruit ripened, in overseeing the making of her jellies, preserves, drying fruit, and preparing them in their fresh state for the fruit-cans, which being hermetically sealed, keep them good the year round.

In regard to Southern fare, I have found it very plain and frugal. Some one has said, "Tell me what a people eat and I will tell you their morals." We will leave Messrs. FOWLERS, and their dietetic school, to expatiate upon this text, but merely remark that the South, according to their reasoning, has the better of us here. Their accustomed diet, at any rate, is more wholesome and healthy than ours. Our table, at Willow Dale, had the best of ham, venison, turkey, birds, fish—*et id omne genus;* with the usual variety of corn-bread and the little wheat-biscuit and butter. Many people North think the famous "hoe-cake," like Venice and Genoa, "lives only in song." They have only, to dispel that error, to come here and find it on the planter's table. It takes its name from its first being baked by the negroes on a hoe. It is about as thick as an Elementary spelling-book, before an urchin gets it, and about as large, cutting the corners off and making it oval. The Sweet Potatoe is cooked whole, or brought on to the table in large flat slices, fried. It is the richest potatoe I ever ate. The usual drink is coffee. One word about pork. Both the ham and bacon must be smoked in order to keep them wholesome. In vulgar parlance, the planter may be said to "go the whole hog." He eats, not only the ham, bacon, jowles and "souse," but the brains, harslet, milt, lights and chitterlings.

This is the plain fare. On extra occasions their tables are a banquet. All the luxuries that can be had at New Orleans, at such times you will find on them. The steamers on the Yazoo and Mississippi are the planters' "careir pigeons." They will stop at the wave of a handkerchief by a negro, and take any message and do any errand for the planter, at Vicksburgh or New Orleans. They also throw off, as they pass by, the daily and weekly Deltas, Picayunes, and other papers, at his residence, along the banks of the river.

## AUTUMN.

"All-cheering Plenty, with her flowing horn,
Led yellow Autumn wreathed with nodding corn."

BURNS.

"Now I imagine you seized with a fine, romantic kind of melancholy, on the fading of the year; now I figure you wandering philosophical and pensive, amidst the brown withered groves, while the leaves rustle under your feet, the sun gives a farewell parting gleam, and the birds

"Stir the faint note, and but attempt to sing.

"Then again, the winds whistle, I see you in the well-known Cleugh, beneath the solemn arch of tall, thick, embowering trees, listening to the amusing lull of many steep, moss-grown cascades; while deep, divine contemplation, the genius of the place, prompts each swelling, awful thought. I am sure you would not resign your part in that scene at an easy rate."

Thus writes Thompson—

"The sweet descriptive bard,
Inspiring Autumn sung."

What a rich inheritance Autumn gives us! What a gift she presents us in this lovely, mellow, golden weather, and the glorious forest standing in it—pensive and dreamy—murmuring and plaintive with leaf-music and the loveliest bird-songs of the year; and soon, too, to be arrayed in hues—Oh! I would give worlds could I describe them—beautiful as those of

———"parting day,
Or the dying dolphin whom each pang imbues
With a new color."

Hues that "mingle into each other, and shift, and change, and glance away, like the colors in a peacock's train." Who would resign a part in such a scene at an easy rate, one so full of the melancholy liveliness of the year? And as if to add more beauty and delight to it—to give the lovely hectic flush to the cheek of dying Autumn, in this region, the roses have commenced blooming again, while those favorites, the crape myrtle and the althæ, continue to do as they have done all summer long—nothing but bloom—bloom—and blossom. Most of the trees—now mid-September—are yet in their summer green—unfaded. The sycamores in front of the negro-cabins, are in their rich olio of colors. Some of the foliage in the woods begins to look old—here and there one in parti-colored leaves, and frequently a bright yellow or crimson bough, radiant in the green tree-top, delights the eye. Death is the lovliest where the most beauty dies. And though we miss here "the living stream, the airy mountain, and the hanging rock," of the North, yet the loveliest of flowers, and a tropical luxuriance, and beauty of foliage, in the grand old forest, are dying. For—

> "Within the solemn woods of ash deep-crimsoned,
> And silver beach, and maple yellow-leafed,
> Autumn, like a faint, old man sits down,
> By the way-side weary."

---

## CHAPTER XVI.

### LIFE AT WILLOW DALE.

"I have pleasant memories of life in this pleasant land."

Willow Dale, so long my home on the Banks of the Yazoo, and where I have spent so many happy and delightful days, is truly a noble mansion and a very pleasant home. I lacked nothing now to make my sojourn in the South truly enjoyable. The pursuit after a school had been the *amari aliquid*—the drop of bitter—in my enjoyment here; that now had ceased, and I was prepared to commence my vocation, and enjoy Southern life. I had a very fine room furnished with everything to make one comfortable—a servant to build my fires, black my boots and do my errands. The family was a very pleasant one. And we had in addition to it, spending the winter with us, two fair cousins. They were thus described by a Yazoo city editor, at a late ball given in that place.

"We noticed the Misses B., of Lexington, ZENOBIA-like in their beauty, and very attractive in the dance." They would be attractive in the court of EUGENIE. The elder—a sprightly Madamoiselle TALIEN—the younger—a graceful JOSEPHINE. To hear the "good night" of the latter, given in the sweet accents of her musical voice, as she glided out of the room in one of her graceful "whirls," impressed you with the charm of its utterance, and her gliding out of the room, you remembered like the beautiful passage of a dream.

Our evenings at Willow Dale were given to amusements. After one becomes acquainted with Southern life, he sees that society here must have them. In other lands, where life has a pursuit, less amusement is required. But here, where one finds its golden leisure, amusements are indispensable. The ladies of our household read, were fond of the works of literature and romance, and among authors they were very fond of SCOTT. He is a favorite of the South. Of the manners and scenes in his novels one is much reminded among this people. Nowhere have I enjoyed reading him so much as in this clime. I have read books here that would have given one the *ennui* to have read at home. Life here has its tranquil repose, and a book in your hand is like a friend, that is entertaining and enjoying it with you. And there is no noise, nor any one to disturb you. A bird-note from a China-tree is sweeter, because you enjoy it unalloyed by any other sound; and the reading of a book is pleasanter, because there is no one to molest or find fault with, and call you indolent or *dellettantish.* The "enjoyment of literature in such a place is like feeding among the lillies in the Song of Solomon."

I have seen Willow Dale so quiet for hours that the birds would stop singing in its trees, in love of its silence. And then, when the sportive laugh or merry shout of the children playing in the yard, sounded out, or the whistle or splashing of a steamer, passing by, or the halloo of a stranger at the gate, and the hounds baying at him, you heard and listened to them with pleasure.

Besides reading, and the light work of the needle, our ladies gave their time to various pleasures—visiting and receiving visits, music, vocal and instrumental, the dance, cards, and *tete-a-tete.* Whist is universally acknowledged a lady's game. But euchre is the game of the South, and by choice, the Southern lady's game. I must confess to predilection for chess, and I always found some one of our evening circle ready to play with me. But they also play whist and the various other amusing games with cards, which here are manifold. To other games, and those above mentioned, and frequent chats about books and authors, our evenings were given.

We often had guests—ladies and gentlemen—from Yazoo city and other places, who sometimes would remain several days with us, and sometimes a planter's daughter would stay two or three weeks. Miss Mollie P., a charming young lady from Virginia, was with us a month or more during the winter. This made life at Willow Dale lively and interesting, and gave our evenings a greater fund of enjoyment.

Then we had moon-light sails on the noble Yazoo. I have no desire to disparage the North—my birth-place and home are there, and I love her. But there is a charm in Southern moon-light that I never before felt, that makes the night exceedingly lovely. It was on one of these lovely nights when—

> "The moon like a rick on fire had risen o'er the dale,"

and the silvery Yazoo flowed murmurless between the deep, heavy foliage of willows that hung over it on each side, like a soft, undulating bank of green, that a party of us at Willow Dale stepped into the boat, with a favorite negro, an adept at the oar, for oarsman, to take a moon-light sail. We were on a serenading trip—were going to serenade Dr. Y.'s daughter at "Rough and Ready"—her home, one mile up the river.

It had been previously arranged that the trip should be wholly romantic—our language poetical, and that all, in unison with everything around us, should be—ideal. Being seated in a fine row-boat, we silently glided up stream. It is beautiful to sail in a light boat "on such a night," when all nature is asleep, and, on a river itself, in a lethean tranquility when no sound is heard but the light dipping and soft plashing of the oars in the water, and the muffled sound of their working in the row-locks. And where the voice has a charmed sound that the night and the water give, and when you are fonder of talking, of music, and musing, and fonder of your own existence.

Thus in love with ourselves and the scene around us, we moved up stream, repeating passages of poetry and snatches of song, that the occasion was full of, and half expressed. And though we repeat some of them here, they seem to lose much of their poetry by not being enjoyed on the spot.

> "Now in the infinite meadows of the heavens, one by one,
> Blossomed the lovely stars—the forget-me-nots of the angels."

To which some one replied, and—

"The moon-light stealing o'er the scene,
Had blended with these lights of eve."

Which one of the party continued by repeating SHELLEY'S exquisite stanza on the moon, from his "Cloud." Another said that though the moon had many brooks and streams, she had but one Yazoo.

To which was replied—

"My soul is an enchanted boat,
That like a sleeping swan doth float
On its silver wave."

Again—

"It is the hour when from the boughs
The nightingale's high note is heard;
It is the hour when lover's vows
Seem sweet in every whispered word."

Yes;—

"On such a night," HERO, from her—
——— ——— tower,
Half set in trees and leafy luxury,"

watched for LEANDER; and "on *such* a night," LORENZO and JESSICA told their loves.

And, another continued, "on such a night," the Hindoo maiden set her wax-taper afloat on the Ganges.

To which some one responded, "on such a night," the Yazoo lover, with his dusky maid, crossed this stream in a bark-canoe.

Thus we were sailing up stream, all poetry and romance, when I thoughtlessly remarked, that the trip was half performed, for we had passed the "old gin-house," standing hard by on the bank.

At which one of the Miss B.'s cried out, "There, you

have broken the spell of romance, by uttering such a vulgar word as *gin-house!*"

I begged her pardon, and told her I would enclose the word in a parenthetical coffin, and bury it in the river; and assured the party that I had been deceived—that it was an old ruined castle, overhung with moss and ivy, which I had mistaken for the above-mentioned building.

To complete the scene of our trip, a magnificent steamer, brilliantly illuminated—the Indian's "Fire Canoe," dropped down stream by us, like a thing of glorious beauty.

When we had reached a point a little above the "Castle" of our lady-fair, we crossed the stream, and silently glided down till we were opposite her abode; when the Misses B., one playing on the guitar, began the serenade. Their voices sounded out on the clear moon-lit air—

> "Soft as the chant of Troubadours,
> Or the rythm of silver bells."

Our lady and her guests came out into the porch of the mansion, which was trellised with honeysuckle and woodbine; but we could not see them—only caught sight of a white handkerchief waving out from behind the trellis-work.

The South has much of romance, but this was truly the most delightful and romantic hour I ever enjoyed. All was the very sleep of stillness; nothing heard but the most delightful singing, or the music of the guitar filling up the pauses in the song, or its light touches, blending with its strains. The party sang three or four songs, then we silently floated away, singing some appropriate piece.

What was very amusing, as we laid by the shore serenading, was to see the negroes peeping out from their cabins, hard by, and some stealing out and peering round the corners of their houses, or, the more bold approaching nearer and looking over the fence at us.

Let us change the theme to our school. It certainly deserves a notice, if for no other reason than its being the termination of my adventures in the South. My walk to it—some over half a mile along on the bank of the gentle Yazoo, was pleasantly shaded by fine trees. It was a very pleasant walk, and I enjoyed every inch of it. There was no snow during the winter—nothing but a few disagreeable sleet-days, and when the walking was bad, which was made so by a little rain, I, if I chose, rode a-horse-back; steamers passing and re-passing me, on my road to and from school. My friends, at home, would scarcely believe me, should I tell them that we had beautiful weather—warm and summer-like all January. During the spring and summer part of our school term, the water was so high in the Yazoo, that it overflowed the banks, and we sailed to school in a skiff—the scholars meeting at eight o'clock in the morning, under the willow-oak on the bank of the river, in front of Willow Dale, and a negro rowed us down stream to the school-house, and came after us at night. These were delightful trips, and long, very long, shall I remember them and the "little crew" with whom I enjoyed them. They were little pleasure excursions from the dull and weary toil of the school-room. When the weather was hot, we would leave the middle of the stream, and sail beneath the shade of the overhanging willows at the side. Writing of these pleasure-trips brings to mind many scenes and incidents connected with them.

Wading along in the edge of the river, his keen eye on the watch for any of the finny tribe that ventured near, and ready, with a quick dart of his long bill into the water, to seize and devour them; or, sitting solitary and alone on some old stub of a tree leaning over the river, contemplating the scene around him, till on the near approach of our boat, he would slowly raise himself on his broad wings, and, as he flew away, pull up his long black legs—his feet sticking out behind like a rudder—and draw in his long neck like a turtle, leaving his head beaking to a point in a long, sharp bill; all of which being done left him about the size of a large white dove; this is the white heron that wades along the margin of the Yazoo.

Occasionally there was rare sport for us, in pulling up the fish-lines that the negroes had set along the margin of the stream, attached to the limbs of the over-hanging willows. The twitching of the bough would invariably tell us whether we should haul up a large buffalo or cat-fish from below. This not only afforded us an amusement, on our little voyage to and from school, but an enjoyment; for the negroes never failed to send in some of the finest of the fish to their master, which were prepared for our table.

And here let me trace a memory to our oarsman, SAM, for the prompt and kind services he ever rendered us, and for ability with his dextrous oars, in managing our little shallop, plying them as a bird her wings, in directing her course; here, avoiding the snags, now, dodging the heavy drift-log, or the ponderous floating raft; or, darting to the shore, as a puffing steamer came upon us; then, with a fearless oar, after it had passed, dashing out into the surging current, letting our little barque, with its precious charge, mount over the crests, and pitch down into the depths of tumbling swells.

And here let me trace another memory to him and the servants at Willow Dale for the very many kind acts and offices they have performed for me.

(Our Academy is within a stone's-throw, by the smallest scholar, of the Yazoo. The river rolls along in front of it. Parallel to this, in the rear of the house, is a bayou. On this peninsular strip of land is situated the school-house. It is built of gum-logs hewn square, and instead of being "chinked up," it is battened on the outside with cypress boards. It has two windows, one on each side. The door is in front, facing the river. It has a broad stone fire-place, at the opposite end, with a stick chimney running up on the outside. The floor is of smooth cypress boards. The one overhead is of cypress-shakes laid from joist to joist, like battened-work. Two strips of desk are nailed against the wall, one on each side of the window, on one side; on the other side is a movable desk of cypress wood, for the teacher. Four chairs, with cow-hide bottoms, and one with a basket bottom, and three smaller ones for the small children, with several blocks of wood, sawed off chair-hight, from a gum-log, are all the seats we had. There is a mantle-piece over the fire-place, and several pegs in the logs on the east side, to hang hats, bonnets and shawls on.

The house stands in a beautiful grove of willow-oaks, and from their branches Southern birds sang their roundelays to us, all winter long. The gum-tree, the persimmon, hackberry, and haw, were also near it. No hollies and magnolias were in sight. The long Spanish moss does not hang so thick from the trees in the valley, as in the up-lands; yet many of its floating tresses waved from the trees about our school-house.

My pupils were seven boys—intelligent, fine lads, three of whom were fourteen or fifteen years old, and two tiny damoiselles, one having a little black waiting maid, who attended her in school and out.

This was my school on commencing it; a month or two later we had three larger scholars. Their studies embraced Latin and the higher English branches. In history I never saw a class of scholars, of their age, that would equal them. I believe the South is ahead of us in giving attention to this study. Are not their Congressmen better informed in history than ours?

But to my school. Although we had the rogue, it is the only school I ever saw without a dunce in it.

At one time the boys had obtained permission to bathe in a little bayou that the high water had formed, a short distance from the school-house. This bayou was separated, by a strip of land about three rods wide, from another larger and deeper one. Two of the boys returned, after a while, and wanted permission to go and tell the overseer to come and shoot the alligators in the "big bayou" on the other side of the path from the one in which they had been swimming.

Startled at such news, I called them all in; when they informed me that they did not see the alligators, till they had been been bathing some time. They expressed no fear from sporting in the water near such terrible play-fellows; merely wished to go and inform the overseer, or some of the negroes, that they might enjoy the sport of seeing them shot—that's all.

It was not a very pleasant thought to me, that, on dismissing school for the day, I should miss two or three of our accustomed "good evenings;" and that, we should miss two or three of our little crew in sailing home. And it was sadder yet to think that we should have to announce to their parents, that they were snatched away and devoured by these greedy American crocodiles.

But with such brave pupils, I had no fears in encountering the difficulties we should meet, in the path of knowledge, nor of passing the "Alps" and "Splugens" of Science.

We would sometimes keep the skiff with us, preferring to row home ourselves at night, that we might steal away from the school-house, during recess at noon, and forget our studies and books, in a fine sail on the Yazoo. We always got our lessons well and were prompt in our attendance; and when recess came, had a spirit to enjoy it. Nothing delighted me more than to see my pupils revel in the enjoyment of their play-hours. They always studied the best after them. On the other hand, had we been exacting and overtasked them, and not allowed them a full pastime—a suitable relaxation—an unbending from hard and wearying study, we would not have had that cheerfulness and eager desire to learn among our little set.

How truthfully and eloquently the school-boy has expressed his dislike to being a little pent-up prisoner with his "slates and books," in that purgatory of his—a school-house.

> "Mother, I am wild for pleasure!
>   No bright angel o'er dull books pores,
> Science and learning are school-walls' treasures,
>   God and beauty are out of doors."

Taking our boat-ride, one day, down the stream from our little Academy, we met a steamer, and rowed out from the river into a little cove of a bayou, and there, beneath overhanging willows, we sat and watched the steamboat passing up stream, while the surging swells almost tossed our little craft out of water. We then ventured out riding the billows—and finally came to a fine place to land, where we moored our boat, and went a-shore.

I left the pupils to ramble out in the woods after berries and wild flowers, while I went over into an adjacent cotton-field, where the negroes were at work, thickly scattered all over the field, some ploughing and some hoeing.

The overseer, a young man with an intelligent look, seeing me, came up, and gave me something of the history of raising cotton. It was up some four or five inches high, looking like thrifty rows of beans, sown in drills, with different shaped and richer leaves. The field was perfectly clean—not a weed could be seen in it.

Seeing a wench ploughing, I asked him if they usually held the plough. He replied that they often did; and that this girl did not like to hoe, and, she being a faithful hand, they let her take her choice.

Returning to the school-house, we saw an alligator sunning himself on a log. At sight of us he dove into the water, and soon came up in another place, just showing his head. We threw sticks at him and he swam off. He was some six or eight feet long. We often saw these laziest of all animals, dozing and basking in the summer sunshine, on old logs in the bayous, doing nothing but snoozing their life away.

The advantage of teaching here, whether in the "old-field" schools—the common school South, or as tutor in a planter's family, or in the academies, is, you have a less number of scholars, and more *time* to devote to each study. The teacher has not got time, he cannot stop long enough by the way, North, to do anything like justice to the various branches he pretends to teach.

Take one exercise for example—that of reading. The class should not only be "taught to read in that graceful and agreeable manner that will make them fond of reading, *but to make them understand what they read, and discover the beauties of the author, in composition and sentiment.*"

We think in words, and pupils that only get the words get the mere husks of ideas. This makes dull scholars. And the reason they are dull, is, they derive no more satisfaction from the lesson, than they would in cracking nuts without having the pleasure of eating the meats. When I see a school-boy whining and complaining over his hard lesson, it reminds me of the squirrel that had unfortunately got a hard nut, and was observed to nibble away at it while the big tears ran down his cheeks.

Much to the credit of our patrons, we mention the very pleasant visits we have received from them in our school, and from their ladies and friends.

We think the little Southron, on the whole, an interesting student, and we must say that we have ever been pleased with the deportment of children in planters' families; and it is a pleasure to walk along the streets in a Southern town, and witness the well-behaved conduct of children. You hear no swearing—no vulgar language. You see no vagrant boys—no wicked little urchins; nothing but the lively pranks and shouts and prattle of well-dressed children.

---

## CHAPTER XVII.

### FRAGMENTS.

"Walk through the garden to the wall of rock
Beyond;—there, in a smoky, dark recess,
Hangs an old lamp of copper;—BRING ME THAT.
I am a virtuoso in such matters,
A great collector of old odds and ends;
And so the lamp, worthless enough to others,
Has an imaginary worth to me."

ŒHLENSCHLAGER.

## A CHESTERFIELD OF A LANDLORD.

"Whoe'er has traveled earth's dull round,
Where'er his stages may have been,
Will sigh to think he still has found
His warmest welcome at an Inn."

SHENSTONE.

Mr. M., late of Vicksburgh, now of Monticello, Mississippi, is a landlord with an exceedingly popular reputation. Such landlords should be multiplied all over the country, not enough to "stale their presence," but so that the way-worn traveler should find here and there in the dull round of his pilgrimage one of those delightful "Lorettoes"—a way-side Inn. But Nature bestows her choicest gifts rarely. Hence a Chesterfieldian landlord like Mr. M., is a gift for which the country cannot be too grateful.

Mr. M., on receiving guests had a certain prelude of civilities to bestow upon them. He treated every man as if he was a gentleman, and every gentleman as if he was a lady, and every lady—a la Dutchess.

A traveler arrived at his hospitable Inn, one day, on whom he bestowed, as he stepped out of the omnibus, his usual round of blandishments. He was then shown his room, where our courteous host soon appeared, to inquire if his guest did not wish some kind act performed for him. Being answered in the negative, he politely bowed himself out. After being the recipient of several of these kind visits, and getting wearied with their very polite interrogations as to his wants, our traveler finally told him that he wanted a servant. One was immediately rung in, when, pointing to our affable host, with an impatient sternness he commanded the servant *to take that man out of his room and put him where he would not molest him any more.*

When Mr. M. was the favorite landlord of Jackson, the capital of Mississippi, the members of the Legislature usually boarded with him. But while officiating as their kind host, he, contrary to his usual practice of having his bills of fare printed, wrote them off, and read them at the head of the table. Being asked about this singular movement, he replied that it was useless to print the bills, "*for the members of the Legislature couldn't read.*"

## THE NEGROES AND THE BEES.

> "As bees
> In spring time, when the sun with Taurus rides,
> Pour forth their populous youth about the hive
> In clusters; they among fresh dews and flowers
> Fly to and fro: or on the smoothed plank,
> The suburb of their straw-built citadel,
> New rubbed with balm, expatiate and confer
> Their state affairs."
>
> MILTON.

Though it was on the Sabbath, it was deemed expedient to save a very large swarm of bees that had just taken wing from one of the old hives, and begun to settle in two different places, on a nectarine-tree, till they hung like a couple of huge pine-apples from its boughs.

We were out in the door-yard with some of the inmates of Willow Dale when we discovered this rare fruit hanging from the tree, upon which Mr. P. ordered two or three of his negroes to gather them, and put them in a new hive. The negroes soon came out with their heads and hands muffled up—accoutered for the task, and began the work of hiving them. The attempt met with some vindictive sorties from the bees, until one of the negroes, contrary to the express orders not to make any hostile demonstrations, began to brush about his head, when—

> "Alarmed at this the little crew,
> About his ears vindictive flew."

At which the other negroes began to box and brush about their heads, till a warm contest arose that resulted in the expulsion of the negroes from the ground.

After waiting for the bees to calm down, a second trial was made by the courageous servants to hive them;—each carrying now a bush in his hand with which to defend himself. By this time the family, as spectators to this scene, were all out in the front grounds about the house, looking on at a distance. It was not long before hostilities were begun by the bees, and which were soon returned by the negroes who were determined to stand their ground, as conquerors in a contest, where the eyes of their master and mistress with their whole household were upon them. But the bees in frantic fury soon beset them; when one of the more timid ran with a halo of them about his head, brushing and plunging among the dense leaves and stalks of the corn-field.

Another ran towards us, to whom Mr. P. cried out—"*Don't come this way! don't come this way!*" The poor negro, in distress, little heeded the command, but on he came, switching and brushing himself, scattering the bees among us, which sent several of the ladies screaming into the house, with a bevy of them buzzing about their heads. Another, like a mad ox, shouting and bellowing with pain, ran into the bushes and shrubs in the yard, head-foremost, to rid himself of half a swarm of these furies.

But poor SAM, the last to leave the field, fought with unparalleled heroism, till he was commanded to retreat;—when, hotly besieged, he first "boused" among the shrubs and bushes, then rolled on the ground—

> "Half blind with rage and mad with pain."

Yet the little winged demons beset him in countless numbers. The family, and the other slaves became alarmed for him; some running up to him and essaying to brush them off; still they seemed "to gather thicker;" when some one cried out—"The *pump*, SAM! the *pump!*" He was there in an instant, and half throwing himself under the spout, the stream was sent gushing over him. But not long; the remaining part of the swarm, in maddened fury, now turned out, and furiously joining in the attack, drove them all from the pump. Poor SAM, nearly victimized, got up and ran for his life, among the rose-trees and shrubs again; jumped over the fence, and, as we thought, was going to take the road, and make a desperate push for freedom. But he was wiser. The next instant we heard a—"*souze*," and looking over the fence, in the direction of the sound—we saw SAM buried in the Yazoo. Here, at least, he had rid himself of these furious "imps." But—*mirabile dictu!* as he raised his head above the water, the little demons that had hovered over it, flew at him frantic and vengeful, till by repeated "duckings" he tired and drowned them out."

## THE NORTH.

In a chat with some of our Southern friends to-day, on the North, we assured them that the North, like the South, could not be *told*. To get an idea of the real North one must visit the winter quarters of old Hiems, where the old Borean Hero sits on his hilly throne, with the "stone before the door of the imprisoned winds," and winter's frosts, and cold, and wrath, and storms, pent up within its vast cavern, ready to let them out as the fit takes him. The North was in that region, with her Hurons and Eries, where

"Strong Niagara's thunder,
Wakes the echoes of the world."

Though not applying to the above, yet the following we trace here as a *bon-mot* of one of the female servants of Willow Dale.

Towards night-fall, to-day, after I had had a lively conversation with Mrs. P. and Miss NELL T., of Michigan, in which we told stories and engaged in *bon-mots*, I remember this punning fling at the North from MARTHA, one of Mrs. P.'s servants.

On arising from our chat, I went to the side-board, in the hall, to get a glass of water, but found the pitcher that usually sat on it, in a temperature of "ninety degrees," and the water in the pitcher—not an iota below it.

I called the servant above-named, and told her to get a pitcher of *cold* water if there was any in the well. She took the pitcher and remarked as she left the hall, "Yes, I will get it from the part you love—from the COLD *North* corner."

At which Mrs. P. remarked, "You must send that to HARPER'S Drawer." As I was not a contributor to HARPER'S Journal, I placed it then in my own, and now it is traced on the imperishable (?) pages of this book, where it will be read, no doubt, when the *bon-mots* of the last HARPER will be forgotten.

## ONE DAY IN A PANTOMIMIC WORLD.

"These, O ye quacks, these are your remedies."
*Corn-Law Rhymes.*

On going down stairs to breakfast this morning, I could not hear my gaiters squeak. They surely did last night. This was strange. Having seated myself in the sitting-room, Miss T. came in, and, as it appeared afterwards, spoke to me, and wondered why I did not answer her; still more when she saw me looking at her, and yet remaining silent. Mr. P. came in with the usual morning salutation, and afterwards spoke to me in a high pitch of voice, yet I said nothing. This was passing strange.

They soon arose and beckoned me into breakfast. The bell had rung, and I had not heard it. At breakfast I ate in silence; not the least noise could I hear. There was no sound to the knife and fork, or dishes; the foot of the servant trod the floor—a step without a sound. All at table talked as usual, but no voice was heard. I had never sat at so still a breakfast-table in my life. Chairs moved—servants pass around us, in and out the doors—opening and shutting them; the family came, sat, chatted, and ate, and went again; yet they had a charmed presence; they came and went in silence. Where was I? Yesterday I was here and heard sounds to it all. To-day everything was the same—yet how changed to me! I saw motions but heard nothing. I was in a pantomimic world. I was *deaf*. I went to the door and looked out—there was this beautiful world of ours, without a sound in it. The birds were voiceless in the trees—the trees without their rustling leaf-music; the river went murmuring on in silence; the steamers went puffing, splashing and whistling by, sending the waves dashing to the shore; yet no sound was heard. As I walked out, Rollo and Bet ran baying to the gate at a strange negro passing by. I never heard them bark so still before.

And as I returned, old chanticleer came strutting by the door raised his head, threw it back, braced out, opened his mouth, flapped his wings—and—that's all. "*Mirabile dictu! vox hæsit in faucibus!*

The turkeys went parading around the yard, spreading

their tails, lowering their wings, and cutting their circling "swells," as usual; but instead of gobbling, they were gulping down mouthfuls of thin air.

But while I stood in the porch leaning my head against one of its posts, and musing on what occurred around me, there were some sounds that I was not sorry to miss. Rollo in his gambols about the yard had routed a bevy of Guinea hens; they, as mad as hornets, flew up into a China-tree, fluttered about, went into hysterics, and poured down upon him a vindictive tirade of harsh notes. I did not regret that I did not hear them.

With a sad step I walked into the house. All that was in-doors, and out-doors, was without sound. The prattle, and laugh, and shout of the children at play about the house, I could not listen to and enjoy. Even little DIDDY went whistling through the hall, and I did not hear him.

I was deaf. Thus sadly I passed the whole day, a day in which all about me was still and silent as death. My foot-steps were so noiseless that I seemed to walk in air. Whatever I touched refused to give a sound; and wherever I went, it fled from me, as the ghost of ACHILLE'S father fled his approach in Hades. There was no voice to anything living, nor could anything inanimate be made to give a sound. I at last tried my own voice—*that too had lost its sound!* I gave up. I went to my couch and laid down. What my thoughts were I never can tell. I remember this impressed my mind—all that I had ever heard in this beautiful world—

"From the vernal showers
On the twinkling grass,"—

to all that was joyous, and sweet, and musical, was now silent to me. Oh! you do not know what it is to hear until you have been deaf!

But you would know the cause of this deafness? *Eighteen grains of quinine.* I had had an attack of the Southern fever, and my physician gave me quinine plentifully. It often has this effect, and sometimes injures the hearing for life. With me it was only for a day. I rejoiced the next morning to hear, once more, old chanticleer's

"Cottage-rousing crow."

## WILLOW DALE IN A RAIN-SHOWER.

"We knew it would rain, for all the morn,
A spirit, on slender ropes of mist,
Was lowering its golden buckets down
Into the vapory amethyst,
Of marshes, and swamps, and dismal fens—
Scooping the dew that lay in the flowers;
Dipping the jewels out of the sea,
To sprinkle them over the land in showers."

ALDRICH.

I love to sit by my window and look out into this fine shower of rain. We have had a series of them to-day. Yesterday I was quite unwell, but to-day I feel the full revivingness of these showers, as well as the "babbling fields of green."

And I love to sit by my window, and look out upon the rich-leafed trees about the house, so lately waving in the breeze, but now standing with their graceful tops rain-bowed and motionless. The tall Lombardy poplars, with their crests of plumes, lately nodding in the breeze, bending over their beautiful heads, dripping with rain. The aspen is twinkling and sparkling with rain-drops that strike its leaves and glance off in glittering sheen. The China-tree is turning off, from strata to strata of its feathery foliage, little gushing streams of rain that come dashing on the ground; and from bough to bough of the dingy, broad-leafed mulberry, it falls in little cascades. The althæ and mimosa are cascatelles, and the rose-bushes —bubbling fountains of rain. The innumerable cotton-rows are all dripping, the vast corn-field gurgling, the grass twinkling, and the river is all a-bubble with rain.

The rain continued to fall all night in copious showers, till I retired to rest. Then I laid and listened to the drowsy poetry of the rain pattering on the roof.

"When the humid storm-clouds gather
  O'er all the stormy spheres,
And the melancholy weather
  Weeps in rainy tears,"
There's a joy to press the pillow,
  Of a cottage-chamber bed,
And listen to the patter
  Of the soft rain over head.
Every tinkle on the shingles
  Finds an echo in the heart,
And a thousand dreamy fancies
  Into busy being start.
And a thousand recollections
  Weave their bright hues into woof,
  As I listen to the murmur
    Of the soft rain on the roof.
  Then in fancy comes my mother
    As she did in days a-gone,
  To survey her infant sleepers,
    Ere she left them till the dawn.
  I can see her bending o'er me,
    As I listen to the strain,
  Play'd upon the shingles
    By the patter of the rain."

## THE LONG-EXPECTED VISIT.

"Soft watch him now the while he opes the packet;
  'Tis from that far-off-land he calls his home,
And there is that within will touch him nearly."

*Some Poet.*

I had been some months in this Southern land, and during the while had not seen one "familiar face" from the "land of the mountain and lakes." And sometimes, a few months with us are a long period. Nothing but letters from home and my correspondents. But it had been quite a long time since I had even received a letter. A lady friend—Miss T., of Michigan, had been promised, and we had been expecting her a long while; she was "due," and waited for, as teacher, in Mrs. C.'s school at Wallachebogue.

This morning, while conversing with Mrs. P. in the sitting-room, she asked me when I supposed my friend from the North would be with them. I replied that I could not tell; she might not come at all, as the time for her arrival had passed.

She then asked me to describe her; which being done, she thought I was not exactly correct, because she had seen a young lady from the North, this morning, who had given her a more truthful description of Miss T., and who, having stood in the hall during the while, listening to our conversation, now presented herself at the door, in whom I recognized an old Northern friend. She informed me that she had lately seen our mutual friend, Miss T., and that she had now given up the idea of coming South. But *she* was like "Miss CAPULET," *id est*—names made no difference with her, she would, with our consent, pass for Miss T.; then there would be nothing lacking, for she would try and make her proxy visit at Willow Dale equal to the one we had been anticipating. The proposal was accepted, and we went in to breakfast.

We informed our friend, at table, that she was now eating the same hoe-cake and corn-dodger, of which Uncle TOM and the immortal TOPSY had once eaten; of the same corn-bread and bacon that old TIFF found by the way-side;

and which he thought, ELIJAH-like, the ravens had brought him; and that after breakfast we would not only show her Uncle TOM'S and TIFF'S Cabins, but the very identical Uncle TOM, TIFF and TOPSY themselves. She was really in the land of heroes, fiction and romance.

Breakfast over, we took a walk out into the garden and about the grounds. Everything seemed so novel, beautiful and tropical; so fresh, fragrant and blooming, to her, just from the cold, leafless and tuneless April of the North; that it was like coming from the scenes in the "Winter's Tale," to those of "Mid-Summer Night's Dream."

I asked her if I had not been fulsome in my description of Southern shrubs and roses.

"No; no. I certainly had not. The roses were more luxuriant and of greater variety than ours. O, they were perfect, radiant beauties!"

Leaving this scene, we mentioned something about going to the "gin-house." She looked at me somewhat surprised, and seemed to say, "What can he mean?"

Guessing the little dilemma that her mind was in, I told her I had not invited her to the "gin-shop," but to the "gin-house," where they separated the cotton-seed from the cotton. O yes, she would go there.

We passed by the negro-quarters, but not without my fair friend's sending many an inquiring look and glimpse, through the doors and windows, into these abodes. We pointed out the celebrated "Cabins" above-mentioned, and their owners, and showed her little TOPSY playing with some negro boys and girls. We went on, getting the key of the overseer as we passed by his house, and went through the "gin-house." But I must waive, or the reader will, I hope, a description of it. Imagine a large barn, hip-roofed, sitting on naked posts some ten feet from the ground, and as for the "*gin-stand*"—I never could describe a machine, it is worse than solving a hard problem in Mathematics.

Our "Miss CAPULET" stayed with us several days, enjoying Southern society very much at Willow Dale. During her visit several of the young ladies and gentlemen in the neighborhood came in to see her.

We took a steamer, at our landing, and sailed up the river to Yazoo City, where Mr. C. found the long-expected Miss T., of Michigan, with whom, in his fine carriage, she went home, to teach in his lady's school at Wallachebogue.

It was the Sabbath. Thinking to hear the Rev. Mr. MARSHALL, of the Methodist Episcopal church, I remained in town, stopping at the residence of Mr. F. B., a very wealthy merchant in this city, and brother to one of the patrons of our academy. The house, though not of itself costly, is embowered in the leafy luxury of the tropics. There was a wealth of trees and shrubs, and a skill and taste displayed in arranging and trimming them that we had nowhere seen in this clime. And among our memories of this pleasant land, none afford us more pleasure than our visits at this delightful rural retreat; and with them will not be forgotten the politeness and kind attention with which we were ever treated by Mr. B. and his lady.

Mr. B. was unavoidably called away as we came in. The room was elegantly furnished. A small, though costly book-case contained splendidly bound volumes, and the walls were ornamented with rich family paintings. While waiting here for church time, we conversed away the pause between the ringing and tolling of the bells, with Mrs. B., and a niece of the famous Colonel HAYS, who was attending a lady's-school in this place, and whom we remember as—pretty, very.

The Rev. Mr. MARSHALL was absent; hence we went to hear the Rev. Mr. MONTGOMERY of the Presbyterian church—a modest, wee-steepled, stone edifice. The congregation had already assembled. A very kind appearing sexton seated me not far from the door, on the wall-side. The audience was two-thirds ladies; and I seated behind them. I don't know why, it was odd and wicked too, but it occurred to me—

You, from this seat, will see more of Southern bonnets than beauty. But, as HAWTHORNE remarks, "one gets a more picturesque view—one of more truth to nature, and characteristic tendencies, and of vastly greater suggestiveness, in the back view of a residence whether in the town or country, than in front. The latter is always artificial; it is meant for the world's eye, and is therefore a veil and concealment. Realities keep in the rear, and put forward an advance guard of show."

I think my view, from this seat, was more picturesque. I found that out, at times, as I got a glance at the front of the "edifices;" I saw handsomer bonnets than faces. But generally, the "front views" in our churches are not only artificial, but rather *picture*sque—"meant for the world's eye."

> "Oh, wad some power the giftie gie us,
> To see ourselves as others see us!
> It wad frae many a blunder free us
> And foolish notion;
> What airs in dress an' gait wad lea 'e us
> And ev'n Devotion!"

Rev. Mr. M. is a man of fair oratorical powers. His sermon had a completeness that one does not often find. You admired it as a finished discourse, as well as for its truths of deep meaning, and instruction enforced by the emphasis of true piety and religion.

The singing, I remember, was miscellaneous. I dislike this way of singing by the church *en masse*, despite WARD BEECHER and his entire church choir. Singing in church, besides being worship, is a musical entertainment. But where all sing, there is no audience to be entertained—none to listen. I would as soon wish that everybody could sing, and that would be extremely absurd, if not awful, as to encourage entire church singing. I am no singer. I sometimes doubt, with HUGH MILLER, whether there is any such a thing as a tune. But yet, "of all noises, music is the least disagreeable to me." In fact, as a listener, I think I am gifted. I enjoy good singing hugely. But a miscellaneous—seventy-four-by-fifty-feet choir, singing to one-or-two, as a solitary audience, is like a "forty-parson-power" employed in preaching to the same solitary one-or-two.

Towards night a servant brought me a horse and saddle from Willow Dale, and I returned, enjoying a pleasant horse-back ride along the banks of the gentle, willow-skirted Yazoo.

## THE NEGRO'S HORSE.

"Here they come, leering and rearing,
Sporting and frisking,
Turning and twisting,
And frolicking round;
Diving and striving,
Biting and fighting,
Darting and parting,
In antic rebound."

SOUTHEY.

The planter has been feeding his mules high, in order to have them in good plight to do his spring work. And, by the way, one word about these animals. They are the hardiest and finest I ever saw. And besides his better qualities, he is an animal that, after a short acquaintance,

"No one could pass without remark."

He may carry you on his back all day long, "up hill and down dale; through bush and brake," safely, affectionately, and without a stumble; but if he can get a chance to kick you at night, he will. He is a snug, compact, hardy, springy, frolicsome animal. He surpasses the horse in frolicsomeness, as much as his master, the negro, does the white man. He is the negro's horse.

This morning I left some thirty-five or forty, running, careering, wrestling, kicking and cutting up all manner of extravagant pranks on the open lawn, before Mr. P.'s mansion.

I was gone, visiting at a neighboring planter's, a large part of the day; and when I returned, they were frolicing as hard as ever. Seeing me approach, some thirty rods off, they all started toward me, with leering heads and open mouths, in as furious an onset as ever a troop of Don Cossacks charged an enemy. Had not my horse been accustomed to them, I should certainly have considered myself in great danger. But he was less molested by them than by the flies that were buzzing about and stinging him.

## OUR NOCTE'S AMBROSIANÆ AT WILLOW DALE.

"Long, long through the hours, and the night, and the chimes,
Here we talk of old books, and old friends, and old times."
THACKERAY.

During this evening, the afternoon here, previous to the accustomed amusements of the latter part of it, I had fallen into one of those moods in which one cannot really please themselves; and in which one longs for something, which is the more unpleasant from the fact that you cannot tell what that something is. I used to love, in such a mood, to wander from room to room of the noble mansion in Willow Dale, all of which had more or less books in them, for Mr. P. had a large collection of many a quaint and rare old volume.

> "The large cypress chambers were crammed in all nooks,
> With tattered old volumes and silly old books,
> With foolish old odds, and foolish old ends,
> And various old things from various old friends."

I loved, I say, to saunter, at such times, about the house, reading by snatches from the various books, till I found something that pleased me, then take the volume and retire to some poetic corner and read.

To-day the volume that satisfied this longing was a book of reminiscences of the last sixty-five years, by a Mr. THOMAS. I had been reading in this while the rest of the company were at whist; till, the latter growing dull, we all changed and took up a topic of conversation that finally led to books and authors; when one of the party instantly declared for BULWER, one for SCOTT, another for G. P. R. JAMES, and I for HAWTHORNE. BULWER first came upon the "tapis." He was handled by some of the ladies rather "tartarly." I believe the last shaft, and the one that "pinned him to the wall," was hurled by a young lady; "a friend of hers had read his novels, 'drugged' with exciting sentiment, till she was afraid of them."

SCOTT, nobody disliked; his wizzard pen charmed all. JAMES, some were fond of; he surely had written enough. But, volume for volume, SCOTT would long outlive him.

HAWTHORNE—I remember the first time I saw his name

in print. I thought of HAWKSWORTH and the old English classic writers. I could not make him seem of our day, and really thought him a cotemporary with SHENSTONE and THOMPSON.

Some did not like him, he was too correct in style—did not unbend enough—nature was not unloosed of her stays—he wanted a little more freshness—something of the "abandon," or carelessness of unstudied nature about his style.

We could not help acknowledging the truth of these remarks, but yet liked HAWTHORNE; for we have, more or less, in him, the style of the old English essayist re-produced.

COOPER, at the mention of his name we thought universal praise would follow; yet one of the party said she disliked him; she must be pardoned for saying so. She gave him genius, but that did not make her like his books.

COOPER is our SCOTT, writing of the feudal days, and brusque chivalry of American Indian life.

But LONGFELLOW, the same lady thought one of our finest poets. Some one replied that *poeta nascitur non fit* had been applied to him.

She thought that his "Psalm and Goblet of Life" had answered that requisition.

We told her that LONGFELLOW troubled APOLLO and the muses; he was so artistical—came so near being one of the "poetic bairns," that they had often favored him in "snatching a grace beyond the reach of art;" by which assistance he has written, as BURNS would say, "a rowth o' rhymes." A share of his poetry is not so poetical as some of his prose. But his chaste and scholarly muse suffers nothing to leave his pen that is not correct and elegant. His best poetry was beautiful. His poorest was always good prose.

Our chat closed with POE'S Raven, which was admired as a thing of beauty. "Beautiful exceedingly"—gloomy, but beautiful. We have not such another poem this side of the Atlantic. BRYANT'S "Thanatopsis," and POE'S "Raven," are worthy of the old English Muse.

But we were not a little mortified when one of the party, referring to a trans-atlantic author of great celebrity, asked us how we liked such a volume of his. We begged to be excused from answering, for we had not read the volume. But we were worse off when the same person rather coolly remarked, "I thought everybody had read that book." I replied that everybody had but me. And I never could account for my not reading it. But this would not do. She continued: You cannot afford to lose the reading of this book. I finally promised my friend that I would read it the first opportunity I had. This soon occurred. And, to-day, we thank our fair friend in the South for the "fix" she got us into; for it was the cause of our reading that most readable of all books—DON QUIXOTE.

But I soon got into a worse situation. Some one asked me how I liked a certain work of a late writer. I, in order to save myself from another expose—for one has a pride in their literary acquisitions—replied, for I was in some doubt about it, that I had forgotten whether I had read it or not. This would not answer for an evasion; for I was plainly told that if I had ever read the work, I certainly could not have forgotten such a thrilling book.

I then resolved to myself that I would read every popular book, ancient or modern, or keep out of literary society entirely, where the continual expose of one's ignorance torments them.

The subject then changed to WORDSWORTH. Perhaps no poet was so "wrapped up in his own poetry, and his own poetical life, as WORDSWORTH. He thinks and observes nothing else. Everything is done with reference to it. He was all and only a poet." And truly he says of himself—

> "To me the meanest flower that blows can give
> Thoughts that do often lie too deep for tears."

He had mused his life away in his most wild, lovely and romantic home, among the hills near Rydal Lake, a spot of all others in the world that he loved the most. "I would not," says he, "give up the mists that spiritualize these mountains, for all the beautiful scenes and sunny skies of Italy."

The story was true that was told in the papers, of his seeing, for the first time, in a large company, some new novel of SCOTT'S, in which there was a notice taken from his works; and that he went immediately to the shelf and took down one of his own volumes and read the whole poem to the party who were waiting for the reading of the new volume referred to.

A few evenings later HUGH MILLER was our theme. Some had read his works, and very much admired him. He was unsurpassed by any writer of the present day, in the descriptive faculty. BUCKLAND said he would give his right hand for it. He was a TITAN among us. A BURNS or SHAKSPEARE hewing stone. And, as CARLYLE would say, the greatest thing Scotland ever did.

One of the ladies present said that while she was living with her uncle, Dr. Y., of Louisville, Kentucky, where she was educated, a celebrated French geologist, in making the tour of the United States, visited her uncle; and he, when asked whether he was a married man or not, replied that he was; he was married to geology—it was his wife and children. She said furthermore that Sir RODERICK

MURCHURSON'S wife was jealous of geology; and that, when Mr. LIELL and his lady were making the tour of the United States, they also visited her uncle, when Mrs. LIELL told her that the wives of geologists were usually jealous of their husbands, and that she, being jealous of her geologic husband, dare not trust him to make the tour of the United States alone.

We, during the evening, asked this lady if she had read Mrs. STOWE'S "Sunny Memories," in which the paintings of the old masters were so severely criticised No; she had not read madam STOWE since she wrote that horrible book of hers—Uncle TOM'S Cabin.

The party this evening were playing euchre, as usual, and requested me, as I did not join them, to act as their tally-man. We thought that that would be exerting a talismanic influence over us to lure us into the game.

I asked my fair friend if playing euchre did not learn —we use learn as a transitive verb; *teaches* here would not be the word—we asked, I say, our fair friend if euchre-playing did not learn ladies to be arch and intriguing? She thought it did; for it was called the game of the evil one by all the good folks.

Another evening while the rest were playing euchre, Miss HATCHIE B. and I were playing chess. We remember, during the evening, that we were interrupted by a servant's coming to us with a server on which were beautiful cut glasses, and rich, scolloped cakes, and some cut in pretty slices. I remember that I took one of the scolloped cakes and one of the glasses in my hand—they were stained glasses—and holding it up to the light, admired its rich, beautiful colors; and that when I put it back again on the server the color had changed. It seemed quite a mystery to me till I solved it. The candle-light when I took up the glass struck it so as to give it those varied colors.

Late in the evening I arose and bid the family good night. Nowhere have I been so pleased, so captivated with a single habit of a people, as with the Southern one of bidding you "good-night" on retiring to rest. To hear the good-night given by them all as they left the room, I always enjoyed very much. It was ever worth waiting for, to hear this last and sweetest word of all spoken. This given, I sought my room, penned a few lines in my journal, then to my pillow, which, like a pretty babe, has a wealth of fringe and drapery about it; and was soon lost in the snowy voluptuousness of my couch.

Misses HATCHIE and MATTIE B., our fair cousins, came home late this evening from the "calico ball," given in Yazoo City. In this ball the ladies all wore calico dresses. It was something plebeian for these patrician ladies. They, the cousins, are tall and graceful figures for the dance, and came home in their full ball-dress, with fine ostrich plumes decorating their heads. They have rich black hair, and the elder, very beautiful black eyes. A fine eye illuminates the intellectual faculties, and lights, like a lamp, the apartments of the mind, showing their wealth, beauty and decorations.

Our topic of conversation this evening was with Miss HATCHIE B., about Northern peculiarities. She thought that she had got much of the peculiarities of the North from an acquaintance with many of its teachers.

She had noticed that our phrases distinguished us as much as theirs did them. A Northerner would be found out before he was in their society twenty minutes, because he could not possibly remain so long without having "guessed" several times. We thought it useless to add that during the same twenty minutes in our society, a Southrŏn would "reckon" an equal number of times.

Now the point at issue was, which was the most correct, to guess or to reckon? The Yankee did them both, he was a guessing animal, and a great reckoner; hence, he had the advantage of the Southron, who only reckoned, but never guessed.

We remarked that we thought Southern ladies more coy of gentlemen's society.

She said, they, in this respect, were more recluse than Northern ladies. But she wished to know what I meant by "country girls." We described as near as we could that "rose-complexioned lass."

Did WILLIS mean one of our country girls in these lines of his:

> "The damsel that trips at day-break,
> Is shod like a mountaineer?"

Yes, and in that line, too, where he calls the same country girl

> "A milk-maid half divine."

The conversation then changed to beautiful women, and finally to POE'S Raven, which we thought surpassed beautiful women. They would fade; but the Raven was a think of beauty and a joy forever. But she did not like it—denied its beauty. We were a little surprised at this, but could not allow her to dislike a thing of so much merit and beauty; hence we undertook the task of making a lady admire a thing she disliked. So we went to noticing some of its rarer beauties and attractions in order to win her over, repeating now and then some of its finest lines.

> "Then I betook myself to thinking,
> Fancy unto fancy linking;"

N

till she finally concluded to like it. We claim no merit in winning so fair an admirer over to POE'S Raven; and only mention ourself as connected with it for the sake of adducing the instance—

> "Merely that and nothing more."

We remember reading SHELLEY'S "Lark" without admiring it, till a poetic friend of ours repeated passages of it to us and pointed out some of its exquisite beauties; and now we shall go admiring it all our days.

We went through the same process with COLERIDGE'S "Ancient Mariner." And now it often holds us, as he with the "glittering eye" did the weddinger,

> "Till its ghastly tale is read,
> And then it lets us free."

And we remember how we came to like SHENSTONE, and CRABBE, and KEATS; and how this passage in Lacon that SHAKSPEARE in his "Winter's Tale" speaks of,

> "Daffodils that come before the swallow dares,
> And takes the winds of March with beauty,"

made us read the "Sweet Swan of Avon." We thought the poet that penned those beautiful lines was worth reading.

But these nights that we have only given an imperfect glimpse of, will be remembered by me and our little group, seated, during the winter and spring, in the sitting-room around the chess-table by a Southern fire-side,

> "Where life is a tale of poetry,
> Told by the golden hours;"

and during the summer and autumn, in the front or rear veranda of the mansion at Willow Dale, chatting and looking out upon the beautiful moonlight scene, and listening to the various insect music about us.

Had I the inimitable pen of Kit North, these nights and their chit-chat should be put in a book, just for ourselves and friends. They would be *our* "Noctes Ambrosianæ."

But now, all the good things we said will be lost. Yes, they will all pass away with the sounds and music of the day—the melodious confusion of bird-tongues, the delicious murmur of countless millions of leaves, the tinkle of hidden brooks, the small talk of squirrels, the whir of partridges; yes, they will all pass away and be lost with the sounds and music of our evening—the monologue of the tree-toad, the harsh notes of the katy-dids, the slender reed of the cicadas, the soft hum, the trills, pee-peeps, and the shrill little pipings of happy insects.

But we will remember these evenings, and in coming years, memory will list to their chit-chat

> "As a sweet tale
> That lulls a listening child to sleep."

## A CYPRESS-SWAMP.

> "Away to the dismal swamp he speeds,
> And his path is rugged and sore,
> Through tangled juniper, beds of weeds,
> Through many a fen where the serpent feeds,
> And man never trod before."
>
> Tom Moore.

Immense swamps of cypress constitute a vast portion of the inundated lands of the Mississippi and its tributaries. No prospect on earth can be more gloomy. Well may the cypress be esteemed a funereal tree. When the tree has shed its leaves, a cypress-swamp, with its countless interlaced branches of a hoary gray, has an aspect of desolation and death. In summer its fine, short and deep-green leaves invest those hoary branches with a drapery of crape. The water in which they grow is a vast deep level, two or three feet deep, still leaving the innumerable cypress knees, as they are called, or very elliptical trunks, resembling circular bee-hives throwing their points above the waters. This water is covered with a thick coat of green matter, resembling buff velvet. The musquitoes swarm above the water in countless millions. A very frequent adjunct to this horrible scenery is the moccasin-snake, with his huge scaly body lying in folds upon the side of a cypress-knee; and if you approach too near, lazy and reckless as he is, he throws the upper jaw of his huge mouth almost back to his neck, giving you ample warning of his ability and will to defend himself.

"I traveled," says FLINT, from whom this sketch is derived, "forty miles along a cypress-swamp, and a considerable part of the way on the edge of it, in which the horse sunk at every step half way up to his knees. I was enveloped for the whole distance with a cloud of musquitoes. Like the ancient AVERNUS, I do not remember to have seen a single bird in the whole distance, except the blue-jay. Nothing interrupted the death-like silence save the hum of the musquitoes."

There cannot be well imagined another feature to the gloom of these vast and dismal forests, to finish this kind of landscape, more in keeping with the rest than the long moss, or Spanish beard; and this funereal drapery attaches itself to the cypress in preference to any other tree. There is not, that I know, an object in nature that produces such a number of sepulchral images as the view of the cypress forest, all shagged, dark, and enveloped in the festoons of moss. If you would inspire an inhabitant of New England, possessed of the customary portion of feeling, with the degree of homesickness that would strike to the heart, transfer him instantly from the hill and dale, from the bracing air and varied scenery of the North, to the cypress-swamps of the south.

## CHAMELEONS, SNAKES, REPTILES AND MIDGES.

> " 'A stranger animal,' cries, one,
> Sure never lived beneath the sun:
> A lizard's body, lean and long,
> A fish's head, a serpent's tongue,
> Its tooth with tripple claw disjoined;
> And what a length of tail behind!"
>
> MERRICK.

It is useless for one to attempt to describe the chameleon—for he would find it something else ere he got through. It is a nondescript in color, or it takes its hue from whatever it is on.

There are many kinds of snakes in this part of the South. The most dreaded are the rattle-snake, moccasin and the pilot-snake, that gets so full of poison in the fall that it grows blind. There are also many scorpions of the lizard species, some venomous, and many lizards of beautiful colors, like those of the East, which TOM MOORE, in his Lalla Rookh, speaks of—there

> "Lay lizards, glittering on the walls
> Of ruined shrines, busy and bright,
> As they were all alive with light."

The aligator is found in the Yazoo River, though the steamers disturb him much, and send him to take his siestas in the more retired bayous, and the secluded swamps and ponds, among which he lazily swims and wanders about, the most detested loafer in the animal kingdom. A dog is a dainty tit-bit for him. If he sees one swimming across the river, or bayou, he springs upon him and instantly devours him.

The chegre, an infinitesimal gnat, often spoken of at the North as being very annoying to one here, I have felt but little of, though his sting awakens one to the memory of hornets or yellow-jackets.

The gnat also, that ephemeral trumpeter, who lights on one with gossamer softness to nettle you with his sting, is very numerous.

The musquitoes in the valley annoy one very much, morning and evening, during the summer. At these hours there is no relief from them, unless you are enveloped, like JUPITER, in a cloud of your own creating. It was even difficult this season to write or read during most part of the day, these imps molested you so. One was glad to retire at night, and, having let down the fine gauze netting about his bed, there was a pleasure—securely freed from their annoyance—in being lulled to sleep by the low hum of their countless wings, and the delicious murmur of their banqueting notes about your couch.

———o———

Our winter culminated to-day, Thursday, February third. The morning gave promise of a fair day. Towards noon the clouds threatened rain or snow; which it would be it was difficult to tell; and in fact, they themselves got into a huff about the matter, and some commenced snowing and others raining, which resulted in the first, real, original compromise, known in elemental strife as sleet.

Friday, February fourth. A beautiful day. Where is

yesterday with its winter sleet? This is a change, and what a change! The sun is out in all its mellow sunshine, the daffodils and hyacinths are out in all their beauty and bloom, the turtles are out on their logs along the beach, basking in the sunshine, the birds are out caroling in the trees, and the negroes are out at work in the field.

## AN OLD SCHOOLMATE.

"When musing on companions gone,
We doubly feel ourselves alone."

SCOTT.

One of my pupils, little WILLIE Y., brought me, this morning, a beautiful orange. His father, he said, came home last night on the "Whiteman," a Yazoo steamer that runs between Yazoo City and New Orleans, and had brought them a barrel of oranges.

The merchants in New Orleans that buy the planters' cotton, usually send by him on his return home in the winter a barrel of oysters or oranges, as a New Year's or Christmas present to their families.

Eating this orange recalls to my mind the memory of JAMES AROSTO DUNCAN, the friend, confident and companion of my life during our academic-days at Kalamazoo, that "Harrow School" of ours, and our college-days at Ann Arbor, Michigan. Who can tell the love of schoolmates?

We had gone during one of the vacations in school to visit some friends in the country. Taking a choice volume of one of the old English poets with us, we were going to read it by the running brook, and enjoy a few days of life among

"The babbling fields of green."

"VAN," said he to me one day—we usually shortened our names, as students always do, preferring to abreviate a schoolmate's name as much as possible, not only for facility of utterance, but they were favorite names—names which our *Alma Mater* had christened us over and given, and by which we were known among ourselves at school, and were ever afterwards remembered. At the time referred to, we had gone a-blackberrying with a party of our friends, and were away in the woods. I had strayed off from the rest, and seating myself on a log was enjoying my musings.

"VAN," says he, as he came up and seated himself on the log by me, some coarse and clownish fellows having joined our party in the woods giving cause to the remark, "We have read much in our Greek and Latin about the '*hoi polloi*'—the 'vulgars;' and in English about the common people—the rabble—and taking me by the hand with his heart full of pure and noble sentiments, continued, "I cannot love the coarse and vulgar in this life of ours—*Amicus Plato sed magis amica veritas.* Why didn't you go out picking berries with the party?" I told him I had got tired and had seated myself on this log and gone into reflection. He had seen me there, and picking a handful of large berries came back from the party, and giving them to me we communed together for some time.

"I thought," said he, "you were lonely and I would come and keep you company."

I replied that I was glad he had, for I had rather converse with him than to scratch myself and tear my clothes for a few blackberries. My thoughts were sweeter than berries to me.

I believe he was as noble a fellow as I ever had for a schoolmate; and how often we two have given the reading of our hearts to each other as we did letters from our friends.

He continued: "VAN, would you not like to leave a good name here, that when you are gone your friends can speak well of you, and praise and remember you with affection and love? O, who does not wish to leave a beautiful memory here on earth that will be like a sweet friend to them when they are gone? It is better than golden epitaphs, or the poet's fame. I should like to leave such a memory when I am gone."

He has gone. He lies here in the sunny South. The magnolia waves and blooms over his grave; but his memory—that beautiful memory of his is here. It is connected with every scene and incident of our school-days. It will never leave me, and when I die I hope that I shall leave a good name, too, that will

"Plead in remembrance of me,"

and there in that better land I shall meet my old schoolmate where we can talk over our past lives and live forever in eternal love in Heaven.

Eating this orange reminds me of him. It is said that by eating one he died. The sharp point of one of the seeds sticking in his throat caused his death.

He lies buried not far from here in Alabama, where he with his young and accomplished wife had gone to teach. How appropriate the name, Alabama, "Here we will rest," to the death of my friend, a stranger far away from home. The following lovely lines that one of England's late poets wrote for his own epitaph, and which my lamented friend had a soul for admiring, and would, no doubt, have selected for his epitaph, as I should for mine, I inscribe here in memory of him.

"He does well who does his best;
Is he weary? let him rest.
Brothers, I have done my best;
I am weary—let me rest.
After toiling oft in vain;
Baffled, yet to struggle fain;
After toiling long to gain
Little good with mickle pain,
Let me rest. But lay me low,
Where the hedge-side roses blow;
Where the little daises grow;
Where the winds a-Maying go;
Where the foot-path rustics plod;
Where the breeze-bowed poplars nod;
Where his pencil paints the sod;
Where the old wood worships God;
Where the wedded throstle sings;
Where the wailing plover swings;
Where the young bird tries his wings,
Near the runlet's rushy springs;
Where at times the tempest's roar,
Shaking distant sea and shore,
Still will rave old Barnsdale o'er,
To be heard by me no more;
There beneath the breezy West,
Tired and thankful let me rest,
Like a child that sleepeth best
On its gentle mother's breast."

## THE YAZOO RIVER AND VALLEY.

Let me notice the view one gets in sailing up the Yazoo. I do wish its waters were clearer, just for its own sake and the sake of its steamers—those stately swans, that they might like those on

"Still St. Mary's lake
Float double, swan and shadow."

The trees in the valley through which it flows are of various kinds, but as you approach the river they have all dropped off, and you see nothing but a border, on either bank, of tall willow-trees, with their rich foliage hanging over the water, and here and there an oak standing among them. While between the trees, from the ground upwards, there is a luxuriant profusion of vine-work and tangle-wood, a rich, green, undulating bank of foliage that rises from the river's edge, and continues till it is lost by mingling and entwining among the boughs of the trees.

River vistas are most always cut off by the winding course of the stream; but where you can catch this holding a straight course long, ere it dodges 'round a bend, or hides among the willows, you have a fine view. A smooth stream of water, some thirty rods wide, fringed with the willow, whose fine foliage, as it recedes from you, has a mezzotint softness, and seems to meet over the water. Sailing down this river on a beautiful moonlight night adds a charm to the scene, and "leafs" one into romance a page or two. At such times I have imagined that this was the stream on which DESOTO met that beautiful Indian Princess—the CLEOPATRA of this region—in her beautiful galley surrounded by her maidens; and I have imagined—but the shrill whistle of a steamer coming in sight, from round a bend, has startled me from my reverie, and started me to my feet, to behold—a floating palace, brilliantly illuminated, pass. us. Heaven bless FULTON "forever and a day," for such a sight!

Some fifteen miles from the mouth of the river, on one of the bluffs that command a fine view of the river and scenery, there are the remains of an old Catholic Church. Tradition says something about its being built by the French. Its history is in doubt, and so is also that of the ruins of an old fort not far from the above-named relics, supposed to have been built by DeSoto. He passed the winter of 1541 on the banks of the Yazoo. But the Yazoo valley, now so blooming a region—rich with its tasseled maize, and snowy with its interminable fields of cotton—according to tradition, was once a bloody ground. Yazoo means the "River of Death;" a tribe of Indians had, undoubtedly, been exterminated here, as the Natchez were below; and since then, while the State was being settled, a band of lawless desperadoes prowled about this region, way-laying and robbing the defenceless inhabitants. One of the Vicksburgh papers has been giving a long tale of murder and crime, laying the scene in the Yazoo valley, and one Dick Mason as the hero. Many of the relatives of these desperadoes are in possession of rich plantations, the true title to which they would be reluctant to trace out.

The river is now very high, and in many places overflowing its banks and killing much corn and cotton. This stream, I believe, is, for its size, unequaled in navigation by any river in the United States. Steamers sail up the Yazoo proper some three hundred miles; and then nearly the same distance up the Tallahatchie, one of its tributaries. This is bringing the Mississippi into this part of the State. The valley has been considered more unhealthy than the uplands, especially in the summer season. Some who own plantations here live "in the hills;" others spend their summers in Tennessee and Kentucky—their winters here. They call this going North. Tennessee, Kentucky and Virginia, and those on their Northern borders, are ranked by them among the Northern States. I have often been pleased to hear them tell of having been North, when they had never crossed Mason's & Dixon's line.

## YAZOO CITY.

This town, viewed from the steamers as you pass up the river, seems as if it was coy of being seen, and had made an effort to hide among the trees and shrubbery, amid which the inhabitants have reared their dwellings. And when you have once got into its strees, you cannot so much wonder at its shyness, for many of its plain and shabby buildings look better half hid. It lies in the embrace, on one side, of a range of bluffs half circling round it, the city sloping down from these to the river that forms the base of this part circle. The side-walks are paved with bricks set edge-wise. The place is quiet, and has an old Spanish air about it. You hear the "clack" of one saw-mill, and the clang of several anvils; and you see the large, lumbering, high-boxed wagons, with their loads of cotton drawn by two or three span of mules, or five or six yoke of oxen, dragging their slow lengths along through its streets. It has four churches—small, decent buildings—Presbyterian, Methodist, Episcopal and Catholic. Rev. C. K. MARSHALL, of the Methodist Church, has the reputation of a fine orator throughout many of the States. He has been traveling so much this summer, that I have not been able to catch him in his pulpit. This town is noted for its two Know-Nothing papers—one the *Yazoo City Observer*, rather an able sheet—the other the *American Banner*, and the only political paper in the United States edited by a lady—Mrs. PREWIT. She is a Northern lady. Her husband formerly edited it, and on his death, she

"Hung out the banner from the outer wall."

The place, though containing some fifteen hundred inhabitants, has no public schools. It has a few private ones. The number of white children is not in equal proportion to a town of the same size in the North. Yet this lack of Common Schools is a sad thing for the place. Private Schools will not answer; they do not gather all in. "Had I as many children," says DANIEL WEBSTER, as old PRIAM, I would send them all to the Common Schools."

## WILLOW DALE PLANTATION.

The plantation proper, that part that is cultivated, is some four hundred acres. I presume Mr. P. has a thousand or two acres in all. He raises usually two or three thousand bushels of corn, and makes three hundred bales of cotton. He is supposed to be worth $100,000. A young widow, a short distance up the river from here, is worth half a million.

A man not only shows his taste, but his wisdom, in his house and its surroundings. I question the economy and philosophy that leaves the house just so it will answer to "stay in"—the grounds about it unadorned and unattractive, and gives all labor and attention to the great field. It is the benevolence that would assist the far-off Greeks when the very Greeks are at your door. Mr. P.'s house is a capacious mansion, sixty-five feet square, two stories high, both verandaed. The grounds about it are finely laid out, and adorned with many rare trees and shrubs. Many a planter with thrice his wealth has a rough log dwelling for his home.

I have said before that the planters built their houses of nearly the same style. Following this out as a hint, I find they are much given to mannerism among themselves.

For instance, you generally find in their houses a large high-posted, heavy-topped bedstead—some cost over a hundred dollars, and are massive and rich. One would think that such a piece of furniture was a relic of feudal days, on which once had couched the chivalrous CUER DE LEON, or WILLIAM the Conqueror, or the lordly inmates of Warwick or Windsor Castle. I might mention other instances.

The family of Mr. P. consists of himself and lady, four children, and an Irish girl as their seamstress. You frequently find poor, white young ladies sewing in their families. Mr. P. is from North Carolina. His lady is from Tennessee. It is considered as honorable to be a Virginian here, as it was once to be a Roman citizen. A good story is told of the North Carolinians, who, feeling all the Virginian's pride of birth, often reply, when asked what State they are from, "From North Carolina, near the Virginia line."

Mr. P.'s slaves were divided into house-servants, carpenter and blacksmith, and field-hands. The servants about the house are well-dressed, and each has his or her respective duty to perform. Aunt BETTY, the cook, is in her "sanctum," hard by the dining room, and during meals a servant is in direct communication with her and the table, who conveys the viands warm to the table, and replenishes them as soon as they get cold.

Where they do not have good mechanics among their slaves, they put out some ingenious one of them an apprentice till he has learned his trade. NATHAN, Mr. P.'s carpenter, is also a preacher, and on Sundays discourses to his brethren and sisters of that better land, far away. The field-hands have their quarters near by the house, some thirty rods to the right. These consist of little frame cabins, boarded with cypress, and white-washed.

They are very often log-cabins; but a planter of pride and taste has everything neat and orderly about him. They are arranged in rows, fronting the road, and shaded by a fine row of cone-shaped cotton-wood and China-trees before them. These are their homes.

They raise their own chickens, and have all the money they can make from selling them and their eggs in market. They often have a patch of corn, from which they gather sometimes five or six hundred bushels. Saturday night they take whatever they wish to carry to town, get a "pass" from Mr. P.—they have no right to sell without it—and put them into a skiff and row up to Yazoo City, six miles, and dispose of them. Besides this, they have all they can make by selling wood to the steamers. An industrious negro can make quite a sum in a year by selling wood. A negro don't like the cold weather. The hottest day in summer suits him better. Last winter they were clearing off a new piece of land. Some of them would bundle up head and ears, though the ground was soft under their feet. Mr. P. remarked to me, as one of the little girls, picking up brush, passed by us with her teeth chattering with the cold,

"I expect to find little LID a lump of ice one of these days."

His negroes have the advantage of having the Word of GOD expounded to them. A little chapel school-house, in a tuneful grove of willow oaks, is the sanctuary for a few planters and their families. The negroes grouped together on seats near the door, the planters and their families are seated within the house. The parson—clergymen are usually called parsons here—standing near the door, so that both parties can hear—JAPHET in his tent, and HAM, his servant, sitting at his door. Our parson is a Methodist, a young gentleman of fair talent. I have pleasing recollections of his acquaintance.

## COTTON PLANTING AND THE CANE-BRAKES.

Some eight or ten negroes with their mule-teams, commenced ploughing to-day, in the field near our school-house. Two of them went ahead and struck the field out into furrows, three or four feet apart. Others followed, turning furrows against these on both sides, till the intermediate spaces between the original furrows were all ploughed up. This forms ridges some four feet apart. After the field is thus ridged, a negro with a single mule, before a small plough, strikes a furrow on the top of each ridge. Another negro follows him with a sack of cotton seed strung around his shoulders, and scatters the seed thickly along in this furrow; he is followed by one of his fellows, with a mule before a small harrow, who drags over the seed, thus covering it up. And finally, to make sure work, a negress follows the last one, with a hoe, to cover up what seed may not have been covered by the harrow. This is cotton planting, which is done on the first of April. Corn is planted the same way, but one month earlier. The overseer is seen walking or riding, here and there over the field, whip in hand, inspecting the work. One peculiarity of the soil in the valley is worthy of notice. It is the innumerable pieces of shells mingling with it. In places you see many acres thickly covered with them, the ground reflecting the sunbeams back in a thousand pearly hues. They are supposed to be the multifold fragments of oyster shells or others, that the Indians have formerly used here. Shells that time, the crumbler, has reduced as a

> "Broken mirror, which the glass
> In every fragment multiplies—and makes
> A thousand images of one that was,
> The same, and still the more, the more it breaks."

The cane-brakes South, and the young and tender cane that is kept down by the grazing of the cattle and deer, is also deserving some attention. The largest grows here to some inch or two in diameter, and some over twenty feet high. It grows five or six years, then dies and commences anew again. Its only use is, pasturage for cattle, and the planters make "pipe stales" and fishing rods of it. Go into the interior of Germany and you will find a small species of cane, the size of a man's finger, and ten or twelve feet high. In the north of Italy, and on the banks of Lago Maggoire, the reed cane is an inch in diameter, and long enough for fishing rods. At Rome and on the coast of Calabra, this cane is two inches thick, and thirty-five feet high, and is substantial enough to be used for fence poles and rafters for the roofs of houses. Go to the East Indies, to Java and Summatra, and there you will find magnificent groves of bambo canes, the joints ten feet apart, the trunks six in diameter. and sixty feet high. The canes are nothing but arborescent grasses—cereals grown up into trees—and belong to the same class of vegetation as wheat, rye, oats and barley, the hay of our fields and the bog-grass used by the inhabitants of Iceland and Shetland to make roads over swamps. It is often stated that grass is rarely seen in warm climates, particularly in the tropics. The green meadows, the grassy lawns and velvet turf, so common, so useful and so healthful in the North, are rarely or never seen within thirty or thirty-five degrees of the equator. But the Creator, adapting means to ends, has turned the grasses into trees. When young, they grow from two feet to two and a-half in twenty-four hours, and in that state are cut like asparagus and used as green vegetables. When full grown the tree and leaves are used for more purposes than hemp, flax, and any six trees of the temperate zones, all put together; making clothing, houses, fuel, furniture, and almost every description of article needed in domestic life."

## A FASHIONABLE CALL SOUTH.

"Hear the pretty ladies talk."
DR. DARWIN.

A servant came to my room and told me that Mrs. P. requested me to come down into the drawing-room. On arriving at the door I was ushered into a drawing-room of ladies with a gentleman in it.

They were all a *tete-a-tete* on some subject; what it was I could not tell; and the longer I listened and tried to catch the theme, the more I got tangled up in their conversation. It appeared to be a Rev. Mr. SOMEBODY, but who he could be, was as mystical as the vagaries of a sleeping girl. I got all of his qualities—his complete portrait was drawn—he was a very clever gentleman, had a mild and pleasant eye, preached good and instructive sermons, had a pretty wife who dressed with good taste, one of the ladies was a schoolmate of hers; and so on, about this Rev. SOMEBODY, his pretty wife, and the sweet little rosette in a love-of-a-bonnet that she wore, till I gave up the idea of ever finding out who he was, and hesitating in the meanwhile to interrupt them by asking, till I grew perplexed and resolved that I never would ask, and really wished not to find out; and to this day I never have, and hope I never shall. I wish to see this Rev. gentleman go down to his grave my "JUNIUS."

After having failed for some time to catch the subject of their conversation, one of the party dropped the theme and began to talk about playing chess; in which I joined, and shortly after some of the rest. Then for a while there was a doubt which theme would claim the attention, the Reverend one, or chess, as the other party still held on to theirs and would now and then essay to bring one of us over on their side. But we check-mated them, and gained the subject, and in a little while it was chess, chess, chess with us all.

This call was a fashionable one in the South. The ladies were dressed in "rings and things and fine array;" sat and chatted with their bonnets on, each with a rich parasol in her hands, occasionally raising its ivory top to her pearly teeth, or pressing it against her lips, or she would lightly tap it against her dress, on the sofa or carpet.

They managed the conversation with vivacity, throwing in now and then a *bon-mot*, uttering no inelegant word, but lisped them with a polite accent, never saying *bun*net for *bon*net, nor *pur*ty for *pret*ty. They were accompanied by a very pleasant gentleman, brother to two of the ladies.

At our gate stood a beautiful span of bays in silvered trappings, before a splendid carriage, with two negro servants in livery, one to hold the horses, and the other to wait on the ladies. When they had conversed the usual time for such a call, they stepped into their carriage and rode some two miles to their homes. This was young Mrs. L., Mrs. M. and her sister's call on Mrs. P. at Willow Dale.

## FOURTEENTH DAY OF WINTER.

This is the fourteenth day of winter, yet our Northern October has a more shriveled forest and colder weather.

The sun is not shining clear this morning. Light, soft clouds are scattered all over the sky; and he now and then peeps out between them, showing his shining, morning face, and gladdening everything with his smile.

I rambled out in the woods to enjoy the soft, balmy air of winter. The hollies and magnolias were in their pure and deep green. These evergreens are of a deeper and lovelier green in the winter. Here in these woods winter merely lets

> "Hoary-headed frosts
> Fall in the fresh lap of the crimson rose;
> And on old HIEMS' chill and icy crown,
> An odorous chaplet of green leaves and flowers
> Is set."

There are many trees in this land that pass through winter in their beautiful summer robes.

This evening at the Ridge House was given to a chat about BEETHOVEN, MOZART, HAYDEN, and HANDEL, and last of all, about SHAKSPEARE. He had written all the poetry we needed for a century or two. He was indeed,

> "Fancy's child,
> "Warbling his native wood-notes wild."

CARLYLE says, "SHAKSPEARE is the greatest thing we English ever did." But England, ere she produces another, must gather new material—must acquire new deeds—historic and romantic life; it must grow old—become the past; and then a new SHAKSPEARE can sing. Major W. intends his daughters shall have a complete education. It will then of course embrace the old masters sublime old bards—all that the ancients said and sung. But a young lady's education, in our schools now-a-days, is complete with what BULWER said and TOM MOORE sung. I do not know why they should not read old HOMER and

SHAKSPEARE. I think they wrote admirably for girls and boys.

## CHAPTER XVIII.

### THE SOUTHERN LADY.

"Of noble race the Ladye came."
SCOTT.

In treating the subject of this sketch one needs to con over his vocabulary as the painter would select his colors, to do with the brush what we would do with the pen, in giving a portraiture of the Southern lady. TOM CARLYLE says, "Show me a man whose words paint a picture, and you have somewhat of a man." We fear that, with all the mimic skill of our pen in word-painting, we shall fall somewhat short of CARLYLE'S man. Doing a picture in words, and one in oils, are two different things. Words and colors differ.

"'Tis as likely for *paint* to be true,
As grass to be green or violets blue."

But the same word may have different hues. Green is always green in painting. The color tells for itself. But the word *written* is more like a chameleon. You may find it light, pale or deep green. It takes its hue from the object to which it is applied.

And we apprehend we shall not be able to give the true meaning to the term, lady—the one at least we wish to give. The origin of the word is lost in the obscurity of the past. WEBSTER, hunting on the trail of its etymology gives it up. But let us take the literary antiquarian's trail and go far away back to the olden time—to the

"Days of belted knight and lady fair,"

when the old ballad word, "ladie" was used instead of our modern lady. We find one of the old poets thus defining lady:

"Our ladye doth as far excede
 Our women now-a-days,
As doth the gillyflower a weede,
 And more a hundred ways."

We find the following in CHAUCER—the "morning star of our poetry:"

"Then say'd he to PALAMON the knight;
Cometh ner, and take your lady by the hond."

And gentle WILL SHAKSPEARE, who created the fairies, calls TITANA, their queen, a *lady*.

"Never harm, nor spell, nor charm,
Come our lovely *lady* nigh."

SPENSER, in his "Garden of PROSERPINE," thus uses this term:

"Here eke that famous golden apple grew,
The which among the gods false ATE threw;
For which *the Idean ladies* disagreed,
Till partial PARIS deemed it VENUS' due."

Here, says JORTIN, he calls the three goddesses, JUNO, MINERVA, and VENUS, that contended for the prize of beauty, boldly but elegantly enough, *ladies*. Again,

"There he a troup of dancing *ladies* found."

Here the same poet calls the Muses and Graces, likewise, *ladies*.

"Fair HELENORE, with garlands all bespread,
Whom their May-lady they had made."

Here SPENSER makes May-lady equivalent to May-queen. The ladies, says TODD, may be further gratified by MILTON'S adaptation of their title to the celebrated daughters of HESPERUS, whom he calls the "*Ladies* of the Hesperides." To all of which LEIGH HUNT remarks: "The ladies of the present day, in whom so much good poetry and reading have revived, will smile at the vindication of a word again become common, and so frequent in the old poets and romancers."

Throughout the whole history of the Troubadours—those lyric poets of chivalry—the term lady is used to denote the noblest and fairest of women—the lady-loves of kings, princes, lords and knights,

> "Who no other care did take,
> Than for their sweet ladies' sake."

We had almost said that the word *lady* originated with *knight* in the age of chivalry."

> "An hundred knights might there with ease abide,
> And every knight a lady by his side."

It was not only the name of their lady-loves, but the term signified their highest conceptions of woman. But, at all events, the term, whether used by fairy SPENSER, with a fairy power, leading his fairy band, in a fairy world, as a fairy name, or whether he uses it singing of love or chivalry, or by CHAUCER, or SHAKSPEARE or DRYDEN, or by the Troubadours and Minnesingers; it is, in a chivalresque sense, the name given to the highest style of woman.

When chivalry, turned into a romance in the minds of those in whose persons the thing itself existed, raised up a fanciful adoration of woman into a law of courtly life, or, at least, of courtly verse; then diamond eyes and ruby lips stirred into sound the lute of the Troubadours and the

Minnesingers, and the famous deeds of war, waked the epic strains of the Troubadours.

> "And ladies left the measures at the sight,
> To meet the chiefs returning from the fight,
> And each with open arms embraced her chosen knight."

Thus having traced this term, if not to its origin, we have at least satisfied ourselves in regard to its definition. To the poet it was the name for the mistress of his heart, whether real or ideal; to the young prince, lord or knight of his real or day-dream love—a name allied to

> "Chivalrie,
> Truth and honor, freedom and courtesie."

Much has been said about the term's losing its import; that it is not synonymous with woman; that the latter is the true, and the other the false and affected term for woman now-a-days. We are not disposed to wrangle about the term's being a misnomer, but we are very much disposed to claim for the *lady*,

> "In these fair *well*-spoken days,"

all that was ever true, and lovely, and admirable in woman. We have an infinite hate for all that "cuckoo croaking" about the falseness of the lady of the present day; it is surely ungallant in the one sex, and very unlady-like in the other. We hate it, because it has a misanthropic obliquity in it. We think that if the *lady* passes at discount in our day, and woman goes at a premium, it is in cases where the false is mistaken for the true lady; not that we disparage the term woman, but we are talking about her in her highest style.

The habits and customs of different lands constitute a different style of the lady without, it may be, varying the essential qualities of either. To designate the two we have in view we shall call one the Saxon, and the other the Norman type of the lady.

In that hyperborean region where the daffodil and hyacinth do not appear till mid-April, womanhood, like the rose, does not bloom till June. But in this half-tropical region, where those flowers appear much earlier, womanhood blooms with the

> "Primrose, earliest daughter of the spring."

The important eras in a Southern lady's life are her school-days; and that poetic age when ballads are made to her eyebrows; the meeting at the hymeneal altar; and the honey-moon; and then her after life, while that orb is

> "Waxing and waning beautifully less."

These periods, or these several acts of their lives constitute the play or melodrama—"As you like it." While with our Saxon lady these several acts of her life may more properly be called an earnest drama of—"As you can make it."

From a cursory glance at the life of the former, one would call them—beautiful idlers. Their life seems to have no apparent purpose. But I have seen those that were as industrious, and that studied economy as much as their Norman cousins. Besides the various lighter employments of the needle, I have seen rich Southern ladies sit, day after day, making cotton-sacks for the negroes.

I don't know how much of the physical beauty of the East belongs to Southern ladies, or whether any mention has been made of it, in speaking of their physique. Climate has some effect upon us. The old Greek poet says

(I quote from memory) of a rough or coarse man prominent among them,

> "One would swear
> That he was bred in coarse Boeotian air."

A poet of a later day says of the Italian ladies, with the glow of enthusiasm, that they are

> "Soft as their clime and sunny as their skies.

We have seen many finely developed women in the South, to whom, from their native independent air and graceful carriage in walking, the "incedit regina" of VIRGIL might be applied. Their dress, of course, is rich and fashionable. They wear hundred dollar bonnets, encase the tiniest of pretty little hands in the richest and softest of gloves, and the tiniest of pretty little feet in the richest and softest of gaiters, as Northern ladies do.

The South has properly no "country girls." The planter lives in the rural districts as the Northern farmer does, but there is this difference in their daughters: the one gets at home a common school education; this generally suffices her for life. The planter educates his daughters away from home—often at the North; hence her society is equal to that of the city lady. You do not see in the country, South,

> "Tripping through the silken grass,
> Down the path-divided dale,
> The rose-complexioned lass,
> With her well-poised milking-pail."

You do not find the "milk-maid half divine," tripping

> "Down the path-divided dale."

No. The little divinity is in the splendid drawing-room, dabbling in a book, or like Lady VERE DE VERE,

> "She left the novel half uncut
> Upon the rose-wood shelf,
> She left the new piano shut—
> She could not please herself."

Or she may be in a "cheek by jowl" with some APOLLO BELVIDERE, or away at the North at school while some Hyperborean gallant is throwing down his offerings at the feet of her goddesship.

I have seen many Southern ladies who have been educated at the North, and in part had Northern manners and habits, and have sometimes thought that if I wished to draw a portrait of a true Southern lady, one of the "manor born," that I should prefer one that had been educated at home. Of course, you find many accomplished ladies among the latter. And I have felt in their society as if I was with the true daughters of the South, on their own native heath, adorned with their own heath flowers. I admire the South because it is really and beautifully the sunny South. If it was like the North I should not admire it so much. And I admire Southern ladies and gentlemen because they are truly Southern ladies and gentlemen. And far distant be the day when distance ceases to keep the enchantment in our Italies and sunny Souths.

But again, one feels in the presence of Southern ladies as if he was overshadowed by the same divinity of beauty as with those at the North; that their eye-shots were just as dangerous, their smile just as winning, their charms—in fine, one feels as if he was with the daughters of EVE, only, from their Utopian lives, that they had got back into the garden again.

The peculiar traits in a Southern lady's character—I have a chronic dislike to characteristics—would actually rather have anything else of one than these mere tangents and angles. They constitute about as much of a person as a minister's notes do of his sermon—the articles of faith of his religion—the accent or brogue of the man.

I would as lief a friend would present me with a dictionary for a history, as the characteristics of a person as having anything of a portraiture of him in them. And worst of all, they are the first thing of a person that is babbled about. And, in fact, they are very often dangerous to have, because they are the most exposed points about one, and easiest assailed by slander. Mine has ever affected me like an unsigned bank-note—like a hole in the meal bag.

That Southern ladies have characteristics is so palpably evident, that in regard to it, I think there is "no hinge or loop to hang a doubt on." So there the matter rests. Furthermore, I have noticed that they are endowed with the power of locomotion, think, act, and even eat as Northern ladies do, but more hoe-cake and corn-dodger; and drink as they do, but more of the flowing cups of Java; that their laugh is just as silvery—some think silverier—and that they talk and sing with all the charm of voice that the Southern throat will admit of. In fine, they look upon life as a rich legacy time has bequeathed them—a luxury to be enjoyed. This, with the other endowments she has, and the "acres of charms" she possesses, is her dower. What most molests her in life is time—the thief; he steals away her beauty, robs her of her charms, and hangs like the *ennui* on her when the various amusements of her life do not baffle him. The hot summer months are the dullest part of the year to her, especially if she does not go North, or spend them on the sea-coast. She is apt to be a bird of passage—spending her summers in another clime, and her winters at home. There is much sunshine to her nature, and want and care not rendering her life sad and gloomy, it ought to have a pleasant shade.

Allow me to half digress from my subject. What I wish to allude to, we have often talked of with some of our fair friends South; hence, we will give them the merit of originating the theme.

There are moods in which woman, especially, exhibits herself truthfully, or phases in which her beauty culminates. CHARLES LAMB—"the gentle and frolic"—looked the most beautiful when asleep. It was the thoughts of disinheriting her son that made the Hungarian queen, MARIA THERESA, the peerless and beautiful conqueror. Lady BLESSINGTON looked the most queenly, and displayed all of her charms sitting in her rich-velveted chair receiving her guests. HAWTHORNE says it was "anger mixed with scorn," or this was the phase in which the beauty of ZENOBIA culminated.

It is not an unpleasant study, that of attitudes and "poses," in which the real woman exhibits herself—phases in which we view her in all her picturesqueness.

I remember a lady in this Southern clime, whom I had seen often, and called her beautiful. I saw her again—a mourner, at the funeral of her brother. I thought her the most beautiful mourner I ever saw, and wished that such ladies could be multiplied, and mourn for our loved and departed friends. "Almost every passion became this lady well,' but sorrow for the dead robed her in lovlier beauty. Here then her beauty culminated.

The same lady overtook me some time after this, in a gallopade, on a proud, champing steed, as I was walking out a little past mid-afternoon in company with a friend. As she reined her horse up to us, I remember remarking to my friend, that she looked with her countenance animated and flushed from her ride, as peerless and romantic as DIE VERNON did when she met "cousin FRANK;" and stopped a moment in the chase to converse with him. She looked the most charming I had ever seen her. She impressed me so at least. I wore this impression for some time, as the finest picture of this lady. It appeared, compared with the other, like one of the old masters' paintings, compared with one of our modern and inferior artists'. But it was not so grief had done the other the best. And I retain her picture, to-day, as a beautiful mourner—a real, genuine REUBENS. This lady had the most perfect command of her features—she could conceal any emotion. She is a true Southern lady, with magnanimity enough to talk on any subject, North or South, as fairly and earnestly as if they were one.

I shall not draw a portrait of a Southern lady *coleur de rose*, or, *coleur de "rouge,"* for the sake of pleasing the South; for I think she would detect the cheat and despise it. Neither shall I keep any merit of hers *sub rosa* on account of the pique that the North may have against her. Their mode of life has tastes, habits, and peculiarities of its own. We might say that their education was different from ours, yet it is like ours; for it is often got in our schools. But they don't *use* it as we do. In fact, in the strict, practical, shrewd, Yankee sense of the word, they don't use it at all. Our utilitarian might think that they wore it as FOUNTLEROY did the beauty of his wife, as a brilliant ornament of display, or admire it as he did his daughter—because she shone.

The appreciation of one's fine attainments North and South is different. Viewed by the keen practical eye of the utilitarian, one with a mind embellished by fine culture, and stored with the riches of classical learning, might be classed by him with, and treated as he treats, the poet GRAY—a poetical drone, writing sonnets between delicious fits of lounges, and noticing the coming of crocuses in spring, or the first appearance of the daffodills and primroses.

The Northern mind is so eminently practical and lucrative, that much that is beautiful in this life is unenjoyed, or passed by, in the haste to secure that which "*will pay.*" The old "iron bedstead" is in use, by which a man is practically measured, and he sometimes finds the most valuable part of him cut off and thrown away as useless. I could never tolerate that school of progressionists that talk about the "mission of the beautiful," as if the beautiful, like the farmer's barrel of beer, must *work*, or it would spoil.

Beauty, as old COMUS says, "is nature's brag." And it is, in the profusion of apple-blossoms, scattered all over this beautiful world of ours. It is very evident that "He who made this world was no utilitarian, no despiser of the fine arts, and no condemner of ornament, and those progressionists and religionists who seek to restrain everything within the limits of cold, bare utility, do not imitate our FATHER in heaven." "The poetic mind is not the progressive one; it has, like moss and ivy, a need of something old to cling to, and germinate upon." It cannot be the practical and lucrative. But one, of late years, would think it could not be anything else. For our poets are half politicians, tradesmen or bankers. It can scarcely be said of them—

> "A primrose by the river's brim,
> A yellow primrose was to him
> And nothing more."

Instead of finding "pansies for thoughts," it is—

> "Dimes and dollars, dollars and dimes."

And when,

> "To tuneful APOLLO
> One of them does hollo,"

it is merely to get his aid in this "Play of philanthropy and progress," or some hints of practical ultility.

But to resume our subject of "poses." The Misses B. were two sisters—"two berries on one stem"—that finely exhibited each other's beauty by contrast. One, I used to think always appeared the most beautiful from this contrast, except when alone some thought animated her, and she was more than usually radiant. I remember her asking a young gentleman "*where* he had rather read his destiny;" and on his replying, "*in some lovely lady's eyes*," the answer inspired her, for she looked the most beautiful I ever saw her, as she turned to him and said, "Why you ought to have a *premium for that*."

The younger sister was statuesque. There was no phase or pose in which her beauty culminated. Some are the most graceful sitting, some standing, and some "can assume a series of graceful positions"—but this young lady was one of the graces. I believe had she been MARY, Queen of Scotts, she could have heard her death warrant read with a countenance unmoved. Grief, care, joy or fear, usually give a betokening shadow from the heart on the face, but not on hers. No thought or emotion of the heart could be traced on it. I have tried to study and decipher her face, but in vain—it was the most beautiful hieroglyphic I ever gazed upon.

Her sister had a countenance of fine phisiological reading. It varied in hues of thought and expression.

> "There is a face whose blushes tell
> Affection's tale upon the cheek;
> But pallid at one fond farewell,
> Proclaims more love than words can speak."

She once remarked to me, after she had been not a little provoked by some of her sister's tantalizing freaks, when she was in the poorest humor to endure it, "Now you have seen Miss H. B. as bad as she really is."

I replied that something might yet lurk behind. "No, you have seen the tigress out of the jungle," which I thought was more beautiful than dangerous, "*my countenance reveals all.*" "But," says she, pointing to her sister who had provoked her to this "expose," "her countenance conceals all, you have got to find her out by her actions and conduct; her face is marble to the feelings of her heart if she has any." The latter stood, the while, tapping her

"Tiny, silken-gaitered foot"

on the carpet, witching us with one of her smiles, and, after she had heard her sister's remarks through, went gliding out of the room singing—

"Hush ye, hush ye, little pet, ye,
Hush ye, hush ye, do not fret ye,
Or the black DOUGLAS will get ye."

The one sister should be painted, to get her finest portrait—at any time; she defied *poses* to make her other than what she was. The other, in her happiest humor, or when some fine thought or beautiful thing inspired her. She had a chivalresque nature, and a finely cultivated mind and taste—was one of the fairest daughters of the South—one educated at home.

Miss MOLLIE P., a friend of theirs—was a young lady from Virginia, spending part of the winter with them. Her buoyant spirits, wit and mirth, enlivened her countenance. If a cloud passed over her heart, nothing but an almost imperceptible change of countenance expressed it;

the next moment she was joyous again; for there was sunshine enough in her nature to chase it away. She was somewhere between the Misses B., but so near the younger, that while her countenance expressed evanescently the emotions of her heart, the latter's did not express it at all.

Miss P. had one of those hearts, the water of whose fountain "wells" or "splashes" up into the eyes if a word of grief or sorrow is dropped into it—it did not remain pent up, but found relief in tears. The chords of her heart were not like the elder Miss B.'s—Æolian, and vibrating long to a touch of grief or sorrow. But there was a counteraction in the joyousness of her nature that stopped the vibrations.

Differing from either of these was Colonel N.'s young and elegant lady—the "cousin LIZZIE" of Willow Dale. She was of that faultless form, step and style of beauty that we rarely meet, but which novelists and poets often do. She was timid and affectionate, with a face that told the simple story of the heart. In the person of Mrs. N. we had the genteel lady.

Here I saw in contrast, if there was any, the Mississippi lady with the Virginian. The peculiarities of expression and habits were nearly one. Let them differ in any other respect, one expression "coalesced" them; that was—"*I reckon.*" But "a Virginian never gets acclimated anywhere else, he never loses citizenship to the old home." It is to him "the Virginia of a place," which the preacher described Heaven to be to a Virginian congregation.

Mississippi is to the other Southern States what the composite order of architecture is to all the other orders. You seldom find two or three ladies together from the same State. It is mostly newly settled, and has but few native planters. Hence, like a mirror, its society reflects the various manners and customs of the other sister States.

But to resume our subject. In regard to the complexion of the fair of this clime, it is merely your Northern brunettes, blondes and beauties done *a la South.* Or, more properly speaking, the former are with corresponding darker shades, done in bronze.

Their eyes, aside from having in them the dreamy beauty of this clime—

> "Are made precisely like the best we know,
> Look the same looks, and speak no other Greek,
> Than your eyes of honey-moons begun last week."

The dreamy, languid East—the pleasant, dreamy South! I don't know but what climates do set one a-dreaming—I rather think they do. And perhaps the daughters of this pleasant clime sleep later in the morning than those of the cold, driving North. Taking labor and business—those pleaders of early rising away, I should think they *would.* We none of us get up early for health. That is too much like labor;—and who ever knew any one to labor for health? Health is the capital we spend for enjoyment. We labor for appetite and passion. Were they not strong, our lives would be day-dreams. But I have heard Southern ladies say that there was such a dreamy luxury—such a poetical drowsiness in their mornings—such a potent charm in poppy-distilling sleep—that a Northern lady could not resist its influence, any more than they could CIRCE'S.

This suggests the question—"How do Southern ladies spend their time?" Oh, they have an easy way of doing it. But let us look over one of their programmes for the day.

After enjoying this delicious symposium of sleep in the

morning, she arises, makes her toilette—servants at her bidding—walks into her room, reads, or engages in a chat with some friend or some one of the family, or, to enjoy the freshness of the morning, takes a walk, by which time she is summoned to breakfast. Here, while sipping the fragrant cup of Java, passes the chat at breakfast-table. The conversation is lively, and probably there is no place where one enjoys the amenities of Southern life more than at their tables. Besides the repast before you, it is really

"A feast of reason and a flow of soul."

A bagatelle for your "Autocrat of the breakfast-table," with his out-of-place, misty, German, metaphysical, indigestible dish of chit-chat, served up as an olla-podrida for the public, but really enjoyed the most by a Miss OLIVER, a school-mistress, and one Mr. WENDELL, a divinity-student, and a certain Mr. HOLMES, the Autocrat who ordered up the dish. Which dish, all the public praise. Yes, all. And there lies the error. You perceive it is just this: a few Savans—the keen-sighted Bell-wethers of the flock—have extolled this olla-podrida, that is, they have leaped over the stick. Now you may take the stick away, but the rest in blind imitation, like sheep, will leap as they did, till the ten thousandth one will be found vaulting over air as the first did over the stick.

But here the conversation is always interesting. And if pleasure and mirth could arrest the flight of time, why, surely here they would beguile the "grey-beard of his pinions." While discussing your venison-steak, your duck or bird, a fresh bit of natural history may bide with them which is narrated by the planter or some one present, recently gathered from the hunt.

But to our lady; breakfast over she retires to her room,

consults the programme for the day, or marks out one; she may have some light work to do, or she may take a short walk. At any rate, she disposes of the morning or forenoon at her pleasure.

The evening, or her afternoon, begins after dinner, which is at two o'clock, and is given to the various needle-work, or she may read a little in a book, or play at whist if she has guests, or she steps into her carriage and takes a short drive, calls on some lady friend, returns, takes supper between six and seven, and the real evening, except in the hot summer months, is given to the various games of cards and other amusements. This programme, of course, is varied in different plaees, but it is nevertheless true.

The following gem from TENNYSON'S "Princess," I append at the close of this sketch of the Southern lady. Let its beauty, if nothing more, make it appropriate here.

"O swallow, swallow, flying, flying South,
Fly to her and fall upon her gilded eaves,
And tell her, tell her what I tell to thee.

"O tell her, swallow, thou that knowest each;
That bright and fierce and fickle is the South,
And dark and true and tender is the North.

"O swallow, swallow, if I could follow, and light
Upon her lattice, I would pipe and trill
And cheep and twitter twenty million loves.

"O, were I thou, that she might take me in,
And lay me on her bosom, and her heart
Would rock the snowy cradle till I died!

"Why lingereth she to clothe her heart with love,
Delaying as the tender ash delays
To clothe herself when all the woods are green?

"O tell her, swallow, that thy brood is flown;
Say to her, I do but wanton in the South,
But in the North, long since, my nest is made.

"O tell her, brief is life, but love is long,
And brief the sun of summer in the North,
And brief the moon of beauty in the South.

"O swallow, flying from the golden woods,
Fly to her, and pipe and woo her, and make her mine,
And tell her, tell her, that I follow thee."

## THE SOUTHERN GENTLEMAN.

"A gentleman!
What, o' the wool-pack? or the sugar-chest?
Or lists of velvet? which is't, pound, or yard,
You vend your gentry by?"

BEGGAR'S BUSH.

Many a wrong and pernicious idea has arisen about the Southern gentleman, from life at Washington—taking that to be the mirror from which our national habits and traits are reflected—both Northern and Southern. It is wrong to judge the South from its Senators and Representatives, who are in a school where the worst and basest passions are brought out. I know, were it put to vote to-day, that the people at large, either North or South, would not be willing to take the characteristics of their members in Congress, as truly characteristic of themselves. Think how perfectly ridiculous a Scotch Reviewer—in BLACKWOOD'S Magazine—made our model Republic and people look, some years ago, by taking a national characteristic from some two or three of our members in Washington.

The term gentleman is the masculine of lady. There has been as much babble about this term's losing its significance, and becoming a misnomer, as about the term lady. I don't know, in fact, but human nature has lost these masculine and feminine qualities, and that we can only find them as fossils in the history of the past. If it were not that they have appeared somewhat later, I should really think that they were beheaded with Sir WALTER RALEIGH, and MARY, Queen of Scotts. Yet they have not come down to us; for our modern DIOGENES has failed, even by the aid of his lantern at noon-day, to find a solitary gentleman, in all this fair land of ours. Still, it is ungallant in us not to claim one. I positively believe that these qualities are indigenous to civilized human nature. If not, as a dernier shift for gallantry, as they are so essential to manhood, depend upon it, Yankee shrewdness and ingenuity would have invented them ere this. But to our theme.

A Southern gentleman is composed of the same material that a Northern gentleman is, only it is tempered by a Southern clime and mode of life. And if in this tempering there is a little more urbanity and chivalry, a little more politeness and devotion to the ladies, a little more *suaviter in modo*, why it is theirs—be fair, and acknowledge it, let them have it. He is, from the mode of life that he lives, especially at home, more or less a cavalier; he invariably goes a-horseback. His boot is always spurred, and his hand ensigned with the riding-whip. Aside from this he is known by his bearing—his frankness and firmness.

There is one trait in a Southron's character which distinguishes him from a Northerner; it is his laconic manner of answering questions. His "yes, sir," or "no, sir," or the more emphatic "I don't know, sir," are given with a positive emphasis, and as unalterable as the laws of the Medes and Persians. You may ask him about any matter, and if there is any doubt in his mind concerning it, his invariable answer is, "I don't know, sir." You are answered once and for all. There is no use asking any more questions about it; you cannot get him to "guess," he will get mad first.

A Yankee, on the other hand, would seem to know something about your affair. If he could not answer you directly, he would at least give you some slight information concerning it. At any rate, if he could do no more he would give you the benefit of a "guess," which might be of some consolation to you. But you get none from a Southron. I early learned to let a Southron alone after I had asked him once about any matter. For on every attempt to ask him the second time I was sure to get his stern, I had almost said, rebuke, "I don't know sir—I have answered you once." He cannot bear quizzing.

> "What he does know, he *does*, and you may depend on't,
> What he don't know, he *don't*, and there's the end on't."

Were you seated in a room of one of our fashionable hotels, you would mark the Northerner—all of them are more or less Yankee—by his peculiar inquisitive look at every person and thing as he came into it. Or were he seated and reading, and you came in, he would eye you askance from his paper—give you a guessing look to find out who you were. You can tell him by his look of shrewd, "acrid, Yankee observation; you know him from the native propensity of his countrymen to investigate all matters that come within their range."

On the other hand, you would know a Southron from the very reverse of this. He comes into the room with as indifferent an air as if there was no one in it but himself, takes a chair, sits down, and takes a paper and reads. Reads as long as he pleases, lays down the paper, and, if he does not choose to converse with any one, walks out of the room, as if he had not noticed a person or thing in it. Yet he has seen, observed and estimated all. The difference in the two is—cool nonchalance and prying inquisitiveness.

You could not be three minutes in a dark room with a Yankee without discovering him. He would, if he could find nothing else to do, be whistling, or whittling—ever trying to bring things to a point.

If he was asleep, pronouncing one word would start his spirits as quick as CÆSAR ever did a Roman's, and that is, *Gingerbread!* Give a Dutchman his "sauer krout," a German his "bonny clabber," a Frenchman his "frogs," a Spaniard his "garlic," an Italian his "maccaroni," but don't deprive a Yankee of his gingerbread.

A word or two about the chivalry of the Southron. The gallantry that would throw its cloak down in the mud that the lady might walk over on it without soiling her feet, I believe, is considered as one of the lost arts. But if we have any RALEIGHS that would be chivalrous enough to do it, perhaps they are in the South. How much of the chivalry of the old world that came to America, sought the South, I do not know. Virginia was founded by that most chivalrous of all adventurers, Captain JOHN SMITH, with his "company of gentlemen," and South Carolina, the HARRY PERCY of the Union, has ever been proud of its chivalrous sons; and many instances of titled families tinged more or less with chivalry, could be adduced, who have sought the South, where they could live more to their desire the old baronial life. One such family of noble blood and proud spirit, gave tone to a whole region. The rest caught honor, pride, and a love of distinction from it. This created a kind of nobility, and many traces of it yet exist.

The two individuals that we have been speaking of in contrast—kith and kin by birth—apparently living the same lives, made up of the same hours, months and years, time ticks alike to both of them, yet one, practically, is the minute, and the other the hour-hand on the dial-plate. The one does not wish to lengthen out the year for the sake of gain, nor to curtail it for the sake of speculation, as the other does. He has time in abundance and never hurries. Nothing would give me more exquisite pleasure than to see a real Southron in WELLINGTON'S situation at Waterloo. I verily believe instead of exclaiming with that hero, "Oh! that night or BLUCHER would come!" he would say something about putting off the issue of the battle till Friday week, and beating Napoleon at his leisure.

After I had been in the South some over two months on expense, and when I began to consider myself as WALTER-the-penniless on my kind friends' hospitality, without employment, I finally secured a situation as teacher; and on my speaking about commencing my school, a Southern friend remarked, "O, I wouldn't take in school yet, I would visit a couple of months or so longer!"

Their clime is so genial, companionable and indulgent that I think a Northerner that goes there needs a sharper spur to prick the sides of his intent. Nature is unloosed of her stays there; she is not crowded for time; the word haste is not in her vocabulary. In none of the seasons is she stinted to so short a space to perform her work as at the North. She has leisure enough to bud and blossom—to produce and mature fruit, and do all her work. While on the other hand, in the North right the reverse is true. Portions are taken off the fall and spring to lengthen out the winter, making his reign nearly half the year. This crowds the work of the whole year, you might say, into about half of it. This is the spur of labor to the different seasons, and this is the Northerner's, and this makes the essential difference between a Northerner and a Southerner. They are children of their respective climes, And this is why Southrons are so indifferent about time; they have three months more of it in a year than we have.

---

## CHAPTER XIX.

### STRAY LEAVES.

"Full many a gem of purest ray serene,
The dark, unfathomed caves of ocean bear;
Full many a flower is born to blush unseen,
And waste its sweetness on the desert air."

GRAY.

#### TO JENNIE B.

"Little JENNIE, haste, we'll go
To where the white-starred gowans grow,
Wi' the puddock flower o' gowden hue,
The snaw-drap white and the bonny vi'let blue.

Little JENNIE, haste, we'll go
To where the blossomed lilacs grow,
To where the pine-tree dark and high,
Is pointing its tap to the cloudless sky.

"JENNIE, mony a merrie lay
Is sung in the rich-leafed woods to-day;
Flits on light wing the dragon-flea,
An' hums on the flowerie the big red bee.

Down the burnie wirks its way
Aneath the bending birchen spray,
An' wimples aroun' the green mass stane,
An' mourns, I kenna why, wi' a ceaseless mane."

"These lines," says HUGH MILLER, "were addressed to a docile little girl of five years, my eldest sister, and my frequent companion, during my illness, in my short walks."

We have written them here because they are so appropriate to a little JENNIE—

"The bonniest little girl in all the border,"

about the same age, and with whom we have taken many a pleasant-remembered walk to school.

In regard to whether you would find the poetry true, to be read along *our* walk, I would say, that the white-starred gowans, nor the puddock flower o'gowden hue, nor lilacs grew along it. But the poetry is just as true and appropriate. It took no time at all to substitue in the place of the above-named flowers those that grew along our walk. To put ours in might have changed the measure of the verse some, but the poetry would have been just as lovely, only it would be fragrant with Southern, instead of Highland flowers, and have the "hum" and "wirk", and "wimple" of Southern "bees and burnies," instead of those it has. The burnie, though, was the willow-skirted Yazoo, that

"Wimpled roun' the green mass stane,
An' mourns, I kenna why, wi' a ceaseless mane."

Few people, it is said, know how to take a walk. But if birds know how to sing, and brooks to tinkle, little JENNIE knew how to take a walk. And I'm sure the "how" never occurred to me in these walks of ours.

The morning was a delightful one. As I walked out in the garden the sun was just rising. His first beams came struggling through a hazy mist, which soon began to glow with their hues, till it became a lovely, golden robe, hanging about the morn. It was AURORA in dishabille.

At the usual hour little JENNIE and I started out for school, a walk of some three-quarters of a mile.

On our going out of the yard, a mocking-bird and oriole were singing from the China-trees, as we passed under them. But every note that the latter poured forth the former caught and re-sung it, till the oriole got provoked and stopped singing. The mocking-bird then went on, but its notes were fitful—he did not finish a single strain. I soon saw the cause: he was angry because we had stopped and were listening to him, and would now and then give a note by way of taunt at us, then, imitating the catbird, he would look at us, ruffle up his feathers, and give a "*squall.*"

We then sauntered out the gate. The road to school first passed a beautiful open wood on our left, the murmuring Yazoo on the right. I really thought nature had studied her toilet with more than usual taste this morn. Had the birds babbled it out that JENNIE and I were going to play truant to-day, and ramble about in the woods, instead of going to school. The forest was in its autumnnal robe, and

> "Like a rich beauty when her bloom is lost,
> Appeared with more magnificence and cost."

In many places beautiful bowers were formed along our walk, by the muscadine and trailing vines that clambered from branch to branch of clustering trees, making a thick thatch-work over head, then fell down in green and graceful festoons, to the ground all around you.

"Oh, what a pretty place to keep school in!" shouted little JENNIE, as we passed one of uncommon beauty. Then she would run on ahead of me—her bonnet in her hand—and snatch a mossy ringlet from the lower limb of a tree, put it around her neck and run on again, as light as a little fairy. Coming to a radiant cluster of crimson leaves in the center of a green bower of grape-vines, she stopped, and clapping both her little hands in ecstasy, shouted—

"Oh how pretty—how pretty! isn't that pretty?" "I wish I had it to carry to school to stick in the wall over my seat." Then again seeing a squirrel run across our path or up a tree, she would clap her hands and shout at the little fellow, who, as if in play with her, would, as he scampered off, raise his tail by way of huzza. We then told her about the Lapland squirrels crossing the river. How they came in large numbers to the bank, where each would get a piece of bark as large as he could carry—"tote" it down to the water's edge, get on it—launch it off from the shore, and trust to wind and wave to drift them on their little crafts to the other side. Hundreds crossed in this way, and hundreds got drowned.

Thus finding topics in scenes and sights around us, we chatted our way to school, little JENNIE as happy and joyous as a bird. Now and then a steamer would come splashing along up or down the Yazoo, when she would stop and point out to me some one of the passengers she knew on board.

After the woods had discontinued on our left, a vast cotton-field, then in all of its snowy bloom, spread out before us. How often I have loitered on my way to school, like a little truant, and got up on the fence, after lifting little JENNIE up, and stood and admired this cotton-field. There is no scene in nature that has so much of gorgeous beauty in it as this. "Beauty," as we have said, "is Nature's brag;" but *here* she must

> ——— "Tax her eulogistic powers,
> And scream and shout—beautiful! for hours."

As far as the eye can reach—*cœlum undique et undique*—a field of mimic snow. If I have any indellible picture of the South hanging up in the gallery of my mind, it is one of her cotton-fields. Why don't some of our CLAUDES or SALVATOR ROSAS give us a scene with a cotton-field in it? A picture with one of their rivers with its wood-skirted banks for its fore-ground—and then through an opening in the willow foliage, catch a view of a fine cotton-field and plantation.

## MISS SALLIE P. AND HER LITTLE BLACK MAID OF HONOR.

> "She sees a little child at play,
> Among the rosy wild flowers singing,
> As rosy and as wild as they;
> Chasing, with eager hands and eyes,
> The beautiful blue damsel-flies,
> That fluttered round the jasmine stems,
> Like winged flowers or flying gems."
>
> MOORE.

Miss SALLIE was a redoubtable little romp, and made a play-fellow of MARY, her little black maid of honor, who was her constant attendant in school and out. She was as much attached to her as she would have been to a sister—she was all the sister she had. In all of her gambols and pranks little MARY was with her. She went with her to school—she went with her visiting—she went with her bird-nesting—she went with her nutting—she went with her berrying—she went with her everywhere. She was in all of her little schemes—shared all the perils and delights of her adventures—climbed with her all the forbidden fences—went in all the forbidden places—waded in all the forbidden brooks—and was siamesed with her in the secret to keep them all from her mamma. Either would have been whipped, and have borne the puishment like a little martyr, ere she would have exposed the other.

If Miss SALLIE had strayed away from her and found anything that excited her curiosity, the "*ho*, MARY!" was sure to be heard as the signal of joy for her to come and share the "*bonny-bouche*" with her.

On leaving the house in the morning it was my custom to give the "ho, for school!" from the veranda, as I went out. It was answered by a shout and halloo by the little folk of Willow Dale, as they sauntered out the hall or gate.

Our some-over-half-a-mile walks to school abounded with their wild gambols und freaks, in which Miss SALLIE was the leader. They made little sorties upon everything they met. The wood-peckers were stoned—the squirrels were chased along the fence—the black-birds were pelted —the geese were routed—and the pigs were cornered and driven into the river.

A venerable old sycamore that stands on the bank of the river along our walk, is memorable in the history of their mad pranks. They had chased a large fox-squirrel, one day, up this tree, into a hole, about mid-way from the ground to its top, and besieged him with a shower of stones till I called them away. But every time after this that they passed this tree, "like the "dog Noble" barking at the "hole in the wall," they would stop and stone this squirrel.

My instructions in regard to Miss SALLIE, during our

recess at school, given me by Mrs. P. were, not to let her pull her shoes and stockings off and wade into the water for craw-fish or minnies, or into the bayou among the alligators; for, she remarked, She is a perfect little naturalist, and is ever straying off, and making explorations.

Miss SALLIE and little MARY were good singers. It was amusing to me to hear them as they walked to school, each carrying by turns the dinner-basket on her arm, sing their little ditties; and among others a famous poetical song of "'56," pleased me most; and of which I remember this verse:

"The Mustang colt has a killing pace,
Du dah, du dah.
And bound to win the White-House race,
Du dah, du dah day.
I'm bound to run all night, I'm bound to run all day,
I'll bet my money on the Mustang colt, will anybody bet on the gray.
Du dah, du dah day."

But there was another association connected with this song that gave a piquancy to its memory. In the "campaign of '56" Senator DOUGLAS addressed a mass gathering of Democrats in Michigan. After he had got through, the applauding crowd called loudly for their favorite orator, JOHN VANARMAN Esquire, whom they played on all great occasions, as the right bower of Democracy in their State. He came forward and made one of his most forcible and telling speeches, during which, in one of his inimitable tirades of wit and sarcasm against the Black Republicans, he scattered fragments of this song, as specimens of the sound logic and argument they used to sustain their cause, closing now and then a glowing period, by way of illustration, with the euphonious chorus—

"Du dah, du dah day,"

till his Rabelias wit shook the sides of the "little giant" with laughter."

Another instance connected with her and her little attendant I never shall forget.

There is a small lakelet lying out in front of the school-house, about as large as a village garden. MARY had thrown some trifle of value to one of the pupils into it, and STANLEY P., Miss SALLIE'S oldest brother, determined that she should get it out again, stood over her—for she had thrown herself crying on the ground—with a whip, about to "lay it on," because she would not wade in and get it out again.

At this moment Miss SALLIE, a little distance off, caught sight of him, and with the bound of a fawn, she sprang towards them, and like a little POCAHONTAS, threw herself on her little waiting maid, and shielding her from the falling blow, looked up and cried—"Strike, my brother! strike your dear sister; but don't you touch my MARY."

I saw all this from my school-room door. The pupils had all stopped their play, and stood looking on with fixed attention. It was a scene worthy of the pencil of a CLAUDE or the pen of a COOPER.

## A ROMAUNT.

"'Tis true—'tis pretty,
And pretty as 'tis true."

Miss FANNIE S. and LAURA W. are daughters of very wealthy parents. The family of the latter is among the first in the South; the other affluent and of high standing. The daughters were young and admired. They were—but I am an odd hand at describing beauty, and, furthermore, the latter will appear in their actions; and for once, let the old adage—"Handsome is that handsome does," have its full meaning out."

There is more beauty in a good deed—more real, essential prettiness, than in all the beautiful coquettes that were ever out-coquetted by their own mirrors;—yes, real brilliancy.

> "How far that little candle throws its beams!
> So shines a good deed in this naughty world."

I am not going to tell a story of charity—a heroic act of a benevolent nature. Let newspapers have the deeds of charity and benevolence, for a while; I am not in that vein to-day. I am to relate—well, a benevolent deed, if you like, with the wild prank of a city-girl in it.

In that most delightful of Southern cities, L., like a thing of picturesque beauty, on the Southern bank of the matchless Ohio—the home of one of our finest poets, and so late the home of that lovely HEMANS of ours—the heroines of my story lived.

The father of FANNIE S. was a banker, and like all of that class of men, he was noted for his shrewd common sense. He loved his daughter because she was the richest jewel in all his possessions. It was during a crisis in the times—a stress in money-matters, and when want among the poor asked alms in the street, after the charities of the mansions and cottages had been sought, that we fix the event of our story. It was a time, too, when, as usually is the case, your charities were often given, not to the poor, but to the lazy and dishonest. Business men are shrewd, but, as we have said, bankers are shrewder.

Mr. S. was not a benevolent man. At least, in his charities, he gave his own limits to the significance of that word. Asking more than that of him, was sure to meet with his imperturable—*No.*

The day before the principal scene in our story was laid, the different committees of many of the charitable societies of the city of L. had been collecting their usual gratuities of the citizens, and as if to test the benevolence of the place, the citizens were almost besieged by the beggars in the streets. It was towards the end of this day—the loveliest part of it, that a group of young ladies were chatting beneath the rural shade in the front grounds of Mr. W.'s noble residence. They were several friends and mates of Miss W., who had been visiting her during the afternoon. After the usual topics incident to such a knot of young ladies had been prattled over and expatiated upon, begging, then so common, was introduced. During the conversation something was said about Mr. S., the baker, of his cold selfishness, at which one of the more sanguine rather eloquently remarked, that she would pay a forfeit of so much to the beggar-girl that would get one penny from this gentleman. Yes, she would defy the shrewdness and deception of a Gipsey beggar, with all of their art at begging, and with even the beauty of his daughter FANNIE to affect his golden heart one farthing's worth. There was no assailable point—no "heel of ACHILLES"—to this banker. He had been completely immersed in the Styx. His heart, like his treasures, was locked up in a salamander safe. This was said in such an earnest manner, and seemed so true that not one of the young ladies seemed to doubt it for a moment. This closed the conference. The young ladies bade their friend, Miss W., good evening, and went home.

It is mid-afternoon, in one of the principal streets of L., whose broad center is alive with drays, carts and carriages, passing and re-passing, and on each side of which, over the solid pavement, flows, fluent and refluent, its usual current of people, with here and there an isolated group standing like an island in either current. To one of these groups I will direct your attention. It is composed of three. The principal figure you recognize is Mr. S. The other two are beggars. They appear to be decent looking young women, but poorly clad. They appeal to Mr. S. for something for their poor sick mother. But they have heard the imperturable *No*, from him, and he is about to go on, when an accent in the voice of one of the females arrests his attention. There is something in the accent—the tone of the human voice, at times, that has the charm of magic upon one's feelings; it awakens the dearest memories of our lives. It is a touch of nature.

WILLIS, who has many felicitous touches in his writings, represents TAGLIONI as being enchanted as she catches, in one of her performances on the stage, strains of music she had heard in her childhood.

And young HARRY BERTRAM, while wandering over the craggy hillside of Ellongowan Hight, catches a strain in the song of a Gipsey girl that is washing by a fountain at the foot of the slope, that awakens the memories of his lost youth. He thinks of a fragment of an old song he once knew—he listens—she sings it. He wonders why it is, that the memories of his chilhood are so vividly brought before him. Why should the song of that Gipsey girl affect him thus?

You see that an accent of this beggar girl's voice has arrested Mr. S.'s attention. He does not know why, but his stoicism begins to relent, and he feels inclined to hear, at least, what she has to say. A few words tell the sad story of their poverty and wretchedness, and ere she gets through, the girl, gaining confidence from the assurance that Mr. S. is more and more interested in what she has to say, raises her head and he catches a full view of her face, which he had not done before. He knew not why, but she seemed to him his beautiful FANNIE, in rags, pleading for bread to carry home to her poor sick and starving mother. This touched his heart. He put his hand into his pocket, and taking out a gold dollar remarked as he gave it to her, "I never saw a girl look so much like my daughter FANNIE as you do. Take this as a compliment to that resemblance, and for your sick mother." And he left them.

In the fine residence of Mr. S., at evening, the family were seated as usual at table. The story of Mr. S.'s giving the gold dollar to the beggar girl was related by himself, and listened to with much interest by the family.

Some time after this the subject chanced to occur in the chat at the dinner-table. Then you think, said Miss FANNIE, that one of the beggar girls resembled me, do you? Her father replied that he did. She then informed him that those two beggar girls were now in two of the most affluent and respectable families in their city, and not only that, they were much esteemed by the inmates of those families. He felt some little pleasure in hearing this; it might be that the gold dollar had been the means of doing something of it. He inquired in what families they were. She would inform him at supper, and as they were to visit BIDDIE, their servant girl, that afternoon, he might have the opportunity of seeing them if he wished.

Miss W. was FANNIE'S guest that afternoon; they were schoolmates, friends, and in love and affection were wedded to each other.

After the usual tea-table chat, something was said by Mr. S. about the conversation at dinner. Miss LAURA and FANNIE had retired to another room, when Mrs. S. replied that if he would step into the other room, she would introduce him to the young ladies of gold-dollar memory. He complied, and was introduced to two young women resembling those he had seen in the streets enough to distinctly recognize them. He addressed them a few words about their sick mother, to which they replied very prettily, that she was well. He then inquired for Miss LAURA and Miss FANNIE. One of the young ladies replied, taking off her bonnet and showing one of the loveliest of faces, and looking at him with all the playful witchery of a pair of charming eyes, "Don't you think, Mr. S., that there is something very FANNIEsque about me?" and then pointing to her friend, who had also unbonneted her head, "and don't you think this young lady looks exceedingly LAURAEsque?"

The surprise had been sprung upon him so suddenly that, for a moment, his mind wavered between a recognition of them and the ruse they had played him, so much so that he wondered who they were.

But while he was thus pondering, it was but the work of a moment, their beggar dresses that they had merely slipped on over their others, were thrown off and Miss FANNIE S., and Miss LAURA W., stood before him.

"Capital! capital!" exclaimed Mr. S., who had now emerged from the unpleasant perplexity the surprise had thrown him into, "this is capital! You deserve a rich 'benefit' for this. But, you witching rogues, don't you babble this about!" There was an exposure of himself about the farce that he did not like, after all.

Miss FANNIE resumed, "My dear father, the play is out. I know it sounds trite, but it is just as true, when I say there is a moral to it. You have met your daughter FANNIE many a time in rags and wretchedness in the streets of this city; her equals in beauty, affection, love and worth. The only difference is, this meaner garb," pointing to the one she had just thrown off, "and this princely mansion, and that wretched hut yonder," referring to the beggar's home. "You were not cheated last week, when Miss LAURA W., and your daughter FANNIE asked alms of you. They were cheated in you—they mistook you for a benevolent man, but found that your benevolence, like the frozen fountain, wanted thawing before it would flow. This is all, save the sequel. Now for that," she cried, as she turned to her friend. "I accepted the challenge so boastingly given the other day, to touch the 'heel of ACHILLES' in my father's heart. I have done it. But others must know it. I understand that there is a pretty reward pledged to the winner of this citadel."

The following note was elegantly penned and sent to the young ladies whom we have noticed in the first part of our story as giving the challenge.

RESPECTED LADIES:

Your ACHILLES has been conquered. The arrow of PARIS has laid him low. I claim your forfeit.

Yours respectfully,

FANNIE S.

Miss JENNIE MAXON.
" EMMA WILTON.
" ANNIE BUTLER.
" MARY CARTER.

This story is true. Should you ever take a trip down the "Great Father-of-waters," one of the finest steamers on that magnificent river would be pointed out to you bearing the name, as a tribute to her worth, of the heroine of our story.

## THE NORTHERN SCHOOL-GIRL THAT WISHED TO BE PUT IN MY BOOK.

"And ne'er did Grecian chisel trace
A nymph, a naid, or a grace,
Of finer form or lovelier face!

* * * * *
And though no rule of courtly grace
To measured mood had trained her pace—
A foot more light, a step more true,
Ne'er from the heath-flower dashed the dew."
SCOTT.

Put her in my book! Why, I could not catch the sylph to put her in. But could I do it, this volume would be more attractive than the Florence gallery with the Medician VENUS in it. It would exhaust the ten thousandth edition, with such an attraction, among the beaux of our land alone. And as many belles would purchase it to attract the beaux. It would be a literary work of the most popular belle-and-beaux style. Everybody would be enamored of it and read it continually. And I,

"As soon as my book appeared in print,
Why, I—should fall in love with the beauty in't."

Why, the pretty will-o'-the-wisp is already the heroine of many an unwritten romance, with their scenes laid in a beautiful rural village in the breezy West, about a pretty cottage peeping out from its wealth of shrubbery; and in and about a school-house with its parliament of girls and boys; with episodes in moonlight walks with her playmate lovers, and May-parties in which she is the Queen Heroine.

But she wishes to be put in my book. Then here she is in five letters—F–R–A–N–K—FRANK, that's all. And there she goes again, romping along the streets with her playmates—the lassie VERNON of the village, always as welcome among her friends as flowers in May.

As I have seen her coming home from school chatting along the way with her schoolmates, as happy as a bird, I have often wondered what she thought of herself. She knew that she was beautiful, for she read it in the lengthened gaze of the passer-by, and the fond attachment of her playmates, and the smiles and caressing words of her teachers. But it did not make her vain. Whom VENUS loves MINERVA slights. FRANK had wisdom enough not to be vain of her beauty. Unlike coquettes, she never got drunk, or even tipsy, over the intoxicating beverages of her glass. Put her in a book!

"I guess it were beautiful here to see
A girl so playful and frolic as she,
Beautiful exceedingly."

"For, loving girl, thou seemest to be
All music, love, and poetry."

"Across thy cheek in thy young glee,
I've watched thy wild thoughts come and go,
Like rose hues on the evening sea,
Or sunset shadows on the snow—
Why thy young soul looked from thine eyes
Like a sweet cherub from the skies.

"Naught ever shades thine eyes' rich hue,
Save those young curls as bright and fair
As if the sunshine, glancing through,
Had chanced to get entangled there.
Ah! nobler hearts than wealth e'er bought,
In those bright meshes will be caught."

## REMINISCENCES.

"Why all this toil for triumphs of an hour?
What though we wade in wealth or soar in fame?
Earth's highest station ends in—'Here he lies,'
And 'dust to dust' concludes her noblest song."

"Speak of me as I am; nothing extenuate,
Nor set down aught in malice."

## OLD GOVERNOR COWLES MEAD, AND AARON BURR.

"There was ae sang, amang the rest,
Aboov them a' it pleased me best."
BURNS.

"Some men are born great, some men achieve greatness, and some men have greatness thrust upon them." Old Governor COWLES MEAD'S greatness may include something of the first and second of these; but the most valuable part of his greatness was rather fortunately thrust upon him by Aaron Burr, with a brief account of which our story bides. It is quickly told.

Fortune often crowds fame enough in one deed for a whole lifetime. She's playing the *multum in parvo* with our acts, when we are not aware of it, and then awakes us, as she did Byron, some morning, to find "ourselves famous!" What we are doing now may one day be history. But to our subject. It is simply this—please dwell on each word, and read it with historic emphasis. "*General* COWLES MEAD *was Lieutenant, though acting Governor of Mississippi, when Colonel* Aaron Burr *chanced to rendezvous on its shores, in the vicinity of Grand Gulf, and by his own order had the said Colonel Aaron Burr arrested.* Though, we say it *sub rosa*, and within parenthesis, (it is asserted as a *fact*, that Colonel BURR merely played IAGO with the old Governor, made him believed he was "*honest*," and he let him go).

The following interesting sketch is the true historical account of Colonel BURR'S capture in the back-woods of Alabama.

"Confident of the aid of General WILKINSON, and of the forces under his command,, BURR continued his exertions, notwithstanding all prospects of a war with Spain had ceased, and in spite of the proclamation of the President, and the efforts of the governors of the various States and Territories of the West, to deter him.

In January 1807, the flotilla of BURR had arrived at Bayou Pierre, on the lower Mississippi. He was there seized by the order of COWLES MEAD, the acting Governor of Mississippi, and conducted to the town of Washington. BURR shortly after managed to escape from custody, and a reward of two thousand dollars was offered for his apprehension. In the mean time several arrests of the supposed accomplices of BURR, were made at Fort Adams and New Orleans. Among these were BOLLMAN—the celebrated deliverer of LAFAYETTE—OGDEN, SWARTWOUT, DAYTON, SMITH, ALEXANDER and General ADAIR, against whom the most rigid and unjustifiable authority was exercised by General WILKINSON, in many cases upon bare suspicion.

Late at night, about the first of February, a man in the garb of a boatman, with a single companion, arrived at the door of a small log cabin in the back woods of Alabama, and inquired the way to Colonel HINSON'S, who resided in the neighborhood. Colonel NICHOLOS PERKINS observed by the light of the fire, that the stranger, although coarsely dressed, possessed a countenance of unusual intelligence, and an eye of sparkling brilliancy. The tidy boot, which his vanity could not surrender with his other articles of clothing, attracted Perkin's attention, and led him truly to conclude that the mysterious stranger was none other than the famous Colonel BURR, described in the proclamation of the Governor.

That night Perkins started for Fort Stoddart, on the Tombigbee, and communicated his suspicions to the late General Edmund P. Gaines, then the Lieutenant in command. The next day, accompanied by Perkins and a file of mounted soldiers, Gaines started in pursuit of Burr, and arrested him on his journey. Burr attempted to intimidate Gaines; but the resolute young officer was firm, and told him he must accompany him to his quarters, where he would be treated with all the respect due to the ex-Vice President of the United States.

About three weeks after Gaines sent Burr a prisoner to Richmond, with a sufficient guard, the command of which was given to Perkins. They were all men whom Perkins had selected, and upon whom he could rely in every emergency. He took them aside and obtained the most solemn pledges that upon the whole route they would hold no interviews with Burr, nor suffer him to escape alive. Perkins knew the fascinations of Burr, and he feared his familiarity with his men—indeed he feared the same influence upon himself. He was actually afraid to trust either his men or himself within the influence of the "exquisitely beautiful Delilah" of his persuasive eloquence.

Each man carried provisions for himself, and some for the prisoner. They were all well mounted and armed. On the last of February they set out on their long and perilous journey. To what an extremity was BURR now reduced! In the boundless wilds of Alabama, with none to hold converse; surrounded by a guard to whom he dared not speak; a prisoner of the United States, for whose liberties he had fought; his fortunes swept away; the magnificent scheme for the conquest of Mexico broken up; slandered and hunted down from one end of the Union to another. These were considerations to crush an ordinary man; but his was no common mind; and the characteristic fortitude and determination which had ever marked his course, still sustained him in the darkest hour.

In their journey through Alabama they always slept in

the woods, and after a hastily prepared breakfast, it was their custom to re-mount and march on in gloomy silence. Burr was a splendid rider, and in his rough garb he bestrode his horse as elegantly as though he were at the head of a New York regiment. He was always a hardy traveler, and though wet for hours together, with cold and drizzling rain, riding forty miles a day, and at night stretched on a pallet upon the ground, he never uttered one word of complaint.

A few miles beyond Fort Wilkinson they were for the first time sheltered under a roof—a tavern kept by one Bevin. While they were seated around the fire awaiting breakfast, the inquisitive host inquired "if *the traitor* Burr had been taken?" "Was he not a bad man?" "Wasn't everybody afraid of him?" Perkins and his party were very much annoyed, and made no reply. Burr was sitting in the corner by the fire, with his head down; and after listening to the inquisitiveness of Bevin until he could stand it no longer, he raised himself up, and planting his fiery eyes upon him, said,

"*I am Aaron Burr;* what is it you want with me?"

Bevin, struck with his appearance—the keenness of his look, and the solemnity and dignity of his manner—stood aghast, and trembled like a leaf. He uttered not another word while the guard remained at his house.

When they reached the confines of South Carolina, Perkins watched Burr more closely than ever, for his son-in-law, Colonel, afterwards Governor, Alston, a gentleman of talent and influence, resided in this State. He was obliged in a great measure to avoid the towns for fear of a rescue. Before entering the town of Chester, in that State, the party halted, and surrounding Burr, proceeded on, and passed near a tavern where many persons were standing, while music and dancing were heard in the house. Burr conceived it a favorable opportunity for escape, and suddenly dismounting, exclaimed,

"I am Aaron Burr, under military arrest, and claim protection from the civil authorities."

Perkins leaped from his horse, with several of his men, and ordered him to re-mount.

"*I will not!*" replied Burr.

Not wishing to shoot him, Perkins threw down his pistols, and being a man of prodigious strength, and the prisoner a small man, seized him around the waist, and placed him in the saddle, as though he were a child. Thomas Malone, one of the guard, caught the reins of the bridle, slipped them over the horse's head, and led him rapidly on. The astonished citizens, when Burr dismounted, and the guards cocked their pistols, ran within the piazza to escape from danger.

Burr was still, to some extent, popular in South Carolina; and any wavering or timidity on the part of Perkins would have lost him his prisoner; but the celerity of his movements gave the people no time to reflect before he was far in the outskirts of the village. Here the guard halted. Burr was highly excited; he was in tears! The kind-hearted Malone also wept, at seeing the uncontrollable despondency of him who had hitherto proved almost iron-hearted. It was the first time any one had ever seen Aaron Burr unmanned.

On Burr's arrival at Richmond, the ladies of the city vied with each other in contributing to his comfort. Some sent him fruit, some clothes, some one thing, and some another.

Burr was tried before the Supreme Court of the United States, at Richmond, for treason, and found *not guilty*, though the popular voice continued to regard him as a traitor. Failing to convict the principal, the numerous confederates of Burr were never brought to trial, and were discharged from custody.

He was defended during his trial by the honorable Henry Clay, on his first assuring him upon *his honor*, that he was engaged in no design contrary to the laws and peace of his country. He was acquitted, owing to the absence of any important witness, and from the fact that the arrest was premature.

After his trial, Burr went abroad, virtually a banished man. He was still full of his schemes against Mexico, and, unsuccessfully, attempted to enlist England, and then France, in these projects. Here his funds failed. He had no friends to apply to, and was forced to borrow, on one occasion, a couple of sous from a cigar woman, on the corner of the street.

But to return: time passed on, and worthy old Governor Cowles Mead lived many years after this remarkable event; but that he had "*taken Colonel Burr*," was ever the pride of his life. The thought ever animated him, when this circumstance was mentioned; and he often found occasion to mention it.

Besides the other good qualities of the man, the Governor was a staunch Presbyterian, and at their Presbyteries, whenever he had anything to say, would be sure to bring in his "taking Colonel Burr." At one of their conventions he rose to speak, when one of the brethren, knowing his Burrish propensity, arose and said he had some objection to brother Mead's speaking, he was so apt to wander from his subject. The chairman gave the necessary precaution about the brethren's confining themselves to the subject, and the rules of the meeting and the Governor proceeded. But, ere he got through speaking, he was cited to an error in one of his dates—the year was wrong. He stopped a moment and reflected—then went on:—"No, I am right, I am confident I am right;—why, said he, there is nothing *surer*, for it was *the same year that I took Colonel Burr*."

## GEORGE M. POINDEXTER.

"He stood growing in his place like a flood in a narrow vale."

"He drew forward that troubled war—but Tremnor they turned not from battle."

"The years that are past are marked with mighty deeds."

OSSIAN.

Among those whose aims, deeds and virtues, are written on the scroll of Southern fame, is that of GEORGE M. POINDEXTER. Although a Virginian by birth, his name and fame are as much identified with Mississippi's early history as that of any other illustrious man. He was a conspicuous actor on the stage when she was comparatively a wilderness; at that stirring and eventful period of her history when the weird and dangerous ambition of BURR urged him to devise schemes for its highest gratification. And, if I remember rightly, he was the United States Attorney who was at Natches when BURR was taken there for examination, after his arrest at Grand Gulf. I do not assert this as a fact.

He was the first territorial Governor of Mississippi, the first Representative in Congress after her admission into the Union; and it was during that great and exciting debate in the House of Representatives, in 1819, on Mr. CLAY'S resolutions censuring General JACKSON for the execution of AMBRISTER and ARBUTHNOT during his celebrated campaign against the Seminole Indians in Florida, that he measured arms with the American CICERO, and proved himself a mighty foe in mental conflict—a proud peer of him who has been justly ranked among the first of his age in oratory and eloquence.

A Southern planter remarked to me: "In early life, I read the speeches of these two great champions," referring to the debate above mentioned, "and I think all intelligent and impartial men would concur with me in the opinion, that for real and genuine power and eloquence, Poindexter's speeches have not yet been surpassed on any similar occasion, by any American orator. At any rate, they gave him a national reputation, and established his fame among the first men of the day as a splendid and effective speaker."

In 1830 he was elected to the United States Senate as a supporter of General Jackson's administration. This was the important era of his life. At that time, the reader will remember, the great contest arose between the old Democratic and Whig leaders in Congress, in relation to the removal of the deposits of the United States Bank.

The measure was put in motion and most strenuously opposed by the Whigs. It was met with an opposition so powerful that the "Old Hero" was afraid of losing a single man. And as he cast his eye over the field where the enemy were arrayed in such a formidable combination against him under those eminent chiefs, Clay, Calhoun and Webster, and ran it along the list of Senators, and saw standing by their side, Bibb, of Kentucky; Chambers, of Maryland; Clayton, of Delaware; Ewing, of Ohio; Freelinghuysen, of New Jersey; Watkins Leigh, of Virginia; Mangum, of North Carolina; Alexander Porter, of Louisiana; William C. Preston, of South Carolina; Southard, of New Jersey; Tyler, of Virginia; he was somewhat alarmed; and when he saw that some of his own chiefs were disaffected, with eager haste his keen eye flashed over his own forces, when with sad disappointment he missed the Roland of his camp—Poindexter—the one in whom his hopes of the South West relied, was not to be found among his chiefs. But instantly

——— "A whistle shrill
Was heard from the opposing hill;
Wild as the scream of the curlieu
From crag to crag the signal flew.
Instant through copse and heath arose
Bonnets, and spears, and bended bows,
On right, on left, above, below,
A chief deserts and seeks the foe."

It is well known that Poindexter sounded the note of alarm summoning the foe to the opposition of this measure, and that he, with many other Democrats, deserted the President, and crossed over, as the Saxons did at Leipsic, to the enemy, and urged with them a fierce and bitter warfare upon him and his measures. But they met a terrible opposition from the Democrats; yet "Tremnor turned not from the battle—he stood growing in his place like a flood in a narrow vale." But what man ever prospered that opposed General Jackson and his schemes? They were doomed men if they incurred his wrath. While in power, Cæsar and his fortunes were with him, and when he retired to his Hermitage,

"Achilles absent was Achilles still."

George M. Poindexter, in this opposition to General Jackson, proved himself a champion in debate—the "Old Hero" and his party found in him a proved and powerful foe.

The brilliant Prentiss refers to him in one of his speeches in Congress, in all the animated glow of his impassioned eloquence, and eulogizes him for his undaunted firmness in this debate—for his proud defiance to the Achillean wrath of the President and the hate of his late friends, the Democratic leaders, in battling for the right. But the enemy were too powerful—they gained the day.

"Ill fared it then with Roderick Dhu."

For in 1833, during the canvass for State election, and when the subject for the United States Senator was necessarily involved, as the Legislature then chosen had to elect one, Robert J. Walker, then residing at Natches, a lawyer of distinguished reputation and acknowledged ability, the same Robert J. Walker, since famous in Kansas history, announced himself a candidate for the United States Senate, in support of General Jackson's policy in regard to the United States Bank; and in opposition to Poindexter, took the "stump," and thoroughly canvassed the State. After one of the most angry and embittered political contests ever known in our borders, he carried the Legislature by a small majority, and triumphed over his distinguished opponent. This so mortified the ambition of Poindexter that he commenced a career of wild and reckless dissipation, sullying very much his well-earned reputation, and alienating, of course, many of his friends and supporters. Seeing evidently that the star of his glory in Mississippi was obscured, if not set forever, he removed to Lexington, Kentucky, to practice in his former profession as a lawyer, was disappointed there, and came back to Mississippi, the theatre of his former glory, broken in health and spirits, and there he died.

> "Such honors Ilium to her hero paid,
> And peaceful slept the mighty Hector's shade."

## SENATOR FOOTE.

> "Such as we are made of, such we be."
>
> SHAKSPEARE.

Every man has, or there is a vocation in life for which every man is exactly fitted. But finding this one among the various pursuits, is not so very easily done, for, in regard to their relation to us, fortune seems to have scattered them about, with the irregularity of sibylline leaves. Yet the secret of success in life is finding this vocation. The ancients believed this, for here it is, "*Gnothi seauton.*" The really finding one's self, is the great discovery of our lives—the true philosopher's stone—the talisman with which men convert everything into gold. Besides this true vocation of one's self, there is one to which men aspire, whether false or true, and for which there is a longing, that, if not satisfied, more or less imbitters their whole lives.

Whether it was the great discovery of Senator Foote's life or not, we do not know, but it is certain that he found himself in the United States Senate, some number of years ago, which discovery to him appears to have been the talisman he sought. For being deprived of this bauble that fortune appears to have given him for awhile to amuse him, there has been an "*amari aliquid*"—a drop of bitter flowing over his life ever since—he has constantly sighed to get the bauble back again.

Senator Foote is a Virginian by birth. He first, on leaving his native State, came to Alabama, but his first location was at Vicksburgh, Mississippi, as the editor of a Democratic newspaper. Soon after he established the *Mississippian*, still recognized as the central organ of the Democratic party of this State. Abandoning this enterprise, he located at Clinton, Hinds county, in the same State, as a lawyer, where he acquired considerable reputation as an advocate. Being of an active and quick mind, well educated, and possessed of a very large fund of general information, he naturally sought every field within reach for a display of his powers. An unusually ready and effective debater, of keen wit and sarcasm, he was rather a formidable adversary, either on the forum or hustings. He commenced his career in Mississippi at a period when that portion in which he lived was attracting much attention as a suitable field for all sorts of men—the cotton-planter, the professional man of all classes, the speculator and the gambler. And at a time, too, when morals were not of a high grade, and excitements and dissipations, always accompanying this condition of things, were universal and rampant. And he being of a mercurial temper, was involved in various difficulties, two of which were with S. S. Prentiss, and resulted in duels, in the last of which he was slightly wounded, and which reconciled the feud between these two distinguished worthies of Mississippi.

Senator Foote's has been a wayward and checkered life. He has been really a political champion, and, for a while at least, has co-operated to some extent with all the political parties that have had an organization in this State. And during this time he was a member of the United States Senate for six years. Halcyon days! But,

> "Gone glimmering through the dream of things that were,
> A school-boy's tale—the wonder of an hour."

Of his career there the reader is well informed. It was while a member of this august body, that he received the cognomen of "Hangman Foote," the origin of which was this: In an exciting debate with Senator Hale, he told him if he ever caught him out of his own State, in Mississippi, he would hang him. To which Senator Hale replied, should he, Senator Foote, ever come to New Hampshire, he would treat him like a gentleman. He was a man of power and influence in the Senate, and Mr. Clay esteemed him highly.

In 1851 he was elected, by a small majority, as the Union candidate, Governor of Mississippi. In the contest of 1853 he declared himself a candidate for the United States Senate, but was beaten by a very decided majority, which so disappointed and mortified him that in a day or two he left the State to take up his abode in California. Here it is said he succeeded in obtaining a large and lucrative practice as a lawyer. But there was the longing for the chief glory of his life—a seat in the United States Senate. His highest hopes and ambition were fixed upon this yet. And here once more, in this new and untried field of action, he essayed his fortunes for the lost bauble—and failed. Despairing of success in this land of gold, he returned to the East, and located in Memphis, Tennessee. And I presume the prospect there for accomplishing the object of his life, or meeting with success as a lawyer, was rather gloomy; for he did not remain in Memphis long ere he removed to Vicksburgh, Mississippi, where he now is, at the foot of the ladder, where he commenced his strangely varied and checkered career, a quarter of a century ago. Truly he can say with the poet,

> "Life is a drama of a few brief acts;
> The actors shift; the scene is often changed,
> Pauses and revolutions intervene,
> The mind is set to many a varied tune,
> And jars and plays in harmony by turns."

Senator Foote is of small stature, though an active, energetic man. In private life he is said to be very estimable, of easy, affable and polished maners, warm and sincere in his attachments and friendships.

## GENERAL QUITMAN.

> "Zealous, yet modest; innocent though free;
> Patient of toil; serene amidst alarms;
> Inflexible in faith, invincible in arms."

> "*Praelio strenuus erat bonus et concilio.*"
>
> SALLUST.

"I have a good deal of faith," says Hugh Miller, "in the military air, when in the character of a natural trait. I find it strongly marking men who never served in the army. I have not yet seen it borne by the civilian, who had not in him, at least, the elements of a soldier."

He likes this trait because a shrewd sense and sagacity are its characteristics. But it has been always considered as never or very rarely to be found with great powers in the Senate, at the bar, desk, or forum. Hugh Miller instances as possessing this "military air," the elder Dr. McCrie, a powerful Scotch minister, who would also have made a good general. We presume John Knox would.

But the two qualities referred to are very hard to be found in the same individual. Hence Sallust says of Jugurtha, "*Quod difficilimum in primis est, et prœlio strenuus erat et bonus concilio.*"*

We have thought necessary to preface our notice of General Quitman with these remarks, from the fact of his possessing these two traits so rarely found combined in the same individual. That he had the military air as a natural trait—that he was "*Prœlio strenuus,*" and proved himself the able general, history glowingly tells. That he was "*bonus concilio*"—good in council—his public services in his own State and in Congress amply prove. Combined with these was another fine and rare element in his character, that was—chivalry. "He was called," says Major W., "the soul of chivalry in our State."

General Quitman was a native of the State of New York. His father was an Episcopalian minister, and he himself was educated for the church, but afterwards studied law and emigrated to Ohio, where he remained but a year or two, and thence removed to Natches, Mississippi, I

*"And what is most especially difficult to find in the same man, he was brave in battle, and good in council."

think about the year 1822, where he rose rapidly in his profession. It was his profound attainments, clear and logical mind, and elevated, manly character, that won for him distinction, for he was what the world calls a poor speaker, both at the bar and at the hustings.

He was several times a member of the Mississippi State Legislature, President of the Senate, Chancellor of the State, and was Major General of the Militia, at a period when men of character and ability alone could attain these positions. During the Texan struggle for independence, upon his own means and responsibility he raised a corps of gallant men and repaired to her assistance. The reader is well informed of his splendid military career in Mexico, as his deeds fill one of the brightest pages of the history of the Mexican war. His flag was the first that was waved, with his own hands, over the walls of the conquered city; and his column the first whose tramp was heard upon its humbled streets; and he the first American General that ever issued his commands from the "Palace of the Montezumas."

Upon his return home he was nominated by a Democratic convention for Governor of his State, and elected by a larger majority than has ever been given to any other candidate. In the Cincinnati convention of 1856, on one ballot, I believe, (my authority here was a member of that convention,) he had the largest vote for the Vice Presidency. He was twice subsequently elected to Congress by an overwhelming majority; and higher honors awaited him in his cherished State, had he been longer spared her.

In all the various stations that he occupied, both civil and military, he acquitted himself with distinguished honor. In person, General Quitman was of medium size, and erect as an Indian chief. In many respects he was the opposite of Senator Foote, firm, steady and unshaken in his opinions and purposes, in manners and bearing always and everywhere plain and unaffected, evincing the dignity and mien of the true soldier. In private life he had many devoted and admiring friends, and his reputation was

"*Sans peur sans reproche.*"

Quitman is dead; but the laurels he won are unfading—his fame will not decay.

"Its lustre brightens; virtue cuts the gloom
With purer rays, and sparkles near a tomb."

## JOSEPH HOLT.

"Others apart sat on a hill retired,
In thoughts more elevate, and reasoned high."
MILTON.

Mississippi is too young to have raised a crop of great men of her own. New York, Virginia and South Carolina have. But her adopted sons, like Plato's pupils, have rendered her name, as well as their own, immortal. She has been the *Alma Mater* that has conferred the degrees on her pupils as they have graduated in her schools. She has not only given their names to the brightest page of her own history, but to fame.

The occasion, it is said, makes the man. She has been the occasion to many of her adopted sons that has made the man. She made a Holt as she made a Prentice.

A friend writing to me says:—"Of Joseph Holt, or Jo Holt, as he is called here, not a great deal can be said, save that he is unquestionably one of the great men of our country. His life affords no rich material for exciting and thrilling biography, but more of calm dignity and splendor."

There was power enough in the word "Solon," as its sound fell upon the ear of the Great Cyrus, to save the life of the Lydian king, who in extreme despair of his own life, was heard to utter it. We do not know how many men in the "Flush and rampant times of Mississippi"—rich as Crœsus in villainy and crime, have saved or lost their lives by the talismanic power in the dissyllable—Jo Holt.

As their friend and advocate at the bar of justice, he was a powerful ally; but as their adversary at the same bar, he was a powerful foe. This name pronounced in the hearing of a Mississippian always arrests his attention. It associates in his mind the profound reasoning—the logical arguments and forensic eloquence of this Webster of their courts. And there is no name that they pronounce with more pride and confidence than—Jo Holt.

Joseph Holt came to Vicksburgh from his native State—Kentucky—at an early day, and soon attained very high distinction as a lawyer and finished orator. In real eloquence and beauty and splendor of style, he had no equal, I suppose, says a friend, in Mississippi. And when he practiced at Vicksburgh and Jackson, there was a splendid galaxy of talent—legal learning and eloquence at the Mississippi bar, with which he had to contend, and which would have ranked high at any bar in the United States.

There were Prentiss, Guion, Gildart, Sharkey, McNut, Tompkins, and others of no common eloquence. Prentiss used to say of Holt, that he "was the most fearful adversary that he ever encountered." He was said to be stern, cold and retiring in his manners; never anywhere seeking for the "bubble reputation." But an enduring reputation he won.

He was a very laborious man, and, I have no doubt, continues the same authority, quoted above, but what he studied well every speech and argument he made in any suit of importance in which he was engaged. He had the reputation, as I have said else where, of being the best lawyer *prepared* that ever entered the Mississippi courts.

I have heard those that were entranced by his eloquence, assert that every word that fell from his lips—he was, though logical, copious and fluent enough—seemed to be the most appropriate and beautiful that the English language afforded, and could not have been improved.

His voice failed him, and he was compelled to retire from the bar, though he had accumulated a large fortune. I have heard his uncle, who assisted in his education, say that he was so retiring and modest at Louisville, where he studied his profession and located, that he was not even known to many members of the profession. And that on one occcasion, when a suit of much importance was to be tried, a friend who knew his ability, insisted that he should make a speech upon it. He consequently prepared himself, and though very able counsel was employed on both sides, so powerful and eloquent was his argument, that the judge, jury and spectators were spell-bound, and when he sat down, the judge inquired, by note, of one of the attorney's at the bar, "*what young man that was.*" That young man is no other than the present Post Master General at Washington—Joseph Holt.

## GEORGE DENISON PRENTICE.

"The flash of wit—the bright intelligence,
The beam of song—the blaze of eloquence.'

BYRON.

Addison makes his "spectator" remark, rather in joke than earnest, "that the reader seldom peruses a book with pleasure, till he knows whether the writer of it be a black or a fair man, of a mild or choleric disposition, married or a bachelor," with other particulars of a like nature, that conduce very much to a right understanding of the author.

That is, there is a certain stand-point from which you get the finest and most picturesque view of a man. One from which he is exhibted as Shenstone exhibited the Leasowes to his guest, always choosing some eligible sight, some commanding point, from which his delightful, rural seat could be seen in all of its charms and picturesqueness.

A very eminent man of our day says of Addison's remark above, "It is literally true;" he understands an author all the better from having seen him.

We have not thus prefaced our notice of this poet and wit, by way of a flourish in introducing a person of majestic mien and kingly bearing; but have merely given them for their suggestive worth in our brief description of him.

The first time we saw this distinguished individual, was from our seat, near the stand of a large lecture-room, which on the occasion, was filled with the intelligence and beauty of one of our Western cities; even the aisle, at the further end of which we caught sight of him, was standing full. We watched him walking down this avenue of citizens, that swayed this way and that, to let him pass along, and now and then like an opposing wave, would surge up before him, stopping his progress, and causing him to use force and energy to "elbow" his way through. He was preceded by the president of the meeting, whom he followed with his hat in his hand. We noticed his step—it was circumspect—his walk showed caution and wariness. We could see as he threaded his way through this crowd, the keen penetration and perception as he met obstacles and unyielding impediments, the wary dodges and subtility of the man.

In this walk down the aisle, we had risen in our seat, and had a fair view of him over the heads of the sitting audience. As he sought his way through the crowd, we thought we saw the man making his passage through life.

While his keen eye glanced ahead to survey the way, and measure opposing difficulties, he lost no attention to things about him, no self-possession, but was prepared to meet whatever opposed him, with a deliberation and strength equal to the demand. This seemed to result from his forecast and remarkable self-possession. Nothing disconcerts him.

My father once walked behind Aaron Burr through one of the streets of Albany. He thought him the softest, stillest, most circumspect walker he ever saw. He was wary. Surprise had no sudden springs—trips or tricks that he could not avoid, or was not prepared to meet. He was your "Cat-a-line" walker.

We did not see Prentice walk in the streets, but, after the lecture was over, we had preceded him in our egress from the crowd, and stationed ourself by the wayside—as Lamertine did to catch a glimpse of Madam De Stael—at the head of the stairs, and after the crowd had passed in a current, by us, and precipitated itself like a cataract down the winding stairway, we saw him walk down the deserted aisle, chatting with the president and two or three other gentlemen. And we thought from his walk, and the glance of his small, keen eye, that he was a man—

"Whom no one could pass without remark."

This may not be acknowledged by all who have merely seen and not studied him.

Though in personal appearance he is different from our day-dream Prentice—we presume Rabelias and Voltaire would be—yet we can read and understand the man better from this view of him.

In person he is five feet eight inches in height, and of full figure. He has light brown hair, a dark, keen eye, and a head of the finest intellectual cast. In his manners he is courteous and gentlemanly in the highest degree.

His voice, as a speaker, though not loud, is forcible—it sends the words home to the hearts of his audience.

The subject of his lecture was the "American Statesman." The lecture itself appeared to be the collected wit, sarcasm—the political wisdom of the man, all concentrated, like a Drummond light, upon this subject. It is not our intention to analyze the lecture, as he analyzed the "common herd of office-hunters," and those who usurp the position of the statesman. It is beyond our power to do it. He portrayed the condition of our country on the verge of ruin. We now were where another mighty Republic had been.

> "Though Cote lived—though a Tulley spoke—
> Though Brutus dealt the god-like stroke,
> Yet perished fated Rome."

He even denied that we had true and honest men in power, that those that were in office did not even assume the virtues they ought to have.

One of the leading Journals of Michigan says of this lecture:

"This very general idea of it is all we can give, after enumerating the manner of treating the various divisions of the subject, the almost infinite number of sparks struck off from the polished steel of his sarcastic wit, the marvelous fluency in the use of terms with which to brand all sorts of meanness and dishonesty—the occasional glow of that fine sympathy with the true and the beautiful, which is the poetical element of the man; the peculiar gratification resulting from hearing for one's self the wit and wisdom of this celebrated character, on this occasion, must be monopolized by those who were fortunate enough to hear him."

I find the following in my journal, penned immediately after hearing him. I give it just as it was penned, because it was written when the full glow and Prentice heat of the lecture was in us:

"I have just listened to a lecture from George D. Prentice. It was a philippic on our government as now managed—a withering invective—it was a Byron giving his English Bards and Scotch Reviewers on the political men and politics of our Republic.

'Fools were his theme, and satire was his song.'

"It was keen with sarcasm—pungent and sparkling with wit, and cruel and withering in denunciation. While with arguments and home truths he dealt the antagonist the sturdy blows of Diomede, his wit and sarcasm, like the arrows of Teucer, unerring and fatal in their flight, flashed out from behind his shield."

The following, written of Hawthorne, is just as true of Prentice: "In ease, grace, delicate sharpness of satire—in a felicity of touch which often surpasses the felicity of Addison, in a subtility of insight which often reaches further than the subtility of Steele—the wit of Prentice presents traits too refined for statement. The brilliant atoms flit, hover and glance before our minds, but the remote sources of their ethereal light lie beyond our analysis,

"And no speed of ours avails
To hunt upon their shining trails."

"George Denison Prentice, the editor of the Louisville *Journal*, is a native of Connecticut, born at Preston, New London county, December 18th, 1802. He was educated at Brown University, studied law, but did not engage in the profession, preferring the pursuit of an editorial life. In 1828 he commenced the New England *Weekly Review*, at Hartford, a well-conducted and well-supported journal of a literary character, which he carried on for two years, when, consigning its management to Mr. Whittier, he removed to the West, established himself in Louisville Kentucky, and shortly after became editor of the *Journal*, a daily paper in that city. In his hands it has become one of the most widely known and esteemed newspapers in the country; distinguished by its fidelity to Whig politics, and its earnest, able editorials, no less than by the lighter skirmishing of wit and satire. The "Prenticeiana" of the editor are famous. If collected and published with appropriate notes, these 'mots' would form an amusing and instructive commentary on the management of elections, newspaper literature, and political oratory, of permanent value as a memorial of the times."

The Louisville *Journal* has been a supporter of the cause of education, and of the literary interest in the West. It has become in accordance with the known tastes of the editor a favorite avenue of young poets to the public. Several of the most successful lady writers of the West, have first become known through their contributions to the *Journal*.

What N. P. Willis is in this respect to the young lady poets and literary writers of the North, George D. Prentice is to those of the West and South West. The *Journals* of these two distinguished literary celebrities and poets, both sons of New England, have been the "*alma mater*" to the young poet and literary aspirant. Mr. Prentice's poetical writings are numerous. Many of them first appeared in the author's *Review*, at Hartford. A number have been collected by Mr. Everest in the Poets of Connecticut. They are in a serious vein, chiefly expressive of sentiment and domestic affections.

## HON. S. S. PRENTISS.

"For talents mourn untimely lost,
When best employed, and wanted most,
Mourn genius, taste and lore profound,
And wit that loved to play not wound;
And all the reasoning powers divine,
To penetrate, resolve, combine;
And feelings keen, and fancy's glow;
They sleep with him who sleeps below.
And if thou mourn'st they could not save
From error, him who owns this grave,
Be every harsher thought suppressed,
And sacred be the last long rest."

SCOTT.

This eminent lawyer, this brilliant orator, this adopted son of the South, was born in the State of Maine, city of Portland, situated on Casco bay, which he called "the fairest dimple on the cheek of Ocean."

We pass by his early life, merely noticing the first reading that formed his taste.

This was from Scott, Cooper, Irving, Byron, and most of all from his favorite Shakspeare. The Bible, too, was thoroughly read, and admired by him. Its sublime passages and figures he often quoted in his speeches.

He read with wonderful rapidity, so much so that one of his classmates once observed, "*Prentiss reads two pages at the same time, one with his right eye, and the other with his left!*"

This is the way he devoured the works we have mentioned, Milton, Bacon, and all the old masters. His classical training, and his familiarity with the Bible, and the great models of English speech, imparted a richness, strength and felicity to his diction, as well as dignity to his sentiment.

He had gathered rich stories from the wild field of fiction and romance; from old classical mythology, and from the whole region of chivalry. Here he got those gems that glittered in his speeches; those thoughts that flew from him in every possible variety and beauty, like birds from a South American forest—those "figures that bubbled up and poured themselves along, like springs in a gushing fountain."

He was fond, in his leisure hours, of hunting and fishing, though he appeared physically incapacitated for such sport, for his right leg was feeble, and it never became so but what he walked with it partly coiled round a stout cane.

The difficulties of his journey South—he was then seventeen, had just graduated at Bowdoin college, he always thought that he graduated too young, and regretted, like Randolph, that he had not stored his mind with more of the riches of books and study—have something of thrilling interest in them as they are narrated by his brother.

Mention is made of this trip by a lawyer of celebrity in Cincinnati, who relates the circumstance of a youth's coming into his office, one morning, and inquiring whether it was a good place for a young man to get into business, and who so impressed him with his worth, and the tones of his voice, and manner, that he never could forget him. And years afterwards when Prentiss became the pride of the South, he felt an equal pride in relating this circumstance, and the incidents of a short acquaintance with him.

Something of trifling importance was the cause of his not remaining at Cincinnati. Hence the brightest page of Mississippi's, and not Ohio's, history is adorned with the name of a Prentiss.

In his passage down the Mississippi, the steamboat was impeded by some cause, and compelled to lay by. He, with a party of others, took their guns and went ashore to hunt. Having wandered away in the woods from the rest, who returned to the boat just as she got out of difficulty, and was ready to start on, he came very near being left to finish his journey South the best way he could; for when he came back to the bank of the river the steamer had gone, but some one on board caught sight of him, and the captain waived the usual habit of the boat, directed it ashore, and took him aboard.

He stopped at Natches, where he not only found himself in a strange place, but penniless. He fortunately found, in a stranger here, a friend, who offered him money which was gladly accepted, and afterwards paid with grateful thanks. He taught school, some ten miles out in the country from Natches, in the family of Mrs. Judge Shields, for some three hundred dollars per year. He afterwards taught in an Academy, then commenced the study of law, in the above-named city.

There is something similar in the history of the two Prentisses—George D. Prentice, the fine journalist, poet and wit of Louisville, Kentucky, and Sargeant S. Prentiss of Mississippi. Both were sons of New England, both early sought their fortunes in the South, both became its adopted sons, and both have dazzled it with the brilliancy of their intellects.

From the first appearance of S. S. Prentiss at the Mississippi bar, in the front ranks of which stood such men as Holt, Boyd, Quitman, Wilkinson, Winchester, Foote, Henderson and others, he was regarded as a sort of mythical personage. No one knew anything of the "limping boy" and his school-teaching in Mississippi; but from obscurity he had emerged into the public gaze so suddenly, and with such brilliant effect, that everybody was envious to know his history. They seized and magnified all the strange stories in circulation about him. Some thought him a disinherited boy—a young Ivanhoe that had wandered away from his home in the North to far off Mississippi.

But when, like an unknown Byron, he appeared among them, the Scotts, and Shelleys, and Wordsworths of law and oratory, if they did not retire in dismay, gazed upon him with wonder and admiration. They considered him *genius itself* that had vaulted, at one bound, into its full pride of place.

One of his cotemporaries at the bar, in after years, writes of him: "His early reading and education had been extensive and deep. Probably no man of his age in the State was so well read in the ancient and modern classics, in the current literature of the day, and—what may seem stranger—in the sacred Scriptures. His speeches drew some of their grandest images, strongest expressions, and aptest illustrations from the inspired writings."

In writing of his life South he says in a letter to his sister Anna, "I owe all my success in this country to the fact of my having so kind a mother, and two such sweet and affectionate sisters as you and Abby are. It has been my only motive to exertion; without it, I should long since have thrown myself away; and often now I feel perfectly reckless about life and fortune, and look with contempt upon them both."

This sounds like Byron, whom he resembled, not only in lameness, but in his genius and in many other respects.

"There was much about him to remind you of Byron: the cast of his head, the classic features, the fiery and restive nature, the moral and personal daring, the imaginative and poetical temperament, the scorn and deep passion, the deformity of which I have spoken, the satiric wit, the craving for excitement, and the air of melancholy he sometimes wore, his early neglect, and the imagined slights put upon his unfriended youth, the collisions, mental and physical, which he had with others, his brilliant and sudden reputation, and the romantic interest which invested him, make up a list of correspondences, still further increased, alas! by his untimely death."

"But," he continues in his letter, "I am solaced only by the recollection that there are true hearts that beat for me with real affection. This comes over me as the music of David did over the dark spirit of Saul."

Mr. Prentiss had scarcely passed a decade from his majority ere he was the idol of Mississippi. While absent from the State his name was brought before the people for Congress; the State then voting by general ticket, and electing two members. "He was elected, but the sitting members, Gholson and Claiborne, refused to give up their seats on the ground that they were elected at the special election ordered by Governor Lynch, for two years and not for the session only."

If he had astonished the Mississippi bar with the sudden burst of his eloquence, like "the Disinherited Knight," he entered the lists in the Halls of Congress with the great champions of debate, and astonished both Houses by his noble defence of Mississippi, and by the power and charm of his oratory.

When congress met, he and Word, his colleague, had not yet arrived. Wise, Webster, Clay and others of their party, held a caucus to see what should be done with the "Mississippi contested election," and they resolved that the two members, Word and Prentiss, should be taken into pupilage and put under a course of training, and that some able member should aid them with arguments and prepare them for their parts.

At this suggestion W. C. Dawson, late senator from Georgia, who knew Prentiss, arose and said:

"Oh, gentlemen, you need to be at no such pains; you have no babes to nurse. One of them is a host in himself, who can take care of Mississippi, and rather help us, to boot, than require our 'pap-spoons.' He is not only full grown, though low in stature and lame in gait, but a giant, who is head and shoulders taller than any man I know, here or elsewhere, for the task of prompting and defending himself. We need not say, *Up-a-diddy* to him."

He did take care of Mississippi. He was admitted to the bar of the House to defend and assert his right and those of his State. He stood there and battled for her like Diomede among the gods. "He delivered then that speech which took the House and the country by storm; an effort, which if his fame rested upon it alone, for its manliness of tone, exquisite satire, gorgeous imagery, and argumentative power, would have rendered his name imperishable."

Preston, Crittenden, Clay, Adams, Webster—*the whole Senate,* came down to hear his speech, and flocked around him, charmed with his eloquence.

Fillmore, then in the House, said—"I never can forget it; it was certainly the most brilliant speech I ever heard."

Webster exclaimed to a senator, on leaving the hall—"Nobody could equal it." Wise grew eloquent in thus speaking of it:

"Prentiss' turn came. He threw himself on the arena at a single bound, but not in the least like a harlequin. He stepped no stranger on the boards of high debate—he raised the eye to heaven, and trod with giant steps. I shall never forget the feelings he inspired and the triumph he won. But there's the speech, or at least, a fragment of it surviving him. There is the figure of the *star* and *stripe;* go read it; read it now that his eye is dim, and his muscles cease to move the action to the word; then imagine what it was as his tongue spake it, his eye looked it, his hand gesticulated his thoughts."

Here is the closing period of that speech that placed him first among the orators of the land.

"But if your determination is taken; if the blow must fall; if the violated constitution must bleed; I have but one request in her behalf to make: when you decide that she cannot choose her own representatives, at that self-same moment blot from the spangled banner of the *Union* the bright *star* that glitters to the name of *Mississippi*, but leave the *stripe* behind, a fit emblem of her degredation."

The house opposed to him as it was in political sentiment, reversed its former judgment, which declared Gholson and Claiborne entitled to their seats, and divided equally on the question of admitting Prentiss and Word. The speaker, however, gave the casting vote against the latter, and the election was referred back to the people.

Prentiss immediately addressed a circular to the voters of Mississppi, in which he announced his intention to canvass the State.

"The applause which greeted him at Washington, and which attended the speeches that he was called on to make at the North, came thundering back to his adopted State. His friends—and their name was legion—thought before that his talents were of the highest order; and when their judgments were thus confirmed—when they received the endorsement of such men as Clay, Webster and Calhoun, they felt a kind of personal interest in him: he was *their* Prentiss. They had first discovered him—first brought him out—first proclaimed his greatness. Their excitement knew no bounds.

"The canvass opened—it was less a canvass than an ovation. He went through the State—a herculean task—making speeches every day, except Sundays, in the sultry months of summer and fall. People of all classes and both sexes turned out to hear him. He came, as he declared, less on his own errand than on theirs, to vindicate a violated constitution, to rebuke the insult to the honor and sovereignty of the State, to uphold the sacred rights of the people to elect their own rulers. The theme was worthy of the orator, the orator of the subject.

"This may be considered the golden prime of the genius of Prentiss.

His real effective greatness here attained its culminating point. He had the whole State for his audience, and the honor of the State for his subject. Not content with challenging his competitors to the field, he threw down the gauntlet to all comers. Some able opponents accepted the challenge. But in every instance of such temerity, the opposer was made to bite the dust.

"Ladies surrounded the rostrum with their carriages, and added, by their beauty, interest to the scene; there was no element of oratory that his genius did not supply. It was plain to see where his boyhood had drawn its romantic inspiration. His imagination was colored and imbued with the light of the shadowy past, and was richly stored with the unreal but life-like creations, which the genius of Shakspeare and Scott had evoked from the ideal world. He had lingered spell-bound, among the scenes of the medævial chivalry. His spirit had dwelt, until almost naturalized, in the mystic dream-land they peopled—among paladins, and crusaders, and knight-templars; with Monmouth and Percy—with Bois Gilbert and Ivanhoe, and the bold McGregor, with the cavaliers of Rupert, and the iron enthusiasts of Fairfax. As Judge Bullard remarks of him, he had the talent of an Italian improvisatore, and could speak the thought of poetry with the inspiration of oratory, and in the tones of music. The fluency of his speech was unbroken—no syllable unpronounced—not a ripple on the smooth and brilliant tide. Probably he never hesitated for a word in his life. His diction adapted itself, without effort, to the thought; now easy and familiar, now stately and dignified, now beautiful and various as the hues of the rainbow, again compact, even rugged in sinewy strength, or lofty and grand in eloquent declamation. His face and manner were alike uncommon. The turn of his head was like Byron's; the face and action were just what the mind made. The excitement of the features, the motions of the head and body, the gesticulations he used, were all in absolute harmony with the words you heard.

"With such abilities as we have alluded to, and surrounded by such circumstances, he prosecuted the canvass, making himself the equal favorite of all classes. Old Democrats were seen, with tears running down their cheeks, laughing hysterically; and some who, ever since the formation of parties, had voted the Democratic ticket, from coroner up to governor, threw up their hats and shouted for him."

Interesting stories are told of the wonder of his eloquence, in this canvass, how he captivated the back-woodsmen, being, in his speeches to them, as profuse of his classical allusions—gems of his own rich fancy, as he would be before a refined and intellectual audience. He gave the unlettered back-woodsman more credit for appreciating these rarer beauties of a speech than is generally done. They looked upon him with as much wonder, in the fascinating and brilliant display of his eloquence, as the Don Cossacks did upon Murat as he appeared before them on his richly caparisoned steed in all his dashing splendor of dress. At one time a caravan and circus followed him wherever he went, in order to get his audiences. They would often give him their tent gratis, when he would mount the lion's cage, for a rostrum, and in some of his most thrilling passages, would stamp on the cage and arouse the "tawny king of the forest" and the other beasts, which he would sieze and apply to the benefit of his cause ;—" Why, don't you see that the lion and the very beasts of the forest are enraged when I mention the unprecedented course of our opponents.."

" His humor was as various as profound—from the most delicate wit to the broadest farce, from irony to caricature, from classical allusions to the verge—and sometimes beyond the verge—of jest and Falstaff extravagance ; and no one knew in which department he most excelled. His animal spirits flowed over like an artesian well, ever gushing out in a deep, bright, and sparkling current."

"The *personnel* of this remarkable man was well calculated to rivet the interest his character inspired. Though he was low of stature, and deformed in one leg, his frame was uncommonly athletic and muscular ; his arms and chest were well formed, the latter deep and broad ; his head was large, and a model of classical proportions and noble contour. Wise said of it : 'His head I saw was two stories high, with a large "attic" on top, above which was his bump of comparison and veneration.' A handsome face, 'He had a face,' says Baylie Peyton, 'of physiognomical eloquence,' compact brow, massive and expanded, and eyes of dark hazel, full and clear, were fitted for the expression of any passion and flitting shade of feeling and sentiment. His complexion partook of the bilious rather than the sanguine temperament. The skin was smooth and bloodless—no excitement or stimulus hightened its color ; nor did the writer ever see any evidence in his face of irregularity of habits. There was nothing affected or artificial in his manner, though some parts of his printed speeches would seem to indicate this. He was frank and artless as a child, and nothing could have been more winning than his familiar intercourse with the bar, with whom he was always a favorite, and without a rival in their affection."

His native bashfulness in the company of ladies, was rather remarkable. He had but a poor opinion of himself in gay circles. He thought himself slighted by them on account of his lameness. He told Judge Wilkinson that "He never could overcome his timidity before ladies, when," said he, "were I let down any moment, suddenly and unprepared, through the roof, into the British Parliament, I could immediately commence a speech without fear or hesitation." Once out of the drawing-room of ladies, before the bar, on the rostrum, stage or stump, and their presence inspired him. Fine stories are told of his speeches changing—becoming more poetical and glowing as some beautiful lady come into his presence.

In his speech at Natches, which is noted for its refined citizens—the little chivalrous Charlestown of Mississippi—"he was," says Peyton, "the hero of romance in real life. He was ever inspired by the presence of ladies and he poured out the choicest gems of his exhaustless fancy." "The ladies, God bless them," he would say—"in the sincerity of my heart I thank them for their presence on this occasion. I wish I were able to say or conceive something worthy of them—gladly would I bind up my brightest and best thoughts into boquets, and throw them at their feet." Speaking of their heroic courage he went on—"The ladies of Poland stripped the jewels from their delicate fingers and snowy necks, and cast them into the famished treasury of their bleeding country."

Speaking of himself, in a letter to one of his sisters, he says,—"I can not write; I never could express myself freely with pen and paper—my thoughts are too quick."

Judge Wilkinson asked him, in the streets of New York, if he did not think his speeches too imaginative, as he had heard said of them. Prentiss replied, "The natural bent of my mind is to dry and pure ratiocination; but finding early that mankind, from a petit jury to the highest deliberative assembly, are more influenced by illustration than by argument, I have cultivated my imagination in aid of my reason."

While on this visit to his home in the North, he was an invited guest to "Old Faneuil Hall," on the occasion of a dinner given to Webster. The great Statesman introduced him to an applauding audience, who had "called him out" to address them. He said in this speech "That if the Government went down, he wanted it to go down administration first—head-foremost."

What he thought of the administration we can gather from this closing paragraph of his speech on "Defalcation in Congress."

"Let the present Executive be re-elected—let him continue to be guided by the counsels of Mephistocles and Asmodeus, the two familiars who are ever at his elbow—these lords, the one of *letters*, the other of *lies*—and it will not be long that this mighty hall will echo to the voice of an American Representative. The Capitol will have no other use than to attract the curiosity of the passing traveler, who, in melancholy idleness will stop to inscribe on one of these massive pillars, "*Here was a Republic.*"

He was toasted, while on a visit to his home in Portland, Maine, as a "Son of Portland, in whose talents and acquirements the vigor of the North was united to the fertility and luxuriance of the South."

He had scarcely been home over two hours, ere he was interrupted while going in to breakfast,—he was really besieged by invitations to address Whig gatherings whenever he went North—by a gentleman bringing him a letter from a Whig Clay Club, to address a meeting. "Why, they seem to think," said he, "it is as easy for me to make speeches, as it is for a juggler to pull ribbons out of his mouth."

He could always find time to write tender and affectionate letters to his brothers and sisters and always wrote one to his "dear mother," on every New Year's Day, which was filled with the love of a true and loving son. In one to his "dear, sweet sister Anna," he says, "I feel very gloomy, and am sorry to find a tendency to melancholy fast overcoming my natural spirits. It is the worse because I can trace it to no practical cause. It broods over me like a black cloud. I sometimes wish I could lie down, go to sleep and not wake."

How truly Barry Cornwall has described this feeling in the following beautiful lines:—

"A deep and a mighty shadow
Across my heart is thrown,
Like clouds o'er a summer meadow
That a thunder wind hath blown.
The wild rose fancy dieth,
The sweet bird memory flieth
And leaveth me alone!"

He never forgot his friends, nor did his love for the North abate—he always cherished her, and in his speeches made beautiful allusions to her.

"Attachment to his friends," says one of his literary associates at the bar, "was a passion. It was a part of the loyalty to the honorable and chivalric, which formed the sub-soil of his strange and wayward nature. He never deserted a friend. His confidence knew no bounds. It scorned all restraints and considerations of prudence or policy. He made his friends' quarrel his own, and was as guardful of their reputation as his own. He would put his name on the back of their paper, without looking at the face of it, and give his *carte blanche*, if needed, by the quire. He knew no jealousy or rivalry. His love of truth, his fidelity and frankness, were founded on the antique models of the cavaliers.

"The same histrionic and dramatic talent that gave to his oratory so irresistible a charm, and adapted him to all grades and sorts of people, fitted him in conversation to delight all men. He never staled and never flagged. Even if the fund of acquired capital could have run out, his originality was such, that his supply from the perennial fountain within was inexhastible.

"It was always a mooted point among Prentiss' admirers, as to where his strength lay. The emiment Chief-justice of the high court of error and appeals of Mississippi, thought that Prentiss appeared to most advantage before that court. Other distinguished judges said the same thing.

"In arguing a cause of much public interest, he got all the benefit of the sympathy and feeling of the bystanders. He would sometimes turn to them in an impassioned appeal, as if looking for a larger audiance than court and jury, and the excitement of the outsiders, especially in criminal cases, was thrown with great effect into the jury box." He was never thrown off his guard, or seemingly taken by surprise. He kept his temper; or if he got furious, there was 'method in his madness.' He had a faculty of speaking I never knew possessed by any other person. He seemed to speak without any effort of the will. All seemed natural and unpremeditated. No one felt uneasy lest he might fall; in his most brilliant flights the 'empyrean hights' into which he soared seemed to be his natural elements—as the upper air the eagle's. I never heard of but one client of his who was convicted of a charge of homicide, and he was convicted of one of its lesser degrees. So successful was he, that the expression, '*Prentiss could'nt clear him*'—was a hyperbole that expressed the desperation of a criminal's fortunes.

"Among the most powerful of his jury efforts, were his speeches against Bird for the murder of Cameron; and against Phelps—the notorious highway robber and murderer. Both were convicted. The former owed his conviction, as General Foote, who defended him with great zeal and ability, said, to the transcendent eloquence of Prentiss.

"Phelps was one of the most daring and desperate of ruffians. He fronted his prosecutor and court not only with composure, but with scornful and malignant defiance. When Prentiss rose to speak, and for sometime afterwards, the villain scowled upon him a look of hate and violence—attempting to intimidate him with a *brutal stare.*

"But when the orator, kindling with his subject, turned upon him a stream of burning invective, like lava, upon his head; when he depicted the villainy and barbarity of his bloody atrocities; when he pictured, in dark and awful colors, the fate which awaited him, and the awful judgment, to be pronounced at another bar, upon his crimes, when he should be confronted with his innocent victims, when he fixed his gaze of concentrated power upon him, and like the ancient Mariner,

"Held him with his glittering eye,"

the strong man's face relaxed; his eyes faltered and fell; until, at length, unable to bear up longer, self-convicted, he hid his head beneath the bar, and exhibited a picture of ruffian audacity cowed beneath the spell of true courage and triumphant genius. Though convicted, he was not hung. Be broke jail, and resisted re-capture so desperately, that although he was encumbered with his fetters, his pursuers had to kill him in self-defence, or permit his escape."

In his defence of Judge Wilkinson, his learned and esteemed friend, who, as the public knows was tried for the murder of the tailor, of whom he had procured a suit of clothes, from a quarrel arising about the suit, he was as profound as Webster in his reasoning, and unusually animated and impassioned in his eloquence; he was defending the reputation and life of a cherished friend. His invective and sarcasm were poured out upon Redding;—his scathing wit upon Oldham. "Surely," says he, "Mr. Oldham is the knight-errant of the age—the Don Quixote of the West—the paragon of chivalry!" &c., &c.

It is said that Holt, his eminent rival at the Mississippi bar, was the greatest lawyer *prepared* that ever appeared in its courts; and that Prentiss was the greatest *unprepared*. Holt said of him that he was the only man he ever met whose performance was equal to his reputation.

"Nature had gifted him with the lawyer's highest talent—the *acumen* which, like instinct, enabled him to see the points which the record presented. His genius for generalizing saved him, in a moment, the labor of a long and tedious reflection upon, and collection of the several parts of a narrative, or subject. An instance is given of this ability in the following anecdote.

"Prentiss was associated with General M., one of the most distinguished lawyers in the State. During the session of the court, at which time the case was to come on, General M. frequently called the attention of Mr. P. to the case, and proposed examining the records, but he deferred it. At last it was agreed to examine the case the night before the day set for the hearing. At the appointed time Prentiss could not be found. General M. was in great perplexity. The case was of great importance—very able counsel opposed them; his client and himself had trusted greatly to Prentiss' assistance. The next morning the case was called up in court. General M., then young, arose to open the case, as Prentiss came in the court-room, made the points and read the authorities he had collected. The counsel on the other side replied. Prentiss then rose to rejoin. His junior counsel could scarcely conceal his apprehensions. But there was no cloud on the brow of the speaker; the consciousness of his power and of approaching victory sat on his face. He delivered a most masterly speech in which he displayed learning—research, reason—even surpassing the expectations of his friends as he surpassed himself.

Genius seemed, at times, to possess him so entirely as to give him the full portrayal of a subject which he had not studied, then to leave him light enough on it to master it in detail, at his pleasure. That fine literary writer, Rev. Mr. Clapp, of New Orleans, gives an instance of this kind, in an address of Prentiss', before a most enlightened audience of that city, on Sculpture; of which his brother says, "besides being a chance orator, without a moment's preparation, he knew nothing at all; but in which he not only surpassed himself but the expectations of his friends."

His address to the returned volunteers of Taylor's army from Mexico, delivered from the portico of St. Charles Hotel, New Orleans, every body has admired. I have seen soldiers who heard it and spoke of it as having the thrilling effect of martial music on the audience. The address was clothed with all the beauty and brilliancy of a Clay or Choate, and the deep pathos and patriotism, and national pride of a Webster.

His address at a New England festival, was still giving

you more and more of the riches of his mind—something rare—a "fresh dish," as he said to his friends, "they must have something new."

But one of the proudest days of his life was in 1844, when he addressed a Whig Mass Meeting of over forty thousand people, at Nashville, Tennessee. What made this day a greater one, he was the orator selected for this grand occasion by five hundred of Tennessee's fairest daughters, of which fact he was informed by their addressing him a beautiful letter of invitation.

As he ascended the platform and saw the mighty concourse before him, and one, too, that had recently been charmed by the eloquent "Harry of the West," he felt the need of all the magic powers of his oratory. While in the midst of his speech, the greatness of the occasion impressing him, he soared in all the glory of his eloquence —swaying the immense crowd with its charmed power; but he had exerted himself too much—he fainted, and fell back into the arms of Governor Jones, who exclaimed, as he received his eloquent and cherished friend—"Die! Prentiss, *die!* you will never find a more glorious opportunity." The mighty throng were touched with deep sympathy for their idol orator, and cried out,—"Let him rest! bring cordials and restore him! we'll wait!" As he began again, Governor Jones cautioned him to speak with less effort, but it was like restraining the flight of the eagle, he soon become as eloquent as before, and finished this most celebrated speech with a grandeur worthy of the occasion, and worthy of the man.

In his speech at Natches, also, in 1844, he gave that enlightened audience who cherished him as their eloquent Bayard, and who, when they heard the "clump" of his cane on the stage, welcomed him with shouts of applause—a splendid eulogy of Henry Clay, extolling him as one of the great ones of the world. He had a lisp in his speech, which, when he become sarcastic, changed into a "serpent hiss." After he had given this splendid portraiture of Clay, he turned round and asked—"Who was James K. Polk?" A breathless pause for an answer—and he replied in his hissing accent "*A blighted burr that has fallen from the mane of the war-horse of the Hermitage.*"

A by-stander says,—"Old Democrats forgot themselves and joined in the general shout, for the plaudits were terrible—out-voicing the deep toned sea."

He said in the same speech, refering to the wide difference between Walker's two Texas letters, grasping and dashing them under his feet—"I wonder, that like the acid and the alkali, they do not effervesce as they touch each other!"

Here is a beautiful passage from one of his last speeches, and we give it as not only one of his last, but as most beautifully applying to the close of his own life. It was delivered to a large gathering of his friends. He was standing between two trees, on a platform at the close of the day. Taking into consideration every thing connected with the close of this speech—the last noble aspirations of a loving spirit, which it breathes — the self-devotion to every noble cause in which he engaged, the admiration which followed, and the charm in the presence of this brilliant orator, and the approach of a near grave glimmering sadly through the whole, there is perhaps no simile in English composition considering the circumstances and feelings under which it was expressed that casts so touching an interest.

"Friends, that glorious orb reminds me that the day is spent, and that I too must close. Ere we part, let me hope that it may be our good fortune to end our days in the same splendor, and that when the evening of life comes, we may sink to rest with the clouds that close in our departure, gold-tipped with the effulgence of a well-spent life."

We have not spoken of his faults, his vices, he had them; but as one of the fairest daughters of the South, speaking to us of them, remarked, his genius and that noble heart of his, would excuse them all.

A fine writer, and one of his eulogists, says of him:—

"At this day it is difficult for any one to appreciate the enthusiasm which greeted this gifted man, the admiration which was felt for him, and the affection which followed him. He was to Mississippi, in her youth, what Jenny Lind is to the musical world, or what Charles Fox, whom he resembled in many things, was to the Whig party of England in his day. Why he was so it is not difficult to see. He was a type of his times, a representative of the qualities of the people, or rather of the better qualities of the wilder and more impetuous part of them. The proportion of young men, as in all new countries, was great, and the proportion of wild young men, was, unfortunately, still greater.

"He had all those qualities which make us charitable to the character of Prince Hal, as it is painted by Shakspeare, even when our approval is not bestowed. Generous as a price of the royal blood, brave and chivalrous as a knight-templar, of a spirit that scorned every thing mean, underhanded or servile, he was prodigal to improvidence, instant in resentment, and bitter in his animosities; yet magnanimous to forgive when reparation had been made, or misconstruction explained away. There was no littleness about him. Even towards an avowed enemy, he was open and manly, and bore himself with a sort of antique courtesy and knightly hostility, in which self-respect was mingled with respect for his foe, except when contempt was mixed with hatred; then no words can convey any sense of the intensity of his scorn—the depth of his loathing. When he thus out-lawed a man from courtesy and respect, language could scarcely supply words to express his disgust and detestation.

"Even in the vices of Prentiss, there were magnificence and brilliancy imposing in a high degree. When he treated, it was a mass entertainment. On one occasion, he chartered the theatre for the special gratification of himself and friends—the public generally. He bet thousands on the turn of a card, and would witness the success or failure of the wager with the *nonchalance* of a Mexican monte-player, or, as was most usual, with the light humor of a Spanish muleteer.

He broke a faro-bank by the nerve with which he laid his large bets, and by exciting the passion of the veteran dealer, or awed him into honesty by the glance of his strong and steady eye. He never seemed to despond for a moment; the cares and anxieties of life were mere bagatelles to him. Sent to jail for an affray in the court-house he made the walls of the prison resound with the unaccustomed shouts of merriment and revelry. Starting to fight a duel, he laid down his hand at poker, to resume it, he said with a smile, when he returned; and went on the field laughing with his friends as to a pic-nic. Yet no one knew better the proprieties of life than himself—when to put off levity, and to treat grave subjects and persons with proper respect; and no one could assume and preserve more gracefully a dignified and sober demeanor."

For the last four years of his life, practice becoming less remunerative in Mississippi, and having mastered the intricate "Justinian code" of Louisiana, he practiced in his profession at the New Orleans bar. He died in 1850, at the residence of his wife's father, near Natches. We have thus given you what we have gathered from the life and speeches, and from those who knew and have seen and heard this eminent orator. "He had," says a friend of his, "the noblest intellect, and the most chivalrous character that the Almighty ever bestowed upon the human form."

This is S. S. Prentiss, the "limping boy" of Maine, who became the Bayard of Southern chivalry, whose eloquence, like the Mississippi—strong and impressive—flowing amid a region attractive with beauty—grand with picturesque views, and rich with genial and gorgeous scenery, so charmed the sunny South.

But he has gone. He lies buried near that noble river, which first, when he was a mere Yankee boy, "caught his poetic eye, and stirred by its aspects of grandeur, his sublime imagination; upon whose shores first fell his burning and impassioned words as they aroused the rapturous applause of his astonished auditors. And long will that noble river roll out its tide into the gulf, ere the roar of its current shall mingle with the tones of such eloquence again—eloquence as full and majestic, as resistless and sublime, and as wild in its sweep as its own sea-like flood:

> 'The mightiest river
> Rolls mingling with his fame forever.'

"The tidings of his death, came like wailing over the State, and we all heard them as the toll of the bell for a brother's funeral. The chivalrous felt, when they heard that 'young Harry Percy's spur was cold,' that the world had grown common-place; and the men of wit and genius, or those who could appreciate such qualities in others, looking over the surviving bar, exclaimed with a sigh:

> 'The flash of wit, the bright intelligence
> The gleam of mirth—the blaze of eloquence
> Set with HIS sun.'"

And this beautiful allusion from Wordsworth was made to him by a loving brother, but which all felt to be as true as beautiful:

> "The rainbow comes and goes,
> And lovely is the rose;
> The moon doth with delight
> Look round her when the heavens are bare;
> Waters on a starry night are beautiful and fair;
> The sunshine is a glorious birth;
> But yet I know where'er I go,
> That there has passed a glory from the earth."

## COLONEL McCLUNG.

> "And, Douglas, I tell thee here,
> E'en in thy pitch of pride,
> Here, in thy hold, thy vasals near,
> (Nay, ne'er look upon your lord,
> And lay your hand upon your sword,)

I tell thee, thou'rt defied!
And if thou saidst I am not peer
To any lord in Scotland here—
Lowland or Highland, far or near,
Lord Angus, thou hast lied!"

The subject of my memoir is a hero; not ono of "Flodden Field," but of Monterey and Buena Vista. Heroes are plentiful in these days—when opportunities for making them are so plenty.

The "pibroch" has but to sound and—

"Belted Will Howards will come with speed
And Williams of Deloraine—good at need."

Had Colonel McClung lived in the days of Charlemagne, he would have been the Roland of his camp. Had he lived in the time of James IV. of Scotland, he would have been a hero of whom Scott would have made a "Marmion"—

"A stalworth knight and keen—"

for his splendid physique

" ———and strength of limb,
Showed him no carpet knight so trim,
But in close fight, a champion grim,
In camps a leader sage."

Had he had a field for the display of his powers—one in which his genius would have culminated, we cannot say what he would have made—but surely nothing short of a hero.

He would have made a splendid Highland chief—a peer of the proudest, that—

"Ever couched a border lance by knee."

For his nature was imperious—he was a lord of the manor born, and ought to have had his true inheritance. He seemed to be an anachronistic to our times—he belonged to the days of chivalry, he was our Ivanhoe, a disinherited knight.

"Human nature repeats itself in adventure." Colonel McClung was a character of the "feudal days," repeated to us. But fortune plays the clown as she plays the hero with us; she spoiled the "acts," cut short the "scenes," and in place of a hero of the "border feuds," or a true drama of the past being repeated, she turned it into a "farce."

She left Colonel McClung as she did Richard on the field of Bosworth, in tragic want. But he instead of exclaiming, like that hero, "A horse! a horse! my kingdom for a horse!" cried out:—"A Bosworth! a Bosworth! my kingdom for a Bosworth."

We said Colonel McClung had an imperious nature; he grew up with it, and in his triumphant progress to manhood, was adorned with every variety of manly dignity and accomplishment.

If he abused them, 'twas through a want of purpose in his life—the opportunity that makes the man. Wanting this, he lacked restraint; the good and evil grew together; and passion, self-willed and imperious as his nature, controled him.

That he had a very warm, generous and rich nature was shown from the richness of its soil, manifested by the "weeds that grew up and flourished in it." And if he was "morose," it was because they choked up the "herbs of grace" and kept the sunshine from it.

But that you may better understand him, we will give you his "traits" as they were given to us, by a chivalrous son of the South, who knew and admired him.

"Colonel McClung was a native of Kentucky. He first located, after leaving his native State, in Huntsville,

Alabama, but very soon after came to Jackson or Vicksburgh, Mississippi, I am not sure which, to practice in h profession as lawyer. But being of dissipated habits—he both drank and gambled—he never attained a very high distinction at the bar. But his splendid intellect, and great powers as a speaker, and highly cultivated mind—with his knightly bearing—secured for him a circle of admiring friends—especially among the Whigs, of which party he was the 'Belted Will Howard.' He was of a stern, morose and overbearing temper, which doubtless was the chief cause of the difficulties which resulted in the fatal duels that he fought.

"He had the port and air of one who seemed to expect and demand homage of those among whom he moved. He was of splendid form, about six feet high, and admirably well proportioned; just such a model as Rome would have chosen for her gladiatorial exhibitions. He had a large head with full animal and intellectual developement, thick, curly, light, sandy hair, locks which he would twist, like a girl, with the fingers of his right hand, when wholly immersed in thought.

"I have looked at him in this attitude, when some thought having aroused his mind, his eye was that of an enraged tiger, he unconscious, the while, that another eye was upon him. I never saw him turn to speak to even a friend, but if approached, he greeted you very politely. He was always in a debauch or deeply buried in his books. He was one of the most powerful political writers in the State, and the adversary that measured lances with him always knew that he had a foeman worthy of his steel. He was Lieutenant Colonel of the first Mississippi regiment, that won immortal honor at Monterey and Buena Vista, and in an assault upon one of the forts was the first to mount the wall and shout defiance to the foe, when he received a severe wound from a ball that carried away two of his fingers and lodged in his thigh. It is said, I believe, that it passed through both of his thighs. His career in Mexico is well known; he proudly won the title of the 'bravest of the brave.'"

After I had left the South, on visiting that most beautiful of Western villages—Kalamazoo, in Michigan, I was informed that an old favorite servant of Colonel McClung's was residing in that place. Anxious to get anything of the private history of this man, from so good a source, I started out in pursuit of this "vein" of information. After some little search, I came across, in the suburbs of the place, a fine looking negro, hoeing in a garden. I asked his name—it was the one I had been referred to. I asked him if he had ever known Colonel McClung, of Mississippi. His eye kindled, at the mention of that name, with animated pride, as he answered—"Yes, sir, I knew him well. I was his *servant*, sir."

He afterwards informed me that he had been Colonel McClung's hired servant for six years, for which services he received twenty-eight dollars per month, and that he often gave him three or four dollars a week as a "bonus" for kind acts he had performed for him.

The following anecdotes and reminiscences of this distinguished character were written down as they were narrated to me by his servant Jo:

"He was at 'Cooper's Wells,' Mississippi, at the table with some 'choice friends;' and, after wine had brought out his shining qualities—the heroic imprint of the man, as heat brings out anew the figures and imprint upon old coin, he began to relate some of the most thrilling events of his life; and every time he came to the culminating point of the story, that, in which his disperate and heroic valor was shown, he would look over to the other side of the table, at a little, inferior sized man, and exclaim with an emphasis that was enforced by striking his hand on the table,—'*I'm a whale, sir! I'm a whale, sir!*'

"The little fellow, thinking he meant to render him insignificant, stood these repeated taunts as long as he could, then gathering himself up into all of his insulted dignity, he rose from his seat, and retorted with all the taunting force of his voice,—'*And I'm no sardine, sir! I'm no sardine, sir!*'

"At this McClung laid his hand upon his pistol and turning to the little fellow with a look that the enraged tiger gives ere he pounces on his victim—paused—paused to consider whether he had not better extinguish such base affrontery at a blow. But his fierce gaze was met by one as fierce and undaunted from our liliputian hero, who gave him 'eye-shot,' barbed with scorn and defiance. That glance gave McClung an idea of the kind of man he was dealing with, for he resumed himself, and in a few moments was round on the other side of the table making the acquaintance of the man. He considered it better to keep such men his friends, and it was well perhaps; for the little hero had a reputation as a duellist.

"While gambling in a faro-bank, in Vicksburgh, some slight disagreement arose between him and the dealer, S., which soon assumed the form of a quarrel. But S. was too drunk to sustain himself in it, and his friend B. took up the dispute for him, which resulted in challenging Colonel McClung to fight him. The parties met on the accustomed dueling ground, secluded in the little woody 'Hoboken,' across the river from Vicksburgh, and exchanged shots in which Colonel McClung wounded B. in the shoulder.

"At 'Cooper's Wells,' in the Summer of 1853, memorable for the raging of the yellow fever in this part of the South, Colonel McClung and a noted gambler by the name of McCoy, had been on a 'spree' for several days when a word of discord was dropped by one of them, that brought on a high dispute in which McCoy challenged McClung to meet him on the *field of honor*; which McClung took in such high dudgeon, that, with his boot, he attacked him 'where it hurts honor the most'—he literally kicked him down stairs."

The following is an instance of his chivalrous nature—one in which he made another's insult his own:

"In an affray," says Jo, "that took place in a coffee-house, in Vicksburgh, I saw a man in a quarrel with a negro, kick the latter out doors, at which Colonel McClung, thinking the negro was highly abused, became so exasperated, that he kicked the man out after him; which he instead of resenting, settled by inviting McClung to drink a flowing bumper with him at the bar. Sometime after this as Colonel McClung was passing St. Charles Hotel, New Orleans, he saw the man of Vicksburgh coffee-house notoriety, kicking some one out of the bar-room of that Hotel, upon which McClung stopped and eyed him with something of amazement, which our hero recognizing, came up to him and familliarly putting his hand upon his shoulder, remarked.—'Ah, Colonel, say nothing about the old affair, it takes *us* to do these things—*you and I know who to kick.*' "

Another instance in which he made a friend's quarrel his own was related:

"A Mr. B., broken in health, and somewhat impaired in mind, got into some dispute with another gentleman, which Colonel McClung, on account of his friend's infirm state of health, took up for him. The parties accordingly met on the 'old duel ground.' There appeared to have been a peculiar or malignant type of hate between McClung and his antagonist, which might have arisen from the former's esteem for his friend, and the idea of his being challenged when not in a proper state of health to defend himself; be this as it may, McClung had some of the 'Achillean revenge' in him, when he came upon the ground, for he most tauntingly asked his adversary to give him, as a memorial of him, a rich diamond pin that glittered on his bosom. This he refused to do. 'Then d——n you,' said McClung, 'I'll blow it through your heart.' The threat did not fail in being executed; he sent the glittering gem through his heart. Thus he left another antagonist dead on the field of honor.

"While listening to a political speech, at New Carthage, from his opponent for the Legislature, Colonel McClung, exclaimed to one of his assertions—'that's a d——d lie.' The speaker paused, left the stand, and swore he would 'whip the man that gave that calumnious fling.' But on being shown the man that had so terribly incensed him—Lo, it was Colonel McClung! He was surprized—flurried and entirely incapable of carrying out his threat. He curbed his wrath, and invited McClung up to a stand, hard by, beneath an oak tree, and—*treated him.*

"Mr. P., a wealthy planter, was called the 'best pistol shot' in Mississippi, and Colonel McClung the next. A challenge passed between this 'Roland and Oliver;' they met and McClung left him seriously, wounded on the field.

"I am confident," says Jo, "it is putting it down low enough to say that he has fought a dozen duels, and in five or six of them, he 'stuck his man on the daisies.'

"The last man he shot was in a Hotel in Jackson, Mississippi. This sad castrophe was the result of a quarrel with this gentleman. He shot him down dead in the bar-room.

"I heard him relate," says my informant, "the following story of his adventures in the Mexican war:

"He was riding out one afternoon, toward sunset, when suddenly, from a dense chaparral, seven guerrillas sprang out, like tigers from a jungle, and fiendishly attacked him with their sabres."

Now

"Good night to Marmion."

"But fear not—doubt not—which thou wilt,
He'll try this quarrel hilt to hilt."

"Seeing himself beset by this hoard, he multiplied himself for the occasion, and dealt them the blows of a *'Ceur de Leon,'* while they plied him with cuts and deadly thrusts on all sides, giving him a deep sabre-wound on his head over his right eye, and two on the left shoulder; yet he fought like the hero of a thousand battles, till five of them were unhorsed and lay dead or wounded on the ground."

"Each stepping where his comrade stood,
The instant that he fell."

"But the two remaining ones fought on with desperation, determined to kill their dreadful foe, till one of them, assured from his fighting that they had a hero to deal with, cried out to his companion, in Spanish,—*'This must be Colonel McClung, for he fights like a bull dog.'*

"At which, McClung, who understood Spanish, cried out,—'Yes, you d——d wretches, I am Colonel McClung, but you will not escape to tell that you ever met him in battle,' saying which, he sent one headlong to the ground with a blow of his sword, and the other took flight and escaped."

"My name," says our narrator, "is Charles La Crouix, but Jo was a favorite name with Colonel McClung, he called all of his servants by that name; it was necessary to be 'Joed' ere they became his servants. He would often, when under the spell of liquor, call out at the top of his voice—'Jo,—Jo,—Jo,'—as if he loved to dwell on that soft monosyllable.

"When he had been drinking I always took care of his money, which would sometimes amount to fifteen hundred or two thousand dollars, and sometimes he had not enough to pay his tavern bills. I have known him, when sober, to be up night after night, doing nothing but walking backwards and forwards, all night long, with two, and sometimes three candles burning."—Here Jo got up and showed me how he walked the room—"With arms folded this way," says he, "like an Alexander, and with the most perfect military tread I ever saw—he moved as straight as a Choctaw. If any one spoke to him while thus walking and talking to himself, he would stop, take off his hat, give you a gentlemanly attention, and having heard what you had to say, would answer you very politely and correctly.

"He lived in Jackson the most of the time when I was his servant, where he owned several houses and lots. He never married but was very fond of the society of ladies."

"Ever the first to scale a tower
As venturous in a lady's bower."

"He would often ride out with them in his carriage, for he was a great favorite with them, and in their society he was a very polite gentleman as he was always when sober, and was never inclined to be quarrelsome or insult any one; and no gentleman could insult him. His maxim was:

"A moral, sensible and well-bred man,
Will not affront me; and no other can."

This is the end of Jo's narrative.

Colonel McClung was twice the candidate of his party for a seat in Congress and twice defeated. He had entertained no doubt of his election in this last contest, and the defeat came upon him like that of Philippi upon Brutus, he was terribly chagrined, and felt from his inmost soul, that:

"Nor poppy nor mandragora,
Nor all the drowsy sirups of the East
Could medicine him again to that sweet sleep
Which he knew yesternight."

That which made his opponent sleep well, had "murdered sleep" for him. "His doom was a sad, though perhaps not a strange one, when the history of his life is impartially reviewed. It was one of violence and blood. In a moment of apparent calmness and composure, he cut short his own life by blowing out his brains."

He has passed through a life of sad reverses to escape which, he finally made a desperate "retreat." And now:

"After life's fitful fever he sleeps well."

But, traveler, stop not to weep over his grave, pass on:

"O, 'tis well the strife is o'er:
Fold his mantle o'er his breast,
Peacefully he sleeps and blest,
Let him rest."

Pass on; and when the ringing of "fame's old bells" shall tell of valorous and heroic deeds in war, think that they rung for *him* once at Monterey and Beuna Vista, when,

"Old Zack! Old Zack! the war-cry rattles,
Among those men of iron tread,
As rung 'Old Fritz' in Europe's battles,
When thus his host Great Frederick led."

## COLONEL JEFFERSON DAVIS.

Of this distinguished son of the South we have no reminiscences, but give the following notice of him by a Northern young lady, who made a trip down the Mississippi with Colonel Davis, as it exhibits a fine trait of the man.

"Senator Davis I like very much, and when I tell you that upon our arrival in Vicksburgh, he went to the officer of the 'McRae'—the boat we took for Deer Creek—and requested him, as a personal favor, to see that everything was arranged for my comfort and convenience during the trip, and that I knew nothing of this until Mr. Porterfield told me, you will acknowledge that he possesses as much chivalry and courtesy for the fair sex as he has credit for in the 'Southern World.'

He is plain in dress and appearance, but possesses great suavity of manner, and is one of the most brilliant conversationalists I ever listened to. The "casket" is rough, but it contains

"A gem of purest ray serene."

On our passage down the Mississippi the passengers, more particularly the ladies, were very anxious to hear his views on the present topics of the day. They hence addressed him a very polite note to that effect, when they received the following from him:

STEAMER J. C. SWAN, MARCH 20TH, '59.

LADIES AND GENTLEMEN;

Accept my grateful acknowledgements of your kind invitation to hear my views upon the public questions which concern the welfare of our common country.

Flattered by the wish you express, and willing at all times to interchange opinions with my fellow-countrymen upon the issues which it devolves upon us to decide, I regret that my physical condition will not permit me to comply with your request in the manner indicated.

In the present posture of affairs, there is much to excite the patriotic anxiety of our people, and to arouse to earnest effort every citizen of the land. Blessed with an inheritance of peculiar value, won by the blood of our ancestors, it requires but a small part of the wlsdom and virtue of those from whom we are descended, to secure the transmission of the institutions we enjoy, to posterity. And I trust, however gloomy our prospects may be, that the cloud will pass as the April shower, leaving to us the sun of our political existence all the brighter for the temporary shadow which obscured it.

Our government was formed to bless the people by the conjoint action of the sovereignties united for the common good. Its powers were defined and restricted so as to ensure its action for the protection of all, and to prohibit the oppression of any. Its benefits, whilst its true theory is adhered to, will fall like the gentle dew. To pervert it to other than the purposes for which it was established, would be treason to our fathers, to our children, and to the hopes of human liberty which hang upon their last best efforts for the maintenance of self government.

With my best wishes for your individual welfare and happiness,

I am your obliged fellow citizen.

JEFF. DAVIS.

# MIKE FINK

THE

# BOB ROY OF THE MISSISSIPPI VALLEY,

AND

## THE LAST OF THE BOATMEN.

———o———

"My foot is on my native heath, and my name is McGregor."

SCOTT.

We are indebted to an old cast-aside, and time-worn volume that we chanced to find among old forsaken books, for much of the following brief sketch of this interesting character.

"Back out! Mannee! and try it again!" exclaimed a voice from the shore.

"Throw your pole wide, and brace off, or you'll run against a snag!"

This was a kind of language long familiar to us on the Ohio. It was a sample of the slang of the keel-boatmen.

The speaker was immediately cheered by a dozen voices from the deck, and I recognized in him the person of an old acquaintance, familiarly known to me from my boyhood. He was leaning carelessly against a large beach; and as his arm negligently pressed a rifle to his side, presented a figure that Salvator would have chosen from a million as a model for his wild and gloomy pencil. His stature was upwards of six feet, his proportion perfectly symmetrical and exhibiting the evidence of herculean power. To a stranger he would have seemed a complete mulatto. Long exposure to the sun and weather on the lower Ohio and Mississippi, had changed his skin; and but for the fine European cast of his countenance, he might have passed for the principal warrior of some powerful tribe. Although at least fifty years of age, his hair was as black as the wing of a raven. Next to his skin he wore a red flannel shirt, covered with a blue capot, ornamented with white fringe. On his feet were moccasins, and a broad leathern belt, from which hung suspended in a sheath a large knife, encircled his waist.

U

As soon as the steam-boat became stationary, the cabin passengers jumped on shore. On ascending the bank, the figure I have just described advanced to offer me his hand.

"How are you, Mike?" said I.

"How goes it?" replied the boatman, grasping my hand with a squeeze that I could compare to nothing but a blacksmith's vice.

"I am glad to see you, Mannee!" continued he in his abrupt manner. "I am going to shoot at the tin cup for a quart—off hand, and you must be judge."

I understood Mike at once, and on any other occasion would have remonstrated, and prevented the daring trial of skill. But I was accompanied by a couple of English tourists, who had scarcely ever been beyond the sound of Bow Bells; and who were traveling post over the United States to make up a book of observations, on our manners and customs. There were also among the passengers a few bloods from Philadelphia and Baltimore, who could conceive of nothing equal to Chesnut or Howard streets, and expressed great disappointment at not being able to find terrapins and oysters at every village, marvellously lauding the comforts of Rubicum's. My tramontane pride was aroused and I resolved to give them an opportunity of seeing a Western Lion, for such Mike undoubtedly was—in all his glory. The philanthropist may start, and accuse me of want of humanity. I deny the charge and refer for apology to one of the best understood principles of human nature.

Mike, followed by several of his crew, led the way to a beach grove, some little distance from the landing. I invited my fellow passengers to witness the scene. On arriving at the spot, a stout, bull-headed boatman, dressed in a hunting shirt, but bare-footed, in whom I recognized a younger brother of Mike, drew a line with his toe; and stepping off thirty yards, turned round fronting his brother, took a tin cup which hung from his belt, and placed it on his head. Although I had seen this feat performed before, I acknowledge I felt uneasy, whilst this silent preparation was going on. But I had not much time for reflection, for this second Albert exclaimed, "Blaze away Mike! and let's have the quart."

My *compagnons de voyage*, as soon as they recovered from the first effect of this astonishment, exhibited a disposition to interfere. But Mike, throwing back his left leg, leveled the rifle at the head of his brother. In this horizontal position the weapon remained for some seconds as immovable as if the arm which held it was affected by no pulsation.

"Elevate your piece a little lower, Mike! or you will pay the corn," cried the imperturbable brother.

I know not if the advice was obeyed or not; but the sharp crack of the rifle immediately followed and the cup flew off thirty or forty yards, rendered unfit for future service. There was a cry of admiration from the strangers, who pressed forward to see if the fool-hardy boatman was really safe. He remained as immovable as if he had been a figure hewn out of stone. He had not even winked when the ball struck within a few inches of his skull.

"Mike has won!" I exclaimed; and my decision was the signal which, according to their rules, permitted him of the target to move from his position. No more sensation was exhibited by the boatmen, than if a common wager had been won. The bet being decided, they hurried back to their boat, giving me and my friends an invitation to partake of "the treat." We declined and took leave of the thoughtless creatures. In a few minutes afterwards, we observed their "keel" wheeling into the current—the gigantic form of Mike bestriding the large steering oar, and the others arranging themselves in their places in front of the cabin, that extended nearly the whole length of the boat, covering merchandise of immense value. As they left the shore, they gave the Indian yell, and broke out into a sort of unconnected chorus, commencing with—

"Hard upon the beech oar!
She moves too slow!
All the way to Shawnee town,
Long while ago."

In a few moments the boat "took the chute" of Letart's Falls, and disappeared behind the point, with the rapidity of an Arabian courser.

Our travelers returned to the boat, lost in speculation on the scene, and the beings they had just beheld; and no doubt the circumstance has been related a thousand times with all the necessary amplification of finished tourists.

Mike Fink may be viewed as a correct representation of a class of men now extinct; but who once possessed as marked a character, as that of the Gypsies of England, or the Lazaroni of Naples. The period of their existence was not more than a third of a century. The character was created by the introduction of trade on the Western waters; and ceased with the successful establishment of the steamboat.

There is something inexplicable in the fact, that there could be men found, for ordinary wages, who would abandon the systematic, but not laborious pursuit of agriculture, to follow a life of all others, except that of a soldier, distinguished by the greatest exposure and privations. The occupation of a boatman was more calculated to destroy the constitution, and to shorten life than any other business. In ascending the river, it was a continual series of toil, rendered more irksome by the snail-like rate at which they moved. The boat was propelled by poles, against which the shoulder was placed; and the whole strength and skill of the individual were applied in this manner. As the boatmen moved along the running-board, with their heads nearly touching the plank on which they walked, the effect produced on the mind of the observer was similar to that, on beholding the ox rocking before an overloaded cart. Their bodies naked to the waist, for the purpose of moving with greater ease, and of enjoying the breeze of the river, were exposed to the burning suns of summer, and the rains of autumn. After a hard day's push, they would take their "fillee," or ration of whisky, and having swallowed a miserable supper of meat half burnt, and of bread half baked, stretch themselves, without covering, on the deck, and slumber till the steersman's call invited them to the morning "fillee." Notwithstanding this, the boatman's life had charms as irresistible as those presented by the splendid illusions of the stage. Sons abandoned the comfortable farms of their fathers, and apprentices fled from the service of their masters. There was a captivation in the idea of "going down the river;" and the youthful boatman who had "pushed a keel" from New Orleans felt all the pride of a young merchant, after his first voyage to an English sea-port. From an exclusive association together they had formed a kind of slang peculiar to themselves; and from the constant exercise of wit, with "the squatters" on shore, and crews of other boats, they acquired a quickness and smartness of vulgar retort, that was quite amusing. Another writer says of them:

No wonder the way of life the boatmen lead, should always have seductions that prove irresistible to the young people that live near the banks of the river. The boats float by their dwellings on beautiful spring mornings, when the verdant forest, the mild and delicious temperature of the air, the delightful azure of the sky of this country, the fine bottom on the one hand and the romantic bluff on the other, the broad smooth stream rolling calmly down the forest, and floating the boat gently forward, all these circumstances harmonize in the excited youthful imagination. The boatmen are dancing to the violin on the deck of the boat. They scatter their wit among the girls on the shore, who come down to the water's edge to see the pageant pass. The boat glides on until it disappears behind a point in the wood. At this moment, perhaps the bugle, with which all the boats are provided, strikes up its note in the distance over the water. These scenes, and these notes, echoing from the bluffs of the beautiful Ohio, have a charm for the imagination, which, although I have heard a thousand times repeated, and at all hours, and in all positions, is even to me always new, and always delightful. No wonder the young who were reared in these remote regions, with that restless curiosity that is fostered by solitude and silence, who witness such scenes so frequently, no wonder that the severe and unremitting labors of agriculture, performed directly in the view of such scenes, should became tasteless and irksome.

But these men thus inured to hardships became, from the frequent battles they engaged in, with the boatmen of different parts of the river, and with the less civilized inhabitants of the lower Ohio and Mississippi, invested with a famous and rather ferocious reputation, which has made them spoken of in this country and throughout Europe.

On board of the boats thus navigated, our merchants entrusted valuable cargoes, without insurance, and with no other guarantee than the receipt of the steersman, who possessed no property but his boat; and the confidence so reposed was seldom abused. And wonderful to relate, these boats were pulled up from New Orleans to Pittsburgh by twenty or thirty half naked Creoles, a laborious task of six months or more. Sometimes they were pulled up by long rōpes hitched to trees ahead, or by hooking long stout canes in the roots of trees on the banks, assisted by men pushing at the pole.

Among these men Mike Fink stood an acknowledged leader for many years. Endowed by nature with those qualities of intellect, that give the possessor influence, he would have been a conspicuous member in any society in which his lot might have been cast. An acute observer of human nature has said, "Opportunity alone makes the hero. Change but their situations, and Cæsar would have been but the best wrestler on the green."

With a figure cast in a mould that added much of the symmetry of an Apollo to the limbs of a Hercules, he possessed gigantic strength, and accustomed from an early period of his life to brave the dangers of a frontier life, his character was noted for the most daring intrepidity. At the court of Charlemagne, he might have been a Roland; with the Crusaders he would have been the favorite of the Knight of the Lion-heart, and in our revolution he would have ranked with the Morgans and Putnams of the day. He was the hero of a hundred fights, and the leader in a thousand daring adventures. From Pittsburgh to St. Louis and New Orleans, his fame was established. Every farmer on shore kept on good terms with Mike; otherwise there was no safety for his property. Wherever he was an enemy, like his great prototype, Rob Roy, he levied the contributions of Black Mail, for the use of his boat. Often at night, when his retired companions slept, he would take an excursion of five or six miles, and return before morning rich in spoil. On the Ohio, he was known among his companions by the appellation of the "Snapping Turtle;" and on the Mississippi, he was called "The Snag."

At the early age of seventeen Mike's character was displayed by enlisting himself in a corps of Scouts—a body of irregular rangers which was employed on the north-western frontier of Pennsylvania, to watch the Indians, and to give notice of any threatened inroad.

At that time Pittsburgh was on the extreme verge of white population, and the spies who were constantly employed generally extended their explorations forty or fifty miles to the west of this post. They went out singly, lived as did the Indians, and in every respect became perfectly assimilated in habits, taste and feeling, with the red men of the forest. A kind of border warfare was kept up, and the Scout thought it as praiseworthy to bring in the scalp of a Shawnee, as the skin of a panther. He would remain in the wood for weeks together, using parched corn for bread, and depending on his rifle for his meat, and slept at night in perfect comfort, rolled in his blanket.

In this corps, while yet a stripling, Mike acquired a reputation for boldness and cunning, far beyond his companions. A thousand legends illustrate the fearlessness of his character. There was one, which he told himself, with much pride, and which made an indelible impression on my boyish memory. He had been sent out on the hills of Mahoning, when, to use his own words, he "saw signs of Indians being about." He had discovered the recent print of the moccasin in the grass, and found drops of the fresh blood of a deer on the green bush. He became cautious, skulked for some time in the deepest thickets of hazle and briar, and for several days did not discharge his rifle. He subsisted patiently on parched corn and jerk, which he had dried on his first coming into the wood. He gave no alarm to the settlements, because he discovered with perfect certainty that the enemy consisted of a small hunting party, who were receding from the Alleghany.

As he was creeping along, one morning, with the stealthy tread of a cat, his eye fell upon a beautiful buck, browsing on the edge of a barren spot, three hundred yards distant. The temptation was too strong for the woodsman, and he resolved to have a shot at every hazard. Repriming his gun, and picking his flint, he made his approaches in the usual noiseless manner. At the moment he reached the spot from which he meant to take aim, he observed a large Indian intent on the same object, advancing from a direction a little different from his own. Mike shrunk behind a tree with the quickness of thought, and keeping his eye fixed on the hunter, waited the result with patience. In a few minutes the Indian halted, within fifty paces, and leveled his piece at the deer. In the meanwhile Mike presented his rifle at the body of the savage; and at the moment the smoke issued from the gun of the latter, the bullet of Fink passed through the red man's breast. He uttered a yell and fell dead at the same instant with the deer. Mike re-loaded his rifle, and remained some minutes, to ascertain whether there were any more enemies at hand. He then stepped up to the prostrate savage, and having satisfied himself that life was extinguished, turned his attention to the buck, and took from the carcass those pieces suited to the process of jerking.

In the meantime, the country was filling up with a white population; and in a few years the red men, with the exception of a few fractions of tribes, gradually receded to the lakes and beyond the Mississippi. The corps of Scouts was abolished, after having acquired habits that unfitted them for the pursuits of civilized society. Some incorporated themselves with the Indians; and others from a strong attachment to their erratic mode of life, joined the boatmen, then just becoming a distinct class. Among these was our hero, Mike Fink, whose talents were soon developed; and for many years he was as celebrated on the rivers of the West as he had been in the woods.

I gave to my fellow-travelers the substance of the foregoing narration, as we sat on deck by moonlight, and cut swiftly through the magnificent sheet of water between Litart and the Great Kanawha. It was one of those beautiful nights, which permitted everything to be seen without danger, yet created a certain degree of illusion, that gives range to the imagination. The outline of the river hills lost all of its harshness; and the occasional bark of the house-dog from the shore, and the distant scream of the solitary loon gave increased effect to the scene. It was altogether so delightful, that the hours till morning flew swiftly by, while our travelers dwelt with rapture on the surrounding scenery, which shifted every moment like capricious changes of the Kaleidoscope—and listening to tales of border warfare, as they were brought to mind by passing the places where they happened. The celebrated hunter's leap, and the bloody battle of Kanawha were not forgotten. The origin of the name of the former to this point is thus given: A man named Huling, was hunting on the hill above Point Pleasant, when he was discovered by a party of Indians. They pursued him to a precipice of more than sixty feet, over which he sprang and escaped. The next morning, visiting the spot with some neighbors, it was discovered that he had leaped over the top of a sugar-tree, which grew at the bottom of the hill.

The afternoon of the next day brought us to the beautiful city of Cincinnati, which in the course of thirty years has risen from a village of soldier huts to a town, giving promise of future splendor equal to any on the sea-board.

Some years after the period at which I have dated my visit to Cincinnati, business called me to New Orleans. On board of the steamboat on which I had embarked at Louisville, I recognized in the person of the pilot one of those men who had formerly been a patroon, or keel-boat captain. I entered into conversation with him on the subject of his former associates.

"They are scattered in all directions," said he, "A few, who had the capacity, have become pilots of steamboats. Many have joined the trading parties that cross the Rocky Mountains, and a few have settled down as farmers."

"What has become," I asked, "of my old acquaintance, Mike Fink?"

"Mike," said he, with a sigh, "ah! Mike was at last killed in a skrimmage. When the 'steam craft' began to usurp control of the river trade, Mike left—his rights were intruded on. But in order to retain him they made him many good offers on board of the steamboats. It was of no use. He said he hated the hissing of steam, and he wanted room to throw his pole. He went to Missouri, and about a year since was shooting the tin cup, when he was corned too heavy. He elevated too low, and shot his companion through the head. A friend of the deceased who was present, suspecting foul play, shot Mike through the heart before he had time to re-load his rifle."

With Mike Fink expired the spirit of the boatmen.

"There beneath the breezy West
Let the untutored Hector rest."

## OLD PETER CARTWRIGHT AND MIKE FINK.

The following anecdote is related by the Rev. James B. Finley, fellow-soldier with this redoubtable Methodist minister who is said to have come off conqueror in all his numerous fights with both "men and bears."

At a camp-meeting held at Alton in the autumn of 1833, the worshipers were annoyed by a set of desperadoes from St. Louis, under the control of Mike Fink, a notorious bully, the triumphant hero of countless fights, in none of which he ever met an equal, or even second. The coarse, drunken ruffians carried it with a high hand, outraged the men and insulted the women, so as to threaten the dissolution of all pious exercises; and yet such was the terror the name of their leader, Fink, inspired, that no one could be found brave enough to face his prowess.

At last one day when Cartwright ascended the pulpit to hold forth, the desperadoes, on the outskirts of the encampment, raised a yell so deafening as to drown utterly every other sound. The preacher's dark eyes shot lightning. He deposited his Bible, drew off his coat, and remarked aloud:

"Wait for a few minutes, my brethren, while I go and make the devil pray."

He then proceeded with a smile on his lips to the focus of the tumult, and addressed the chief bully:

"Mr. Fink, I have come to make you pray."

The desperado rubbed back the tangled festoons of his blood-red hair, arched his huge brows with a comical expression, and replied:

"By golly, I'd like to see you do it, old snorter!"

"Very well," said Mr. Cartwright, "will these gentlemen, your courteous friends, agree not to show foul-play?"

"In course they will. They're rale grit, and wont do nothing but the clear thing, so they wont," rejoined Fink indignantly.

"Are you ready?" asked the preacher.

"Ready as a race-hoss with a light rider," answered Fink, squaring his ponderous person for the combat.

The bully spoke too soon; for scarcely had the words left his lips when Cartwright made a prodigious bound toward his antagonist, and accompanied it with a quick shooting punch of his herculean fist, which fell crushing the other's chin, and hurried him to the earth like lead. Then even his intoxicated companions, filled with involuntary admiration at the feat, gave a cheer. But Fink was up in a moment, and rushed upon his enemy exclaiming:

"That warn't done fair, so it warn't."

He aimed a ferocious stroke, which the preacher parried off with his left hand, and, grasping his throat with his right, crushed him down as if he had been an infant. Fink struggled, squirmed and writhed in the dust, but all to no purpose, for the strong, muscular fingers held his windpipe, as in the jaws of an iron vice. When he began to turn purple in the face, and ceased to resist, Mr. Cartwright slacked his hold, and inquired,

"Will you pray now?"

"I doesn't know a word how," gasped Fink, "because you're the devil himself."

The preacher then said over the Lord's prayer line by line, and the conquered bully responded in the same way, when the victor permitted him to rise. At the consummation the rowdies roared three boisterous cheers, and Fink shook Cartwright by the hand, exclaiming,

"By golly! you're some beans in a bar-fight. I'd rather set to with an old he-bar in dog-days. You can pass this crowd of nose-smashers, blast your pictur!"

Afterwards Fink's party behaved with decorum, the preacher resumed his Bible and pulpit."

This anecdote is undoubtedly true, only, Mike Fink's hair, instead of being "blood-red," was as black as the wing of a raven; and years before the event of this story transpired he had "passed that bourne whence no traveler returns"—all the rest is true.

---

## FAREWELL TO THE SOUTH.

"How oft, within yon pleasant shade,
   Has evening closed my careless eye;
How oft, along these banks I've strayed,
   And watched the wave that wandered by;
Full long their loss shall I bewail;
Farewell thou beauteous, sunny vale.

"Good-bye to all! to friend and foe!
   Few foes I leave behind;
I bid to all, before I go,
   A long farewell, and kind.

"Here's a health to thee, fair South,
   In a parting cup of wine;
Farewell to thy sunny vales,
   'Land of the myrtle and vine.'"

PIKE.

Spring came with many new bird-songs and "bokies." The summer followed, with her warm sunny months; and then came autumn—dreamy, rich, golden and glorious autumn—which we enjoyed exceedingly till past mid-October, when we concluded to return home. We did so with regret, but our illness, which we thought would be more serious, would not, on the subject of staying, be compromised with; and to Dr. Hanlin of Satartia, whose kind services were given to me for over two week's sickness, free of charge, and to Dr. Leet of Yazoo City for his gratuitous and generous aid in sickness, let me here trace a grateful memory. And now, courteous reader, we are to take our leave of you and the sunny South at the same time. You have followed us in our adventures here, and sojourned with us in this pleasant land; and in taking our leave of you, we return many, very many thanks for the favor you have shown us in the perusal of these jottings. Coleridge once saw a volume of Thompson's Seasons lying on a table in a wayside Inn, in Wales, and remarked, "This is fame." We are not eager for fame, but were we assured that the reader had been interested in persuing these jottings, we should be half inclined to solace ourselves with the reflection—"This is fame." But are you going to take your leave without saying a word about Slavery? Why not give us a protrait of it South—as you have seen it South? My dear friends, once on a time Apelles, the celebrated painter of Greece, subjected a fine portrait to the criticisms of the people. You know the result; he had to withdraw it, or the critics would have spoiled it.

But in bidding this sunny land farewell, we could not consider it a final one. We felt like leaving a country and people whom it would be pleasant to visit again. There is so much nature South, and she is so much in bloom, and in her smiling summer time, that she has fairly wooed and won us. No where have we seen so little winter, and no where have we heard so little grumbling about the weather as in this clime.

The reader will pardon us, if we scatter a few ideas from the writings of a celebrated tourist in Italy, among those of our own, about this Italy of ours. With the exception of the Indian summer, and here and there through the spring and the hot months, there is no weather tempered so finely, North, that one would think of passing the day in merely enjoying it; but life is spent by those who have the misfortune to be idle or invalid, in more continual dread of the elements than here. The atmosphere, at the North, is the first of the necessaries of life. In the South, it is more the first of its luxuries. You breathe without thinking of this common act, but as a means of arriving at happiness. Here, to breathe and to walk abroad are of themselves happiness. Day after day, week after week, month after month, you wake with the breath of flowers coming in at your window, to look out upon a sky of serene and lovely blue, and mornings and evenings of heavenly beauty. The few rainy and unpleasant days are forgotton in the long halcyon months of sunshine. It is surely the country for the idler and the invalid—the wholesome fare of the tables, and the healthful air of the houses, are a specific remedy for the latter. Then it is delicious here to do nothing—delicious to stand an hour and let the loveliness of the weather, and the charm of scenery impress you. It is delicious to sit away the long silent noon in the shade of the verandah, or China trees; delicious to be with a friend without the interchange of an idea; to dabble in a book, or to fall into one of those delicious fits, "like dozes in sermon time," and no where, as you seek your couch for the night, is it so delicious to have sleep shed its poppies over you. This appears like describing a Utopia. But it is what the South seemed to us.

Life may be the reverse of Monsieur Jourdan's talk—all poetry, but one may live ignorant of it, while another may enjoy it all, if not alloyed with too much anxiety and care. Life South has a value so different from one in the colder Northern regions, one of so much less care that you seem to like to live it more, and there is no more need of your being deprived of its enjoyment than of the deliciousness of Southern peaches. Often have I thought of the lovely day in mid-October, when I bade my friends in the Yazoo valley adieu—stepped on board the steamer "Home," and as she pushed off from the shore, bade this Southern clime farewell—leaving one of the happiest years of my life in this "land of the myrtle and vine," but carrying home with me the most pleasant memories of its beauteous snowy vales and sunny hills, its companionable seasons, its lovely skies and Italian sunsets.

My trip home is too uneventful for detail; it would be merely reading a trip down the Mississippi turned northward. The perils I encountered on the commencement are the most exciting part of it. The yellow fever was not only raging at Vicksburgh, where I must stop, perhaps, a day or two, in order to get a Mississippi steamer that might have it aboard, for St. Louis; but it was also liable to be on any of the Yazoo steamers—and the "Home," the one I did take, was reputed to have lost recently one of her hands by this disease. In our present illness, we not only had this fear of disease, but an anxiety to get home to worry us. A day and night's sail down the Yazoo, and we were at Vicksburgh, eight o'clock in the morning. Here, of course, I was to "belay me" till a steamer bound for St. Louis came along. In the event that none did come, ere the "Home" left, which was at noon, I was to go back with her a few miles up stream, rather than to risk my life by exposing it to this terrible disease, and stop with some planter on the banks of the Mississippi and there wait till I could hail a steamer bound for St. Louis. This was the safe advice of my gentlemanly and worthy friend, Captain M———, to whom I am indebted for the kindness and attention he has shown me, and also to his very gentlemanly clerk. Captain M——— is a Northerner, and while we send such worthy citizens to her, the South cannot hate us without some noble exceptions.

His excellent steamer, "Home," is the favorite of the Yazoo Valley. But as soon as we got to Vicksburgh, imagine me seated on the hurricane deck, looking down the "Great Father of Waters" that swept by me with its restless current on, and onward to the ocean, for a steamboat to come in sight. And then again, as Ulysses seated on a commanding point, on the Island of Ogygia, looked with a longing desire towards his dear Ithica, and thought of his beloved Penelope and Telemachus, imagine me gazing up the Mississippi, and thinking of my dear North, and the loved ones at home. Thus, for two hours, I, in pensive musing, sat watching. Now and then I would look up into the city, and think how many of those beautiful and happy homes were mourning the loss of some loved one, that had fallen a victim, in all the joyousness of life, to the dreadful disease now raging in and around them. Then again as I turned and looked to the other side of the river, the Hoboken of Vicksburgh, I could imagine, just beyond those clumps of trees, parties grouped together, listen to their low but distinct talking about something of intense interest—hear

"That strange, quick jar upon the ear,
The cocking of the pistol———."

then the dreaded word given, then the sharp report; and, "ah, woeful then," I could see, had I not closed my eyes, but

"My eyes make pictures when they're shut,"

and the scene went on, despite me, to its tragic end. One of the group lay dying on the green earth, which he had so lately trod in all the glory of manhood. The rest stood in mute sorrow around him. As I turned from this imaginary scene and looked down the river again, a small white cloud, just rising above the tops of the trees, among which the river wound out of sight, caught my gaze. Soon I could see white, nodding plumes come tossing up in sight, and then, not an army with banners, but the top of a steam-pipe, then another, and then the hulk of a steamer came puffing round a bend in the current—

"Then felt I as some watcher of the skies,
When a new planet swims in his ken,
Or like stout Cortez, when with eagle eyes,
He stared at the Pacific———."

The glass was brought, and she was pronounced to be the Wm. H. Morrison. My trunks were got ready, and I was soon, with all my effects, aboard of her, and introduced, by the kindness of Captain M., to her officers. I found her to be equal to her reputation—the elegant steamer Wm. H. Morrison. She has a fine set of passengers, many of whom contributed much to making my trip interesting. She was gentlemanly officered, and had a *posse comitatus* of Irishmen, who made wood piles on the banks, cotton-bales, and all the variety of freight on the boat and wharf, disappear with an Alladin dispatch. They are sad looking fellows, and lead a sorry life of it. To see them carry wood aboard, of which cords without number are "toted". up a narrow plank—sometimes so steep that it would be hazardous for any one but an Irishman to walk unencumbered—one thinks of the mules packed to ascend the Andes; only the former, loading himself with three or four sticks of four feet wood—trots, instead of walking, up the steep ascent, then "dumps" his load in a running whirl, and scampers down another plank to the pile again. Their fare is like their work—hard. They sit on the floor and eat; each has a mug of coffee, then in the center is a dish of hard biscuit and beans. This is their usual fare. Night and day they are in a revolving "freight-chain," loading and unloading the steamer. Now and then they catch an hour which they appropriate to dozing, on cotton-bales, or stretched out at length on the canvass over the freight, or on the floor of the fore-castle, and in a few moments of slumber, forget the hard toil of their lives.

The river, in many places, was making sad havoc with the bank, often eating under so that the trees were continually falling into the stream. I have seen them nearly two feet through, standing erect at the water's edge, some ten or fifteen feet below the top of the bank where they grew. These trees, embedded in the sand in the river, with their tops swaying up and down by the force of the current, are called "sawyers." A "snag," is where the trunk of a tree, or log, thus embedded, leaves part of its length sticking above the water. A "tow head" is an island of sand in the current, often crowned with young cotton-wood trees.

"And the mighty river, brown with clay and sand,
Swept in curves majestic through the forest land,
And stuck into its bosom, heaving fair and large,
Many a lowly cypress that grew upon the marge;
Stumps, and trunks, and branches, as maids might stick a pin,
To vex the daring fingers that seek to enter in.
O travelers! bold travelers! that roam in wild unrest,
Beware the pins and broaches that guard this river's breast;
For danger ever follows the captain and the ship,
Who scorn the snags and sawyers that gem the Mississip."

The flood had subsided and left the water in the river just high enough to secrete the sandbars and many of the snags, making it more difficult for the pilot to find the true current. Some nights we laid by in the fog, a dense one usually rests on the lower Mississippi; but on moonlight nights we sounded along, while the ringing of the alarum bells as we struck a sandbar, that brought the man with the line to his post; and his monotonous drawl of "five feet twain! quarter less twain!" would ever and anon wake us from our slumbers, or steal in as a part of the fantasies of our dreams. Thus struggling over sandbars, or up rushing chutes, or stopping at a town or wooding station, we eked out five long days in our passage to Cairo. We remember getting a glimpse of Memphis by daylight, through the narrow roads cut through the high bluffs on which it is seated, and of its roofs and gables over the bluffs. New Madrid is a little Memphis. We staid all night at Cairo.

"Glad to see it—glad to leave it—glad to hurry on."

The next morning we in-*car*-cerated ourself aboard the Illinois Central Railroad train. Then ho! for a drive again over the heaven-wide prairies of Illinois. This was a speedier route than by St. Louis. We caught sight of Chicago, about noon the next day, some twelve miles off, as we were flying to it, over an adjacent prairie. It was situated on a higher point of ground, that sloped down towards us. We had seen it before they told us it was Chicago, but we did not think it a city, or any place of habitation; we could think of nothing but water dashing in white foam caps among dark projecting rocks. Coming nearer to this rapidly growing, new place—we write of the part we saw of it—we were somewhat surprised to see so decent, and even neat looking buildings, on the extreme verge of the city. Nowhere could we see any indications of poverty, or want. The ragged edge of the city, if it has any, must certainly be on the other side. Chicago disappoints one; "it has opinions of its own." You may have heard it described, but you find the city does it much the best. There is a general idea that the lower part of the city is muddy because low; it is as solid as granite. It makes no difference to Chicago what St. Louis has been, and is to her; but it may to St. Louis, what Chicago is and will be to her. It is a miracle of a new place.

At 5 P. M. we took the Michigan Central Railroad train for home. Night was soon upon us. But here are those splendid sleeping-cars. Ha! ha! ha! they have achieved it at last! The steamboat state-room is left behind! You can ride now over the land, reposing on couches of Ottoman ease. Once more in Michigan; once more at home; once more my eyes are glad with the sight of our beautiful farm-land. How imperfectly a late tourist has recently described Michigan. We wouldn't give her, to-day, for his "prairie Illinois," than which, he avers, there is not so rich a portion of land on this round world. Why, we have got prairie Illinois scattered all over Michigan, besides the rich burr-oak plains, and the delightful oak openings, that have inspired the pen of the great American novelist; and the rich farm-land of timbered soil; and her marshes—those natural meadows so luxuriant in grass; with worlds and worlds of grand forests. Then think of the surface of our State, beautifully diversified with hill, valley and plain; of our Arcadian streams, Loch Lomonds, Goguacs and St. Marys. If this, because penned by a resident of Michigan, seems too glowing, take the following from a stranger, though a celebrated writer, author and tourist: "Sometimes you would come out suddenly upon little plains of soft verdure, broken by lovely groups of oak trees; these are the oak openings, and riding in and about them, is like voyaging in a pleasure-boat among a thousand fairy isles. This is in Michigan, one of the gardens of the world."

"Gentles, my tale is said."

www.ingramcontent.com/pod-product-compliance
Lightning Source LLC
LaVergne TN
LVHW020224110826
845151LV00003B/824

* 9 7 8 1 4 2 5 5 3 1 2 8 7 *